5.00

DELAWARE, from the best AUTHORITIES. 1796
Scale of Miles
PENNSYLVANIA
PHILADELPHIA
Moorestown
Gloucester
Haddonfield
Derby
Chester
Woodbury
WEST
NEW
JERSEY
Wilmington
Newport
Newark
Newcastle
Christiana Bridge
Salem
St Georges
Port Penn
Reedy I.
Middleton
Warwick
Appoquinimink
Duck Cr.
Bombay Hook
Greenwich
Fairfield
Fortescue
Egg I. Flats
Little Creek
DOVER
Camden
Canterbury
Lewisville
Frederica
Mother Kill
Mispillion
Milford
Cedar Creek
DELAWARE BAY
Cape May
Over Falls all broken Ground from 6 to 8 Feet
St. Johns
Lewis town
Cape Henlopen
Light House
SUSSEX
Broad Kill
George town
Rehoboth
Indian River
False Cape
Dagsbury
Baltimore
Little Creek
Mineral Spring
ATLANTIC
OCEAN
Fenwicks I
MARYLAND
Meridian
Meridian of Philadª.

DELAWARE

To Dawn Esther Williams Stitzel and Mark Thomas Williams,
natives of the First State.

Pictorial Research by Carolyn Stallings

American Historical Press
Sun Valley, California

DELAWARE

THE FIRST STATE

For Brett Ashley

AN ILLUSTRATED HISTORY
BY WILLIAM HENRY WILLIAMS

Bill Williams 12/4/99

Cover Illustration
Robert Shaw (1859-1912) was one
of Delaware's most talented artists. A
resident of Penny Hill, he won fame
for his many etchings, as well as book
and magazine illustrations. This
exacting work led to temporary
blindness. Upon regaining sight,
Shaw took up watercolors, capturing
some fine landscape scenery.
Courtesy, Historical Society of
Delaware

Endsheets
This map of Delaware, drawn in the
early 1790s, shows its network of
waterways, roads, and towns. The
population at that time was
approximately 60,000, evenly divided
between the three counties and towns
clustered along the inlets and creeks
flowing into Delaware Bay, since
water transportation was easiest and
cheapest. Courtesy, Historical Society
of Delaware

Photograph Credit Corrections:

From: To:
Bank of Delaware   PNC Bank
Delaware State Archives   Delaware Public Archives

Published 1999
Printed in the United States of America

Library of Congress Catalogue Card Number: 99-76386

ISBN: 1-892724-03-0

Bibliography: p. 258
Includes Index

CONTENTS

Preface   8

CHAPTER   I
Red and White on the Delaware   10

CHAPTER   II
Europeans Establish Permanent Settlements   22

CHAPTER   III
From Dependence to Independence   34

CHAPTER   IV
Revolutions of Different Kinds   48

CHAPTER   V
Delaware in the Nineteenth Century   70

CHAPTER   VI
The Age of DuPont   96

CHAPTER   VII
Towards a More Democratic Society   118

CHAPTER   VIII
Closing out the Century   158

CHAPTER   IX
Chronicles of Leadership   178

A Timeline of Delaware's History   254

Bibliography   258

Index   260

THOMAS R. CARPER
GOVERNOR

Dear Friends:

When 30 delegates to the state's convention unanimously voted to ratify the U.S. Constitution in 1787, Delaware became the "First State" -- the state that started a nation. The tenets of freedom, equality and justice that we've embodied in the constitution first took root with Delaware's ratification and positioned our state at the forefront of the new nation. In some ways, little has changed since those colonial times -Delaware strives to remain on the cutting edge.

As Governor, I am proud to be a part of the illustrious history of the "First State" and I am pleased to welcome you to the pages of *Delaware The First State: An Illustrated History.* Thanks to the outstanding work of author William Henry Williams and pictorial researcher Carolyn Stallings, this book promises to serve as a definitive historical resource of all things Delaware.

As someone who's traveled the length and breath of this state thousands of times, I know full well the historical diversity Delaware has to offer. Whether it's in the rolling hills of northern New Castle County, or the stately capital in Kent County, or the expansive beaches of southern Sussex County, Delaware has been blessed with natural beauty and rich history.

Whether you're a lifelong resident or your introduction to Delaware starts with this book, I urge you to learn some of the many things which make Delaware a terrific place to live, work, and raise a family. With *Delaware The First State: An Illustrated History* in hand, you can discover for yourself -- or discover again -- just how special the First State is.

Sincerely,

Thomas R. Carper
Governor

Painted on glass, the Delaware state seal exhibits a bright, luminous quality. Courtesy, Delaware State Archives

PREFACE

Throughout most of its history, Delaware has been tagged with a number of labels including: The Diamond State; The First State; and, more recently, The Small Wonder. Because each captures something of the unique flavor of Delaware, each is appropriate. And yet the Delaware story is far too complex to be captured by a clever label or epigram.

Part of the Delaware story supports Voltaire's observation that "history is little else than a picture of human misfortunes." For most of the First State's past, its Indians, blacks, and even its white women were exploited. Indeed, the Delaware story is often about ruthless ambition, greed, and prejudice. The figures who move across its stage include the corrupt, the shortsighted, and the inordinately selfish. But Delaware's history is also about altruistic sacrifice, empathy for the less fortunate, and hope for the future. It embraces visionaries, public servants, and many others who concern themselves with the public good. Above all it is a history of a state that, despite its small size, is really a microcosm of the United States.

Extending only 110 miles from north to south and only thirty-five miles at its widest from east to west, America's second smallest state incorporates in its past most of the major themes of American history. The clash between native Americans and Europeans, the development and exploitation of the land, the struggle for political independence, the rise of political parties, the popularity of religious revivals, the agony of slavery and the staying power of racism, the problems and possibilities created by industrialization and urban growth, the impact of immigration and the implica-

tions of suburbanization, have all been central to the development of both the First State and the United States. And yet, for those with an appreciation of the unique, Delaware's past also offers a fascinating array of singular personalities, events, and developments.

By its very nature, this short history must omit many of the important people and events that helped shape the First State. For this reason it is my hope that the reader will next turn to the books and articles of John A. Munroe, Harold Hancock, Carol E. Hoffecker, Clinton Weslager, Bill Frank, Richard Carter, Roger Martin, and others for a more detailed treatment of Delaware's past. Indeed, this history of Delaware draws extensively from their seminal works.

I am grateful to Dr. Munroe, Dr. Hoffecker, Dr. Barbara Benson, Richard Carter, and Helen Williams for reading the manuscript for chapters I-VII. Manuscript readers for chapter VIII included Richard Carter, Celia Cohen, and Helen Williams. In addition, more than 65 other Delawareans have contributed to this book in a variety of ways. Institutions too, such as the Historical Society of Delaware, the Delaware State Archives, Morris Library of the University of Delaware, and Betz Library of Delaware Technical and Community College, Georgetown, were helpful in meeting the author's needs. Brenda Baker typed most of the manuscript.

William Henry Williams
University Parallel Program
Georgetown, Delaware
1999

In "Return Day—Georgetown,
Delaware, 1796," artist Robert E.
Goodier captures a historic tradition which lives on to the
present time. Until the early
1800s, Sussex County voters had
to travel to the county seat to
cast their ballots. Since the trip
was an arduous one, they remained in Georgetown to await
the electoral results. Booths, food
stalls, and the gathering of candidates all added color to the
scene. Courtesy, Bank of Delaware

The Lenni Lenape, whose name roughly translated to "common people," inhabited Delaware, Pennsylvania, and New Jersey until the late seventeenth century. Tribal wars, European settlement, and disease reduced their numbers, and the survivors migrated westward. Courtesy, Historical Society of Delaware

CHAPTER I

RED AND WHITE
ON THE DELAWARE

On December 2, 1632, two Dutch-owned ships commanded by David de Vries beat their way northwest towards Cape Henlopen and the Delaware Bay. While still too far away to see land, northwesterly winds carried the fragrance of burning herbs and sassafras to the two Dutch ships. De Vries had been told that this sweet aroma filled the air at the beginning of every winter, when Indians set fire to thickets and underbrush to make hunting easier.

On December 5, Indians were still much on De Vries' mind as he sailed the smaller of his two vessels along the south shore of Delaware Bay. Dropping anchor at one point, the Dutch commander spotted a whale near his ship and commented on the pleasing prospects of the region with "the whales so numerous—and the land so fine for cultivation." The next morning, De Vries' small force, heavily armed and anticipating an Indian ambush, moved up Lewes Creek. There the terrible news, which had reached the Netherlands ten months before, was confirmed. On the west bank lay the burnt remains of a fort, and scattered about were the bleached bones of thirty-two Dutchmen, as well as the skeletal remains of their horses and cattle. The first act in the drama of white-Indian relations in the present state of Delaware had ended in a decisive victory for the native Americans. But there were other acts to follow and they would have a different ending.

Native Americans have lived in Delaware for at least 10,000 years. When Europeans first sailed into Delaware Bay and up the Delaware River, the Indians they encountered called themselves Lenni Lenape which, loosely translated, meant "common people." The English called them the Delawares because they lived along the bay and river named for Lord De La Warr (Thomas West), who had been appointed Governor of Virginia in 1610. Ironically, Lord De La Warr never did see the bay, river, Indians, and state that would perpetuate his name.

The Lenni Lenape occupied the land on both sides of Delaware Bay and on both sides of the Delaware River as far north as its headwaters. They lived in small, self-governing villages that seemed independent of any central authority. What unity existed among the Lenape seemed to rest on a shared language and the sense of being a separate people.

The largest concentration of Lenape villages was north of Delaware in what is now southeastern Pennsylvania. Evidently, northern Delaware was primarily used as a hunting and fishing ground by Lenape warriors and for temporary campsites by their accompanying families. Further south, Lenape settlements seemed more permanent. The land from Bombay Hook south to Cape Henlopen was claimed by a branch of the Lenape called Sickoneysincks, described by a Swedish observer in 1654 as a "powerful nation rich in maize plantations."

Lenape men hunted and fished while their women cultivated corn, beans, squash, pumpkins, and tobacco. They lived in one-room bark huts or wigwams and dug silo-shaped pits in the ground in front of their dwellings to store the bounty from their fields. On fishing and hunting expeditions they paddled dug-out canoes rather than the birch bark variety popular further north. Probably monogamous, the Lenape nevertheless seemed willing to offer the sexual favors of their wives and daughters to European visitors as a hospitable gesture. Indeed, it was the warm hospitality of the Sickoneysincks that caused the Dutch to name present day Lewes Creek, Hoerenkill or Whorekill (Whore's Creek).

The Lenape were about the same physical size as contemporary Europeans with Lenape men averaging

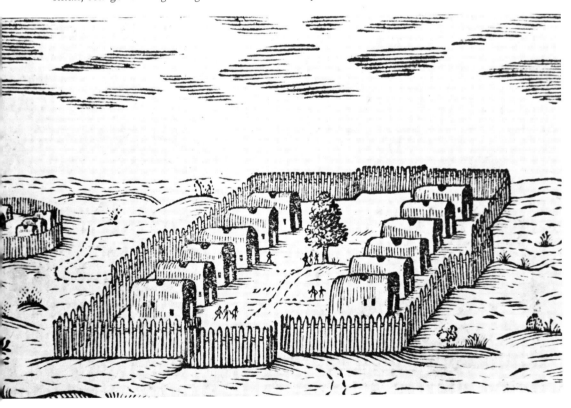

Left
A peaceful, sedentary tribe who practiced agriculture, hunting, and fishing, the Lenni Lenape lived in autonomous villages near freshwater streams. Each village of several hundred people was led by a chief, but no central government united the Lenni Lenape tribes. Courtesy, Historical Society of Delaware

Facing page
Delaware Indians constructed canoes of hollowed-out logs and used these vessels for fishing, trading, and transportation to neighboring villages. Courtesy, Historical Society of Delaware

between 5'7" and 5'10" in height. Ranging in color from light to dark brown, Lenape faces rarely exhibited beards. When facial hair did appear, it was pulled out by the roots with hinged clam shells. (Smooth faces were easier to paint for special occasions.) Older men allowed their hair to grow long, but young males shaved their scalps, leaving only a small lock on top. Bear grease was used by both sexes for hair dressing and for insect repellent.

Because the Lenape lacked a unified central government and were generally peaceful prior to the arrival of Europeans, they were often victimized by more aggressive Indian neighbors to the north and west. The Susquehannocks, or Minquas as the Lenape called them, often left their villages in the Susquehanna Valley to invade Lenape lands. When Dutch fur traders appeared on the Delaware in the early seventeenth century, the Minquas increased military pressure on the Lenape because the latter were seen as commercial rivals who occupied the key geographic location. To cross into the Delaware Valley to get at the Lenape, the warlike Minquas used the Christina and Appoquinimink rivers so often that the Dutch called both water-

ways Minquakill. Later in the seventeenth century, after English fur traders made their way into the northern Chesapeake, the Minquas lost interest in attacking the Lenape. But by that time, however, the Lenape were facing a much more serious threat.

When Europeans first sailed along the Delaware coast, they noted that the land was abundant with such wildlife as black bears, wolves, elk, and deer, and that the streams teemed with fish and beaver. In the past, a natural balance in the wildlife population had been maintained because the Lenape killed only what they needed for food and clothing. The European fur trader changed all of this by cleverly creating insatiable appetites among the Lenape for such imported products as guns, metal utensils, cloth, beads, and liquor. Driven by their newly developed thirst for European goods, the Lenape soon exhausted the beaver and deer population of Delaware in order to meet the fur trader's bartering price.

But even more significant to the Lenape than the change in hunting habits and the deplorable resulting impact on Delaware's wildlife, was the real possibility of cultural suicide caused by an increasing dependence on

Highly regarded for his knowledge of the Delaware Bay and River, Henry Fisher of Lewes (1735-1792) was called upon to choose the site of the first Cape Henlopen lighthouse in 1765. The lighthouse stood at this location until 1926 when it fell into the sea, the victim of a spring storm and shifting sands. Painting by Robert E. Goodier. Courtesy, Bank of Delaware

When Europeans first explored
what was to become the First
State, they encountered Lenni
Lenape villages adjacent to
freshwater streams on both sides
of the Delaware River. The land
boasted an abundance of wildlife
which settlers hoped to turn
into a profitable fur trade. Courtesy, Historical Society of Delaware

A small group of Nanticoke Indians preserves its heritage
through membership in the
Nanticoke Indian Association.
Most members of the original
tribe left Delaware in the 1750s,
but a few remained. This unidentified Nanticoke from Millsboro was photographed in Indian dress about 1920. Courtesy,
Delaware State Archives

products made in Europe. Along with their brothers in
the Delaware Valley to the north, Delaware's Lenape
had to make a traumatic choice: they might be allowed
to remain in Delaware if they were willing to surrender
their native American lifestyle for that of the white
man, or they could leave Delaware and move west beyond the white frontier where they might live again
like their ancestors. Decimated by the white man's diseases and bewildered by his concept of private property, Delaware's Lenape joined the Indian migration to
central Pennsylvania and then to the Ohio country. By
the last quarter of the seventeenth century, there were
only a few Lenape remaining in Delaware.

South of the Lenape region, a small number of other
Indian people spilled over into Delaware from their tribal homelands on Maryland's Eastern Shore. Among
these were the Nanticokes whose villages extended up
the Nanticoke River as far as a site on Broad Creek

just west of Laurel, Delaware. Despite the ravages of a smallpox epidemic, the Nanticokes seemed to be more successful than the Lenapes in surviving white encroachments. In 1742, however, the increasingly frustrated Nanticokes joined with remnants of a few neighboring tribes in an aborted plot against nearby English settlements. The failure of the uprising caused the discouraged Nanticokes to follow the earlier Lenape example and leave the Delmarva Peninsula. Initially settling in Iroquois country along the upper Susquehanna where they gave their name to Nanticoke, Pennsylvania, the tribe was soon pushed further west and became a scattered people.

In 1705, under pressure from white settlers, a party of Assateague Indians moved north from their home in Worcester County, Maryland to the south bank of Indian River in Sussex County. Some of them joined the ill-fated plot of 1742 and subsequently left Delaware, while other Assateagues remained behind.

Despite the exodus to the West and the heavy toll taken by white man's diseases, a few Indians continued

Henry Hudson sailed his ship, the Half Moon, *into Delaware Bay, and then left to explore the Hudson River, as illustrated here, hoping to find a northwest passage to the Orient. In 1609, he became the first European to view the Delaware. Courtesy, Historical Society of Delaware*

to live in Delaware. Today two "mixed blood" communities, the Moors of Cheswold, northwest of Dover, and the Nanticokes of the Oak Orchard area, on the north bank of the Indian River, are at least partially descended from the remnants of Delaware's native Americans. In the case of the Moors, the Indian ancestors were probably Lenape, while modern-day Nanticokes may actually have as much Assateague, Choptank, or Lenape as Nanticoke blood in their veins. Delaware's Nanticokes are particularly active in claiming their Indian ancestry. To celebrate their heritage, each September they put on a powwow with the

Left
The seal of New Netherland, decorated with a crown and a beaver, reflects the importance of the fur trade to the Dutch colony. Courtesy, Historical Society of Delaware

Right
The Dutch West India Company established trading posts at New Castle and Fort Nassau to strengthen their claim to these lands. Colonists trapped and traded with the Indians for furs to export to Europe. Courtesy, Historical Society of Delaware

proceeds going to the development of the Nanticoke Indian Museum near Oak Orchard.

On August 28, 1609, the *Half Moon,* a Dutch ship commanded by Englishman Henry Hudson, rounded Cape Henlopen to become the first European vessel to enter Delaware Bay. Hudson was searching the eastern coast of North America for a northwest passage to the Pacific and he hoped that Delaware Bay was his route. But Delaware Bay proved to be full of dangerous shoals and, after dropping anchor overnight, a disappointed Hudson was convinced that the sought after passage lay elsewhere. The next day he sailed back into the Atlantic and turned north towards the mouth of the river that would one day bear his name.

On August 17, 1610, Englishman Samuel Argall, an employee of the Virginia Company of London, commanded the second European ship to enter Delaware Bay. While sailing from Virginia to Bermuda, Argall was blown off course and took refuge from the storm in the placid bay behind Cape Henlopen. It was Argall who named the bay in honor of Lord De La Warr, Governor of Virginia.

Despite Argall's visit, over the next three decades the

Dutch, rather than the English, were the most visible Europeans north of Cape Henlopen. By 1616 a Dutch ship had sailed north into the Delaware River, and in subsequent years other Dutch vessels rounded the Cape, bent on commercially exploiting the region beyond. There was, of course, good fishing to be had north of the Cape. A Dutch ship testing Delaware Bay's marine life in 1632 found that one cast of a net brought up enough fish to feed thirty men. But in Europe the beaver hat was the rage, and no matter how fecund the marine life of Delaware Bay and River, it was the presence of that flat-tailed, buck-toothed mammal that really sparked Dutch commercial interest in the region.

Initially, however, the Dutch didn't seem to be all that interested in the new lands claimed for the Netherlands by Henry Hudson. In 1621 the Dutch government granted a charter and monopoly rights on all commerce and colonization in the New World to the Dutch West India Company. Because the Netherlands was at war with Spain to secure its newly won independence, Dutch privateers made fair game of Spanish merchant ships plying the waters between Iberia and

David Peter de Vries, Dutch explorer and trader, was a partner in the Dutch West India Company. He sailed to Delaware in 1632, only to find all the inhabitants of the fledgling colony of Swanendael massacred during an Indian attack. De Vries proved unsuccessful in establishing another colony in Delaware. Courtesy, Historical Society of Delaware

Spanish America. Obsessed with the spoils of war to be found in the Caribbean, the West India Company's efforts to colonize the Hudson and Delaware valleys were only half-hearted. Somehow Dutch trading posts at the present sites of Albany and New York survived. But in the Delaware Valley, the two Dutch settlements established near present day Philadelphia in the 1620s were soon abandoned.

By the end of the 1620s, however, the Dutch West India Company belatedly recognized the profit potential of the fur trade in general and beaver pelts in particular. Fearful of losing its commercial monopoly in the Delaware and Hudson valleys to English interests, the company decided that new, permanent Dutch settlements in both regions must be established. In 1629 the government of the Netherlands enacted a series of measures to entice its citizens to cross the Atlantic and strengthen Dutch claims in the New World. One government measure allowed any West India Company stockholder to purchase an extensive tract of land from the Indians, provided that he would pay the transoceanic passage of fifty adults.

Shortly before the Dutch Government's initiatives

were publicly announced, three stockholders sent seaman Gillis Hossitt to procure Indian land along the Delaware Bay. In exchange for "cloth, axes, adzes, and beads," the Sickoneysincks sold a tract that started in the vicinity of present day Lewes, continued north for thirty-two miles along Delaware Bay, and extended two miles inland. Hossit and his men then exchanged their remaining trade goods for furs trapped by the Indians. The furs proved equal to approximately one-twelfth the value of the annual imports of the Dutch West India Company.

In the spring of 1631, Gillis Hossitt returned with twenty-eight men and, after deciding on a site along Lewes Creek, constructed a brick building with a surrounding palisade. The presence of many swans in the area caused the new colony to be called Swanendael (Valley of the Swans).

Now joined by other Dutch partners including David de Vries, the three stockholders who had commissioned Hossitt's venture addressed the legal obligations mandated by their government in 1629; if they wished to legalize their purchase of Indian land, they would have to transport a sizeable number of new settlers to Swanendael within four years. The Dutch stockholders expected that their tiny colony would prosper and send back to the Netherlands valuable animal pelts and whale oil. With a little luck, the returning ships might even add to their cargoes some of the spoils of war, pirated from the Spanish shipping lanes in the West Indies.

Initial results were disappointing. The West India Company liked the idea of a Dutch settlement inside Cape Henlopen, but was unwilling to allow the Swanendael investors to challenge its own monopoly of the fur trade. Accordingly, West India Company agents watched Hossit like a hawk to prevent the exportation of a second valuable cargo of animal pelts from Delaware Bay. Whaling also was a failure, as it produced only a small amount of oil. To add to the chagrin of the partners, the Walvis, an eighteen-gun ship which returned to the Netherlands from Swanendael, didn't even bother to detour through the West Indies where it could have filled its empty hold with the treasures of a captured Spanish merchantman.

At this point Swanendael seemed a losing proposition. Nevertheless, Samuel Godyn, one of the partners, talked his associates into outfitting another expedition with partner David de Vries, an experienced seaman, in command of its two ships. De Vries was directed to first explore the abundant possibilities to be found in the Caribbean and then to turn north for Swanendael.

There were no Indians in sight when De Vries finally reached the site of the Swanendael massacre on December 6, 1632. The next day, while on the east side of Lewes Creek, De Vries instructed his cousin to fire a fowling piece at a flight of seagulls passing overhead. Across the creek behind bushes, two or three Sickoneysincks furtively watched the Dutch. When a seagull was knocked out of the sky while in flight, the astonished Indians jumped up and shouted their appreciation. De Vries quickly established verbal contact. By the following day his reassurances that the Dutch wanted peace rather than revenge caused one Indian to explain why and how the massacre had happened. From the Indian's explanation De Vries put together the following story:

Because native Americans along the Atlantic Coast didn't know how to smelt ore, they were eager to acquire metals brought to America by Europeans. At Swanendael the Dutch coat of arms had been painted on a piece of tin and nailed to a pole. Aware of the flexibility of tin and unaware of the significance of a coat of arms, a Sickoneysinck stole the piece of metal to make tobacco pipes. Gillis Hossitt, the chief official in Swanendael, angrily scolded the Indians, no doubt

pointing out that the Dutch government had been insulted. Concerned about good relations with the Dutch, some of the Sickoneysincks killed the thief and brought back "a token of the dead"—perhaps his ears, scalp, or even his head—to Hossitt. The horrified Dutch official told the Indians that they had gone too far and that all he really wanted to do was to sternly admonish the culprit not to steal again.

Sickoneysincks who were friends of the slain thief demanded revenge against the Dutch, blaming Hossitt's complaints for the death of their comrade. Intent on wiping out the entire colony of thirty-two men (evidently three additional settlers had joined the community), a band of warriors approached the unguarded fort and found almost all of the Dutch working in their fields outside the palisade. Gillis Hossitt and a large, chained dog were standing near the brick building, while inside lay a sick man. According to De Vries:

Three of the bravest Indians, who were to do the deed, bringing a lot of beaver-skins with them to exchange, asked to enter the house. The man in charge, [Gillis Hossitt] went in with them to make the barter; which being done, he went down from the loft where the stores lay, and in descending the stairs, one of the Indians seized an axe, and cleft the head of our agent [Hossitt] who was in charge so that he fell down dead. They also relieved the sick man of life; and shot into the dog, who was chained fast, and whom they most feared, twenty-five arrows before they could despatch him. They then proceeded towards the rest of the men, who were at their work and going among them with pretensions of friendship, struck them down.

Realizing that revenge was not only pointless but also bad for business, De Vries re-established friendly relations with the Sickoneysincks. He then set some of his men to whaling on Delaware Bay. The harpooners were inexperienced, however, and only seven of the seventeen struck whales were captured and processed. The total amount of oil was small and the expedition that headed back to Holland in the spring of 1633 represented yet another loss to the investors. By 1635, the Dutch partners were happy to sell their land and privileges to the Dutch West India Company. The collapse of the Swanendael venture left the intermittently occupied Fort Nassau, a small Dutch post located on the east bank of the Delaware nearly opposite present day Philadelphia, as the only European settlement along the Delaware Bay and River.

Two Swedish ships, the Kalmar Nyckel (Key of Kalmar) *and the Vogel Grip* (Griffin) *landed in 1638 at "The Rocks," near present-day Wilmington. Their crew members formed Delaware's first permanent European settlement. Courtesy, Historical Society of Delaware*

CHAPTER II

EUROPEANS ESTABLISH PERMANENT SETTLEMENTS

t was early October, 1664 and two English ships lay anchored in the Delaware, their restless skeleton crews eyeing Fort Casimir on the West Bank and, next to the citadel, the wooden buildings of the town of New Amstel (New Castle). On a pole towering above the fort, where only yesterday a Dutch flag had been visible, the insignia of England rippled in the breeze.

Ashore English soldiers and sailors, intent on enjoying the spoils of victory, had just looted the fort's storehouse of cloth, shoes, clothing, and liquor. Drunk on Dutch wine and brandy, the enlisted men ignored the commands of their officers as they plundered the homes of New Amstel's Dutch burghers and drove off their livestock. Whatever his riotous troops didn't pillage, the English commander later confiscated for himself and his officers. As for the captured Dutch soldiers, they were summarily packed off to the Chesapeake and sold as indentured servants to English

Left
Queen Christina of Sweden, only seven years of age in 1632 when she inherited the throne, established a Swedish colony in the New World as her father had hoped to do. Courtesy, Historical Society of Delaware

planters.

The sacking of New Amstel marked the beginning of the English phase of Delaware's history, but only after the Swedes, and then the Dutch, enjoyed their day in the sun.

Paradoxically, it was the Dutch drive for commercial profits that brought the Swedes to the New World. Although Sweden was the dominant military power along the Baltic, the Dutch dominated commercial activity in that region. When some Dutch merchants became unhappy with the New World monopoly granted to the Dutch West India Company by their government, they turned to Sweden for a charter that would challenge the Dutch West India Company's dominant position.

In 1637, the New Sweden Company—made up of Dutch and Swedish investors—was chartered with the right to trade from New Foundland to Florida. The *Key of Kalmar* and the *Griffin*, two Swedish-owned vessels commanded by the Dutch former governor of New Netherland, Peter Minuit, set out from Gothenburg, Sweden in the late fall of 1637. Minuit's goal was to establish a Swedish colony in America on territory previously claimed by the Netherlands. Stopping in Holland for repairs, some cargo, and a few passengers, the expedition arrived in Delaware Bay in mid-March, 1638.

Moving up the Bay into the Delaware River, Minuit made contact with five Lenape chiefs. The tribal leaders then sold to the New Sweden Company all of the land on the west bank of the Delaware from Duck Creek in the south to the Schuylkill in the north and stretching westward indefinitely. The Indians, of course, didn't understand the European concept of land ownership and thought that they had merely given the Swedes the right to share in the use of this tract. No wonder there would be future misunderstandings between the Lenape and Europeans!

But at that moment Minuit was more concerned with building a fort and planting crops. He constructed

Left
Settlers set sail from Gothenburg, Sweden, during the fall of 1637 and landed at the confluence of the Christina and Delaware rivers almost six months later. Their arrival marked the beginning of limited and rather short-lived Swedish colonization in the New World. Courtesy, Historical Society of Delaware

Below
Here, a Swedish artist of the late 1600s depicted various aspects of native American life. Three types of dwellings—as well as an Indian burial ceremony and a battle scene of tribal war—are shown. Courtesy, Historical Society of Delaware

Fort Christina on the north bank of the Christina River, approximately two miles from the Delaware on a site presently part of Wilmington's east side. Both the river and fort were named for Queen Christina, the reigning monarch of Sweden, who at the time was only twelve years old.

The future of New Sweden seemed very promising. Subsequent ships brought additional settlers, including Finns living in Sweden and Dutch farmers whose request to come to the New World had been rejected by the Dutch West India Company but accepted by the New Sweden Company. The Indians continued to trade valuable furs, and the first two ships to leave New Sweden for Europe carried a combined total of 1,769 beaver pelts and the skins of 314 otters and 132 bears. Moreover, in 1654, the valley of the Christina was portrayed by the visiting Peter Lindestrom as "suitable for all kinds of agriculture and the cultivation of all kinds of rare fruit-bearing trees." The Christina River, deep and "rich in fish," could "be navigated with sloops and other large vessels a considerable distance." So fertile was countryside along the river, wrote Lindestrom, "that the pen is too weak to describe, praise and extol it." Indeed, "on account of its fertility it may well be called a land flowing with milk and honey."

But even a land "flowing with milk and honey" can be unproductive if mismanaged. By the mid 1640s, intensive trapping had almost exterminated the beaver

population along the lower Delaware, forcing the settlers to turn from the nearby Lenape to the more distant Minquas for pelts. Because New Sweden proved less profitable than anticipated and because certain pressures were brought to bear in the Netherlands, within a few years the Dutch investors sold their shares of the venture, leaving New Sweden as a wholly Swedish undertaking. Since the Swedes had no previous experience in overseas colonization, New Sweden was often badly managed.

In 1643, Lieutenant Colonel Johan Printz, a native of Southern Sweden and the heaviest chief executive in Delaware's history, arrived at Fort Christina to govern New Sweden. A tall man possessing an immense girth (which led the Lenape to call him "Big Belly" and the colonists to dub him "The Tub"), Printz weighed in the neighborhood of 400 pounds. The appointment of this Swedish military officer as governor was significant because it reflected a temporary increase in interest and involvement by the Stockholm government in the struggling colony along the Christina and the Delaware.

For a few years after Printz's arrival, New Sweden took on new vigor, causing those connected with the colony to be optimistic about its future. Through further purchases from the Lenape, the Swedish settlement now claimed the land on both sides of the Delaware Bay and River from Cape Henlopen and Cape May in the south to the falls of the Delaware at present day Trenton on the north. Furs acquired from the Minquas to the west and tobacco purchased from English settlers on Maryland's Eastern Shore were exported to Sweden, while incoming ships brought European-made goods to the Delaware.

Throughout the Swedish occupation of the lower Delaware region, Fort Christina continued to be the chief seaport and commercial center. But Fort Christina's location, two miles from the Delaware, rendered it less valuable in controlling commercial traffic than military posts situated directly on that river. To remedy the problem and strengthen Swedish influence in the entire region, Printz set about building three forts: the first on the east bank of the Delaware just south of the mouth of Salem Creek, the second in the vicinity of the Schuylkill River, and the third on Tinicum Island in the Delaware just south of present day Philadelphia. Printz also made Tinicum Island the capital of New Sweden by constructing his own residence there.

The Swedish colonists adapted well to their New World environment. Their cultivated fields, which dotted the lower Christina Valley and the west bank of the Delaware as far north as the Schuylkill, produced

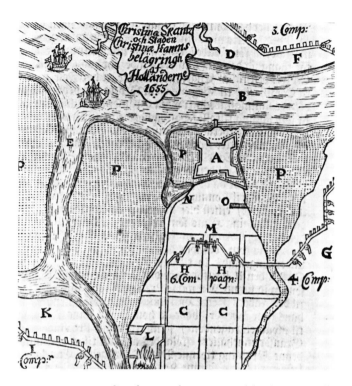

grains native to Sweden, such as rye and barley, as well as the North American Indians' corn and tobacco. Nearby, increasing numbers of livestock grazed. Local Finnish colonists previously had been steeped in the pioneer tradition. While living in Sweden, they had carved out farms from some of that nation's most remote forests. Having built their Swedish homes of logs, they continued to do so in America. The log cabin, first introduced along the Christina and lower Delaware by the Finns, became the standard home of the American pioneer. It was only when the frontier pushed beyond the Mississippi into the treeless Great Plains, that the log cabin gave way to the more practical sod house.

There were also spiritual needs to be met in New Sweden. By 1640, the first Lutheran services in America were being conducted by a Swedish pastor at Fort Christina. The Indians, of course, were regarded as heathens, but settlers always hoped that they could be converted to Christianity. One Lutheran pastor, Johan Campanius Holm, was particularly interested in working with the Lenape and even translated the Lutheran Catechism into the Lenape tongue. Campanius' fascination with the natives' language was partly due to his desire to show its affinity with Hebrew, thereby proving that American Indians were descended from the ancient Israelites.

Despite accomplishments in many areas, New Sweden's existence remained precarious. Increasingly the colony fell under the control of the government in Stockholm where its needs were generally ignored.

From 1648 until 1654, for example, no supply ships or instructions reached New Sweden from the mother country. Without supplies from home, the struggling colony had to make do with goods provided by English and Dutch traders. Yet, the presence of these foreign nationals was an unsettling reminder that both England and the Netherlands regarded the Swedes as trespassers in the Delaware Valley. Despite prior claims to the region, both nations were willing to tolerate the Swedish presence, but only because the three nations were allies during the Thirty Years War in Europe (1618-1648).

A rapidly growing population, fed by shiploads of new immigrants from the Baltic, would have strengthened the Swedish claim to the Delaware Valley. However, the passing of six years without the arrival of one Swedish vessel seriously limited population growth. Indeed, at no time were there more than four or five hundred colonists in all of New Sweden.

Seemingly abandoned by the mother country, surrounded by potentially hostile Indians, and eyed by resentful English and Dutch settlements, New Sweden's survival depended on Governor Printz's ability to maintain good relations with its neighbors. Although he worked hard and was successful at external diplomacy, Printz's authoritarian nature quickly surfaced when faced with internal challenges. In 1653, for example, the leader of a group of twenty-two settlers who were critical of the Governor's rule, was summarily arrested and executed.

While the frustrated Johan Printz grew increasingly apprehensive about the future of New Sweden, only a hundred miles to the northeast on Manhattan Island, an equally authoritarian Peter Stuyvesant waited impatiently for the opportunity to add New Sweden to his domain. The peg-legged governor of the Dutch colony of New Netherland was forbidden by his country to attack New Sweden, but was directed to insist on the maintenance of Dutch rights in the Delaware Valley.

In 1651 Stuyvesant ordered the periodically occupied Dutch base at Fort Nassau to be moved downriver to the site of modern day New Castle. Strategically obstructing the Swedish settlements' access to the Atlantic, the new Dutch post was called Fort Casimir. Although Fort Casimir's garrison was too small to immediately threaten New Sweden, its close proximity to Fort Christina was upsetting to Printz. Realizing that he must raise a relief expedition to reinforce his isolated colony, Printz sailed for Europe in 1653. On his arrival in Sweden, he was pleased to meet an expedition, under the command of Johan Rising, about to set sail for the Delaware.

Rising's fleet arrived on the Delaware River in 1654 and promptly captured the weakly defended Fort Casimir. But that initial Swedish victory gave Stuyvesant the perfect excuse for direct military action against New Sweden. Soon after the capture of Fort Casimir, the Swedish fleet sailed for home, leaving New Sweden unprotected. In late August of 1655, seven Dutch ships—carrying 317 soldiers under Stuyvesant's person-

Facing page
Swedish soldiers and settlers built the garrisoned Fort Christina soon after their arrival. A wall surrounded the small, square fortress ("A" on the map), and the village of Christinaham was laid out in a grid pattern a short distance away. Courtesy, Historical Society of Delaware

Left
Old Swedes Church (1698) served the Lutheran congregation led by Erick Bjork and remained a community center long after Sweden lost its New World claims. English language and customs gradually replaced Scandinavian ones, however, and the Swedes assimilated with the larger population of Wilmington. Courtesy, Historical Society of Delaware

al command—rounded the Delaware capes and beat their way north towards New Sweden. Stuyvesant's superior forces landed between Fort Casimir and Fort Christina, surrounded both Swedish strongholds and then forced each to capitulate.

The victorious Dutch proceeded to integrate the former Swedish colony with New Netherland. The Swedish settlers along the Delaware were offered the choice of returning to the mother country or remaining under the Dutch flag. Only thirty-seven decided to return to their native land. Under Swedish rule the capitol had first been at Fort Christina, then Tinicum Island, and finally, after Printz left, it was moved back to Fort Christina. Under Dutch rule the capitol for the Delaware Valley became Fort Casimir. Alongside Fort

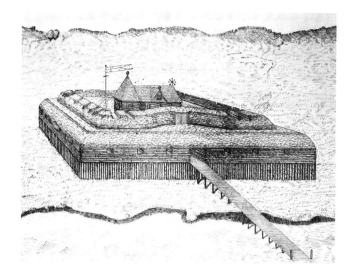

Above
Located on the site of present-day New Castle, Fort Casimir was at the center of a struggle between the Swedish and the Dutch in the New World. In 1651 the Dutch built Fort Casimir a few miles from the Swedish Fort Christina. Minimally protected, the Dutch fort fell to the Swedes before being reclaimed in 1655. Courtesy, Historical Society of Delaware

Left
Dutch settlers laid out the village of New Amstel (now New Castle) near the site of Fort Casimir during the 1650s. The enterpising Dutch traded tobacco, obtained from English colonists, on the world market. Courtesy, Historical Society of Delaware

Casimir, the victorious Dutch laid out streets for the town of New Amstel (present-day New Castle) which, within a few years, contained 110 homes and was the commercial center for the entire Delaware Valley. Despite the fact that the Dutch flag now flew over the region, a new influx of Finns and Swedes joined with immigrants from the Netherlands to swell the population. As labor needs increased, Dutch ships also brought in black slaves, often by way of the Caribbean island of Curaçao.

Initially the settlements along the Delaware were owned and administered by the Dutch West India Company. In 1656, however, the company sold the area south of the Christina River to the Dutch city of Amsterdam. In practice there were now two Dutch colonies on the Delaware, separated by the Christina River.

The Dutch had tolerated the Swedish foothold in America so long as an alliance with Sweden in Europe was necessary. Similarly, the English tolerated the Dutch foothold in North America as long as a European alliance with the Netherlands was useful. With the ending of the Thirty Years War in 1648, English-Dutch relations underwent a remarkable change and the two former military allies became commercial rivals. Indeed, this commercial rivalry became so intense that it led to three Anglo-Dutch wars over the next twenty-five years.

In 1664, James, Duke of York and eventual heir to the English throne, received a grant from his brother, King Charles II, to all lands between the Connecticut and the Delaware rivers. In making this grant, Charles II was obviously claiming for England all of the Dutch

Although Peter Stuyvesant re-captured Fort Casimir from Swedish commander Johan Rising, the victory proved costly. It strained Holland's colonial coffers, and Stuyvesant learned that the Indians were attacking Dutch settlements on the Hudson. Courtesy, Historical Society of Delaware

When landing at New Castle on October 28, 1682, William Penn established his claim to Pennsylvania and the "Lower Counties Upon Delaware." The proprietor was given two gifts symbolizing the transfer—a piece of turf and a porringer of water. Courtesy, Historical Society of Delaware

holdings in North America. And yet, through perverse oversight or inexact knowledge of American geography, the grant didn't include the settlements under Dutch sovereignty on the west bank of the Delaware. But this rather important omission didn't stop the Duke of York from claiming the west bank for himself.

Nor did the fact that Britain and Holland were officially at peace in 1664 deter the future James II from sending a fleet of four ships and 450 soldiers to occupy his new domain. The Duke's fleet struck first at Manhattan Island in late August and then, after the theatrical Peter Stuyvesant was forced to surrender, two British ships headed for the Delaware under the command of Robert Carr. Once in the Delaware River, the English sailed right by New Amstel in order to meet with and win over the upriver Swedes and Finns. After being assured of cooperation, the British moved against New Amstel and the Dutch garrison at Fort Casimir. Outnumbered 130 to 30, Fort Casimir's defenders were quickly overwhelmed by an assault on the rear of the fort which coincided with cannon barrages from the

two English ships stationed in the river. In the brief battle, three Dutch defenders were killed and ten wounded. The English emerged unscathed.

Except for a brief Dutch reoccupation (1673-74), the British ruled the Delaware Valley from 1664 to the American Revolution. New Amstel quickly became New Castle and served as secondary capital to New York City for the Duke's holdings in the Hudson and Delaware valleys. (The Duke gave New Jersey to two of his friends.) For a number of years the Swedes and Finns continued to be the dominant ethnic groups north of the town of New Castle, while the Dutch prevailed in and around it. More importantly, the English element, fed in part by tobacco planters and their slaves pushing east from Maryland, steadily grew. But as British institutions and attitudes were slowly introduced, disputes concerning overlapping land claims contributed to considerable uncertainty among the populace.

To repay a loan, Charles II granted Pennsylvania to William Penn in 1681. It was decided that the southeast-

ern border of Pennsylvania be at least twelve miles from New Castle—a measure initiated to protect the Duke of York's land claims to the south. For the first time Delaware stood as a separate entity from Pennsylvania, and this seventeenth-century decision provided the basis for the present boundary with the Keystone State. Although initially surveyed in 1701 by drawing a circle with a twelve-mile radius centered on the town of New Castle, the precise location of this border was not finalized until 1750.

William Penn was very pleased with the size of his land grant, yet he was greatly concerned about Pennsylvania's lack of direct land access to the Atlantic Ocean. Penn brought his concern to his old friend, the Duke of York. In 1682 the sympathetic Duke turned over to Penn his own claim on all land lying south of Pennsylvania.

This generous gift of the future state of Delaware did not go unchallenged, however. According to the Calverts, the proprietors of Maryland, all of the land south of Pennsylvania belonged to them and, therefore,

was not the Duke of York's to give away. When Charles I granted Maryland to Cecilius Calvert in 1632, the King's charter stated that the eastern boundary of Maryland extended to the Delaware Bay and River, except in those places previously cultivated by Europeans. But a year earlier the doomed Swanendael settlers had plowed and planted fields along Lewes Creek, thus providing legal grounds for denying the Calvert claim to present-day Delaware. Moreover, because the heir apparent to the English throne lay claim—dubious as it might be—to the west bank of the Delaware River and Bay, the Calverts were somewhat cautious about pressing their own territorial ambitions. Between 1670 and 1682, however, Cecil Calvert did make some forty-seven land grants in what is now southern Delaware, causing great confusion.

Despite years of political maneuvering and litigation by the Calverts, William Penn and his descendants successfully held on to Delaware until the American Revolution. In 1685 the English Privy Council ruled that because of the Swanendael settlement, Delaware was not part of Maryland. The Privy Council also ruled that Delaware's southern boundary would run west from Cape Henlopen until it reached a point midway between the Atlantic and the Chesapeake, and then north to intersect with the Pennsylvania line. Unfortunately for Maryland's proprietors, the map used by the Privy Council placed Cape Henlopen at Fenwick Island, almost twenty-five miles south of its present location. As a result, the Calverts were eventually forced to surrender their claim to most of what is now Sussex County.

In spite of the 1685 decision, boundary disputes between Maryland and Delaware continued into the mid-eighteenth century. Finally, the southern border of Delaware was precisely drawn by two Maryland and two Pennsylvania surveyors in 1751. Plotting Delaware's western boundary line, however, proved too difficult for local surveyors, and Englishmen Charles Mason and Jeremiah Dixon were called in to complete the job. In 1765 the two Englishmen finished their Delaware assignment and then turned to marking the boundary between Pennsylvania and Maryland which became the famous Mason-Dixon line.

As soon as they were set off from Pennsylvania in 1681, the west bank settlements comprising the future state of Delaware needed a distinctive geographic label. By late 1682 William Penn was calling them the "Lower Counties." Subsequently, "Lower Counties," "Territories," or even the cumbersome "Counties of New Castle, Kent, and Sussex on the Delaware" were common. Just plain "Delaware" found occasional usage, but it was not until the American Revolution that the name actually stuck.

By contrast, Delaware's three counties officially received their present names at a much earlier date. Initially, under the Duke of York, the only court and public officials in Delaware were stationed at New Castle. But population growth in the southern and central portions of the colony soon created the need for a court and public officials at two other locations.

In 1659 the Dutch established a garrison along Lewes Creek, the first European settlement in the area since Swanendael. Four years later the Lewes settlement—then called Whorekill—was reinforced by forty-one Mennonites from Amsterdam under the leadership of Peter Plockhoy. Despite the sacking of the Dutch fort and Mennonite homes by British soldiers in 1664, population growth continued. The English consequently set up a court in Lewes six years later, with jurisdiction stretching north to include the Saint Jones River Valley. Because "hazards and perils both by land and water" made the trip to this distant court quite difficult, in 1680 farmers along the Saint Jones successfully petitioned for a court in their vicinity.

The jurisdictional areas of these three early courts became the basis of Delaware's three counties. In 1682 Penn gave the two southern counties their modern names of Sussex and Kent, while the town of New Castle lent its name to the northern county. The town that the Dutch had called Whorekill and the English named Deal in 1680, was renamed Lewes (after the county seat of Sussex, England) by Penn two years later. In 1683 Pennsylvania's proprietor directed that a new town named Dover—presumably after Dover in Kent County, England—be built somewhere along the Saint Jones River as the seat of Kent County. Initially, the Kent County court met in a private home at Town Point, near the mouth of the Saint Jones River, before moving seven miles northwest to a tavern located on the future site of Dover. It wasn't until the mid 1690s that a courthouse was completed, however, and it wasn't until well into the eighteenth century that the town of Dover actually appeared.

Penn wished to keep the three "Lower Counties" and Pennsylvania united under one General Assembly, but powerful forces urged their separation. The older town of New Castle, for example, was very jealous of newly-founded, but more rapidly growing, Philadelphia. Furthermore, Anglican leadership, which was dominant in the "Lower Counties," disagreed with the Quaker elite controlling Pennsylvania.

On their part, Pennsylvanians found close political ties with the "Lower Counties" quite objectionable. Although rapidly falling behind in population, the "Lower Counties" had the same number of representatives in the General Assembly as Pennsylvania's three counties and, therefore, could block legislation deemed essential by Pennsylvania.

By 1701 mutual hostility had reached such a point that the representatives of the "Lower Counties" walked out of the General Assembly. Needing American support for his constant struggle in England to maintain his proprietary claims along the west bank of the Delaware, a concerned William Penn persuaded the representatives of the "Lower Counties" to return to the General Assembly. But first he granted them and their Pennsylvania counterparts the right to establish individual assemblies in the future. Consequently, the first separate assembly of the "Lower Counties" met in New Castle during the fall of 1704. Although Delaware would continue to share with Pennsylvania an allegiance to the English crown and would acknowledge the same proprietor and his appointed governor, Delaware was now a separate colony.

Above
Cape Henlopen in Delaware Bay, pictured in this 1780 illustration, formed a safe haven for ships, and the nearby town of Lewes became a home for sailors who regularly maneuvered their vessels up the shallow, rocky waters of the Delaware River to New Castle and Philadelphia. Courtesy, Historical Society of Delaware

Left
Built in about 1722, the New Castle Courthouse served as the seat of government for William Penn's "Three Lower Counties Upon Delaware." It later housed the colonial capitol of Delaware. Courtesy, Historical Society of Delaware

In a scene recreated by Wilmington artist Howard Pyle, members
of the Continental Congress
leave Independence Hall in Philadelphia to listen to the first
public reading of the Declaration of Independence. Only New
York's abstention marred a
unanimous vote, though Delaware previously had been divided on the issue. The heroic all-
night ride of Caesar Rodney
ended this deadlock in the Delaware delegation. Courtesy, The
American Revolution: A Picture
Sourcebook (New York: Dover,
1975)

FROM DEPENDENCE TO INDEPENDENCE

*A*curious and excited crowd filed into St. Peter's Anglican Church in Lewes on the afternoon of October 31, 1739. Inside, George Whitefield, a slender, blue-eyed, light-skinned Englishman of twenty-four rose to speak. Despite his relative youth, Whitefield was already a famous evangelist in England and Wales, and his reputation had spread to the American colonies. Although he had arrived by ship from Europe the previous day and had intended to leave directly for Philadelphia, a small delegation of Lewes' leading citizens persuaded him to remain long enough to preach a sermon.

The congregation first noticed the extraordinary force and power in Whitefield's voice—Benjamin Franklin later estimated that it could be heard by as many as 30,000 at a time—and then his crossed eyes, which seemed to mesmerize as they searched the faces of his audience. Finally there was that unmistakable message which warned his listeners that they were "half beast and half devil," and that their only hope for avoiding an eternity in hell was to be reborn in Christ.

William Becket, the Anglican rector at Lewes, was unhappy with Whitefield because he sensed that the great evangelist represented a threat to the Church of England and its staid ways. Whitefield subsequently justified Becket's concern by pointedly criticizing the Anglican Church. In doing so, Whitefield challenged an important English institution and helped set in motion a process that would lead to further suspicion of all English institutions.

The influx of different races and nationalities into Delaware, which had begun in the 1600s, continued throughout the next century. Newcomers so radically altered the ethnic makeup of the population that by the eighteenth century, only a minority of Delawareans could point to a Swedish, Finnish, or Dutch ancestry. According to one estimate, even as early as 1790, descendants of these three ethnic groups together represented less than 6 percent of the state's total population.

The migration of tobacco growers from the played-out fields of Maryland's Eastern Shore to the virgin lands of Sussex, Kent, and lower New Castle counties brought thousands of Anglo-Saxons and their black slaves to Delaware. In 1790 an estimated 50 percent of Delaware's population claimed English descent while, according to the U.S. Census of the same year, 22 percent of the state's population was black.

Although only part English and far wealthier than most, Samuel Dickinson was one example of the Anglo-Saxon immigrants from Maryland's Eastern Shore. Dickinson left his soil-depleted tobacco fields in Talbot County, Maryland to the children of his first marriage in 1740. He then turned to developing approximately 3,000 acres in eastern Kent County, Delaware. In 1741, Samuel, his wife, and two sons by his second marriage—one of whom was John Dickinson, later known as the "penman" of the American Revolution—and his slaves moved into their new plantation on Jones Neck, Southeast of Dover.

Large numbers of Scotch-Irish settled in Delaware during the early and mid-eighteenth century. Primarily descended from lowland Scots who moved to northern Ireland in the 1600s, many came to North America in the next century in search of better economic opportunities. Their primary port of entry was Philadelphia, but thousands disembarked at New Castle. Although

the majority eventually moved west in pursuit of cheap land, enough Scotch-Irish remained in Delaware to give New Castle County a decidedly Scotch-Irish flavor by the mid-eighteenth century. Referring to lower New Castle County in 1741, one observer wrote of the "multitudes" arriving "from the North of Ireland." Some Scotch-Irish even formed communities in central and southern Delaware, causing the Reverend William Becket of Lewes to note, as early as 1728, the many Scotch-Irish "families that are settled in Sussex."

Although poor and obliged to finance their Atlantic crossing by agreeing to serve for a time (generally three to seven years) as indentured servants, the Scotch-Irish were usually better educated than other Delawareans. As a result, Scotch-Irish names such as Killen, Tilton, Alison, and McKinly soon became prominent in Delaware's medical, legal, and educational circles. Of considerable significance was the distrust and resentment of English institutions that these newcomers brought with them from Ireland. Anti-English sentiments led Delaware's Scotch-Irish to enthusiastically support the rebel cause during the American Revolution.

Other nationalities settled in Delaware during the eighteenth century, but in far fewer numbers than the

English, Africans, and Scotch-Irish. Thousands of German immigrants poured into the Delaware Valley but, because they were from outside the British Empire, they were denied entry at New Castle and had to disembark at Philadelphia. Intent on finding cheap land and living with other German-speaking people, most Germans moved west and only a few pushed south into Delaware.

More numerous were the Welsh. After spending two years in Pennsylvania, in 1703 fifteen or twenty families moved into the Welsh Tract, a 30,000-acre grant from William Penn which began just below Newark along the Maryland border and extended south for several miles. Subsequently, additional Welsh settled into the Welsh Tract and other parts of Delaware.

Almost all of the newcomers were English-speaking, albeit in some cases with Irish or Welsh accents. This factor made it difficult to distinguish individual ethnic groups from each other and from the older residents of Delaware. But on Sundays, distinct differences did surface as each nationality celebrated its own peculiar religious heritage. Indeed, it seemed that church affiliation more than language kept alive a sense of ethnic identity in eighteenth-century Delaware.

The Dutch, who were never numerous in Delaware, soon intermarried with Swedes, Finns, English, and finally, the Scotch-Irish. Because Delaware had no Dutch Reformed churches during the eighteenth century, some of the Dutch joined the Presbyterian Church in New Castle, a natural occurrence considering that both faiths shared a common theology based on the ideas of John Calvin.

By contrast, many of the Swedes and Finns along the Christina River continued an allegiance to the Lutheran Church which was the official religious institution in both mother countries. Construction on Old Swedes Church began in 1698 in what is now east Wilmington, and Lutheran pastors from Sweden filled the pulpit throughout most of the eighteenth century. By 1767, however, English language services were being

Facing page
The famous English evangelist, George Whitefield, preached to an excited audience in Lewes on October 31, 1739. In the years that followed, Whitefield converted thousands to his enthusiastic brand of religion. Courtesy, Library of Congress

Left
The original Saint Peter's chapel in Lewes, where Whitefield spoke, was replaced in 1858 by this Gothic-style structure. Perhaps the evangelist's greatest achievement was that he truly challenged the beliefs and attitudes of his audience. Courtesy, Historical Society of Delaware

The Wilmington Society of Friends built this meetinghouse in 1816 on a site where they had congregated since 1748. Quaker families dominated the state's mercantile, milling, and shipping economy; later, many spoke out for the abolition of slavery. Courtesy, Historical Society of Delaware

conducted on alternate Sundays. The last Swedish pastor departed and Old Swedes Church became Protestant Episcopal in 1791.

Delaware's Anglo-Saxons were drawn to their ancestral church, the Church of England. But Anglicanism in Delaware faced some extraordinary difficulties. Unlike Virginia and Maryland, Delaware's Anglican Church was not tax-supported. This meant that all Anglican pulpits were filled by clergymen sent and partially financed by the Society for the Propagation of the Gospel stationed in London. Furthermore, the Anglican insistence on an educated ministry produced a clergy that had difficulty relating to the concerns of the vast majority of Delawareans.

Most colonial Delawareans lived lives marked by poverty, disease, violence, and early death. Moreover, only a minority could read and write. Sussex Countians, for example, were described as:

a people without learning, which proceeds altogether from their extreme poverty. There is not a grammar school within the county and it is a thing extremely rare to meet with a man who can write a tolerable hand or spell with propriety the most common words in the English language.

Such people found it difficult to respond to a clergy that, in the eighteenth century Anglican manner, read learned sermons on the significance of moral responsibility but did little to address their deepest needs and concerns.

Other hindrances to Anglican success included the lack of a bishop in America and, more particularly, the scattered nature of the population. Delaware was overwhelmingly rural; most of those descended from English stock lived considerable distances from Anglican churches and chapels. Moreover, at no time during the colonial period were there more than five Anglican clergy to serve Delaware's widely dispersed population. As a result, although a large number of Delawareans of English background gave nominal allegiance to the Church of England, only a few took communion, and

not many regularly attended services.

A number of English Delawareans continued traditional family connections with the Society of Friends. As the eighteenth century progressed, Quakers increasingly abandoned the emotionalism that marked them in the seventeenth century for a quiet mysticism which reflected their rise in social status. This new Quaker image was not very effective in attracting new members. Despite limited numbers, however, Quakers would dominate the economic and civic life of eighteenth-century Wilmington. Some Anglo-Saxons along the Kent-Sussex border were drawn, in the 1760s, to an emotional variant of Quakerism founded by Kent County native Joseph Nichols. But by the end of the century, only a few Nicholites (as Joseph Nichols followers were called) remained in the state.

Several Roman Catholic families lived in colonial Delaware and they too tended to be of English ancestry. Thanks to the ambiance of religious tolerance established by William Penn, some Catholics felt comfortable in joining other Marylanders in their migration to central and southern Delaware. By 1762 there were five or six Catholic families in Kent County, and priests from the Eastern Shore of Maryland conducted religious services on a regular basis in the Dover and Odessa areas.

Just as most Anglo-Saxons tended to identify with the Church of England, the Scotch-Irish maintained their Old World Presbyterianism. In 1723 one observer noted that almost 200 families had recently arrived in the colony from Northern Ireland and "they are generally Presbyterian." Although Delaware's Presbyterian Church traced its roots back to the 1600s, by the mid-eighteenth century it had taken on an overwhelmingly Scotch-Irish tint and this caused friction between Presbyterians and Anglicans. George Ross, Anglican rector at Immanuel Church in New Castle labelled the Scotch-Irish, "the bitterest railers against the {Anglican} Church that ever trod the American ground." Eventually the animosity between Scotch-Irish Presbyterians, strongest in New Castle County, and Anglo-Saxon Church of England members, most numerous in downstate Delaware, led to the formation of an "Irish party" and a rival "church party" to contest Delaware elections prior to the American Revolution.

Unlike the Scotch-Irish, the Welsh did not have a nationalistic commitment to any one Protestant faith. As a result, their names could be found on the rolls of Anglican, Quaker, and Presbyterian congregations in Delaware. In the Welsh Tract, the Pencader Presbyterian Church and the Welsh Tract Baptist Church, which was the only strong Baptist congregation in Delaware during the colonial period, had almost exclusively Welsh congregations.

But despite the variety of religious choices open to them, most colonial Delawareans remained unchurched. In Kent County, for example, approximately two-thirds of the population had no church attachment in the 1760s and many who did seemed rather passive in their commitment. Although some blacks were baptized and a few might attend church or chapel with their masters, the religious needs of most of them went unattended.

This religious lethargy was briefly challenged by the Great Awakening, a revival that swept through the American colonies in the 1730s and 1740s. From New England to Georgia huge crowds turned out to hear charismatic preachers, such as George Whitefield, who

Religious gatherings, sparked by evangelism, were compelling social events to the overwhelmingly rural population of early Delaware. Probably nine out of ten Delaware families lived on farms during the colonial period. Although holdings varied in size, New Castle County's farms averaged slightly more than 200 acres. Often only a small part of a Delaware farm was actually cleared of trees and brush. This particularly held true in Kent and Sussex where individual land holdings were generally larger than in New Castle.

Soil fertility and, to a greater degree, location dictated the value of these farms. Most New Castle County farm land, for example, was more expensive than land further south because the cash crops produced in northern Delaware had such easy access to the market

urged them to save themselves from the fires of hell by being born again in Christ. While touring Delaware, Whitefield most often visited New Castle County, speaking to thousands at a time. Eight to ten thousand stood in the cold and rain at White Clay Creek, for example, to hear him preach on December 2, 1739.

By the 1750s, however, the enthusiasm created by the Great Awakening had given way to the lethargy of earlier years. And yet, this remarkable outpouring of religious fervor demonstrated beyond doubt that the spiritual needs of many weren't being met by Delaware's churches in general and the Church of England in particular. Indeed, the religious fires may have died down but some hot coals remained to be fanned by itinerant preachers of the future.

towns of New Castle and Philadelphia. In Kent and Sussex, the costliest acres were situated along navigable streams such as Duck Creek, the Broadkill, St. Jones, Nanticoke, and Indian rivers, which afforded a cheap means of transporting produce to distant urban trade centers.

At the beginning of the eighteenth century, tobacco was the chief cash crop in Kent and Sussex. But declining prices and the loss of soil fertility, caused by years of tobacco culture, forced Sussex farmers to turn to corn by mid-century. Both corn and wheat proved a profitable replacement for tobacco among Kent County planters, while in northern Delaware wheat had been the main cash crop almost from the beginning. In fact, the fine quality of New Castle County wheat of-

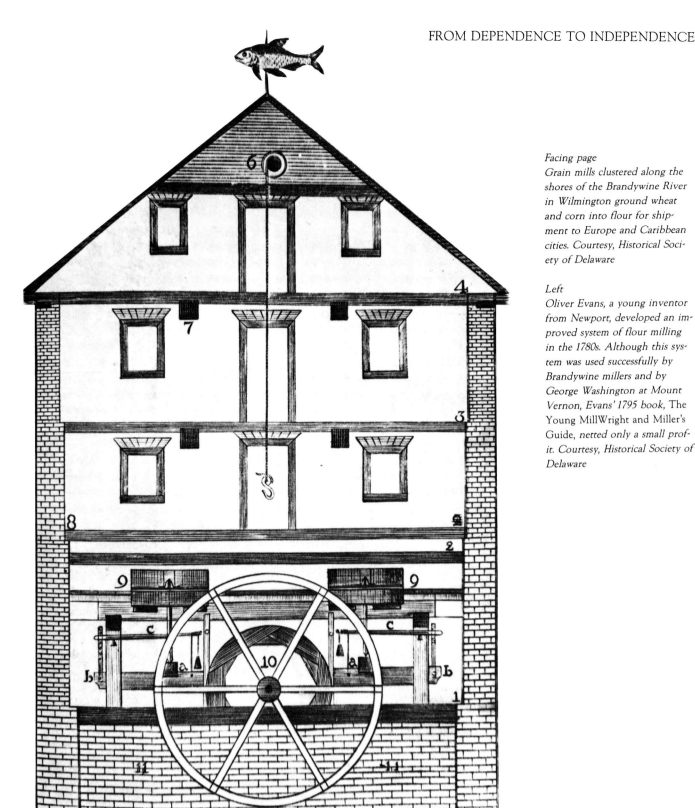

ten commanded a higher market price than wheat grown elsewhere.

Beside one or two cash crops, Delaware's farms also produced a large enough variety of vegetables, grains, fruits, and livestock to be virtually self-sufficient. Farm families ate the bounty of their fields and pasture land, and grew flax, sheared sheep, and treated animal hides so that they could manufacture their own clothes. In general, Delaware's farmers were most prosperous in New Castle County and least prosperous in Sussex.

The flourishing agricultural economy created a demand for mills to grind corn, wheat, and barley into flour. The first mills appeared in New Castle County during the Swedish period. By the mid-eighteenth century, they were scattered throughout all three counties, but the most important concentration was along the fast flowing lower Brandywine River. By 1770, for example, eight large, commercial, grain mills were clustered along a quarter mile stretch of the lower Brandywine.

Other economic activities included the tanning of hides and iron production, with one furnace located just south of Newark at Iron Hill and a second at Middleford in Sussex County. Rehoboth Bay was dredged for oysters, and the many streams leading into the Delaware were fished for herring and other species. Wooded lands, particularly in Sussex, produced boards and shingles that often yielded more income for their owners than did cultivated fields. A number of Delawareans also were artisans, especially in the area of a new but rapidly growing town on the Christina.

For decades the small Swedish hamlet built alongside Fort Christina showed little sign of economic vitality or population growth. In the 1730s, about a mile west of the somnolent Swedish settlement, a fledgling community called Willingtown began to rise from the farms and woodland that sloped down to the north bank of the Christina. This location proved ideal for mercantile activity because the Christina served as a commercial highway to and from the rich agricultural regions of western New Castle County and southeastern Pennsylvania. Farmers from the north and west shipped their grain down river to Willingtown where it was ground at the nearby Brandywine mills and shipped via the Christina to Philadelphia or to the West Indies. The farmers then purchased supplies from Willingtown merchants to take back home.

In 1739 Willingtown received its charter of incorporation and was renamed for Spencer Comptom, Earl of Wilmington, who was lord president of the King's Privy Council and perceived as an ally of the Penns in their struggle over proprietary rights with the Lords Baltimore. As Wilmington grew from about six hundred people in 1739 to more than twelve hundred by 1776, it surpassed New Castle as Delaware's largest community.

Despite the growth of Wilmington and the presence of New Castle, Lewes, and a few other towns, the vast majority of colonial Delawareans lived out lives dictated by eighteenth-century rural values. Such mores demanded, among other things, that considerable deference be shown to the gentry, the landed aristocracy. Because it was expected of them, Delaware's gentry quite naturally filled most local and colony-wide political positions. When a political office was hotly contested, it was because the gentry had split into two competing factions rather than because other elements of the population were using the political process to protest aristocratic domination. Obviously, in important decisions concerning Delaware's future—such as what, if any, ties should be maintained with Great Britain—the "middling and lower sorts" would look to such gentry as Caesar Rodney and John Dickinson for guidance.

Politically, the "Lower Counties" enjoyed considerable independence after separating from Pennsylvania in 1704. Delaware's colonial legislature, which met in the town of Newcastle, contained a single body of eighteen assemblymen, six from each county. These officials were elected by white males, twenty-one years of age or older, who owned fifty acres (at least twelve of which were cleared land) or possessed other property worth £40. Probably a majority of Delaware's adult white males met these suffrage requirements.

The Delaware assembly was a very powerful body. Unlike the legislature of Pennsylvania and most of the other thirteen colonies, its enactments were not reviewed

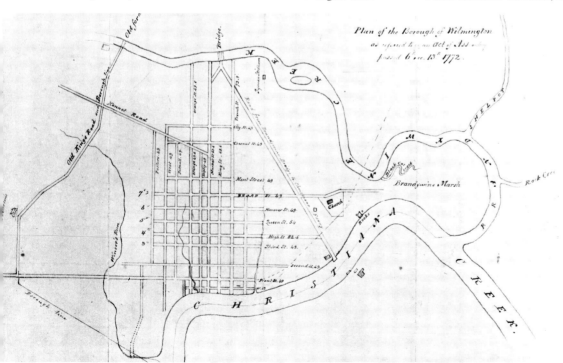

Wilmington's growth was owed to its location at the confluence of three rivers. The swiftly-flowing Brandywine could power dozens of mills; the slow-moving, highly navigable Christina formed a great water highway; and the wide Delaware (not shown) offered commercial and cultural ties to Philadelphia. Courtesy, Historical Society of Delaware

in Great Britain because of confusion over the Penns' proprietary governing rights and the relative obscurity of the "Lower Counties." Only the joint governor of Pennsylvania and the "Lower Counties" (appointed by the Penns) clearly had the power to veto legislation passed by Delaware's colonial assembly; and the governor was usually cooperative because Delaware's assembly annually voted funds for part of his salary. As a result, only Connecticut and Rhode Island enjoyed more self rule than the "Lower Counties" in the mid-eighteenth century.

The English ancestry of approximately two-thirds of Delaware's white population and the general veneration for English "liberties" caused many to value ties to the British Empire. To those who thought deeply about things political, it was self-evident that the powerful Delaware assembly represented part of the ongoing evolution of representative government which dated back to the Magna Carta.

Just as self-evident was the vulnerability of Delaware

When his term as Governor of Pennsylvania expired in 1785, John Dickinson returned to Wilmington and built the city's largest private house at the corner of Eighth and Market streets. Like other members of the gentry, he provided political and social leadership for the new state. Courtesy, Historical Society of Delaware

to attack by sea and the consequent need for the protective umbrella of the Empire. Pirates ransacked Lewes in 1698 and a French raiding party looted the town a few years later. In 1747 two plantations on Bombay Hook, about ten miles northeast of Dover, were attacked by either French or Spanish raiders. Delawareans recognized that only the might of the British fleet kept such incursions to a minimum.

Delaware also appreciated its tie to proprietary gov-

TO THE
Delaware Pilots.

WE took the Pleasure, some Days since, of kindly admonishing you *to do your Duty*; if perchance you should meet with the *(Tea,)* SHIP POLLY, CAPTAIN AYRES; a THREE DECKER which is hourly expected.

We have now to add, that Matters ripen fast here; and that *much is expected from those Lads who meet with the Tea Ship.*----There is some Talk of A HANDSOME REWARD FOR THE PILOT WHO GIVES THE FIRST GOOD ACCOUNT OF HER.----How that may be, we cannot *for certain* determine: But ALL agree, that TAR and FEATHERS will be his Portion, who pilots her into this Harbour. And we will answer for ourselves, that, whoever is committed to us, as an Offender against the Rights of *America*, will experience the utmost Exertion of our Abilities; as

THE COMMITTEE FOR TARRING AND FEATHERING.

P. S. We expect you will furnish yourselves with Copies of the foregoing and following Letter; which are printed for this Purpose, that the Pilot who meets with Captain *Ayres* may favor him with a Sight of them.

Committee of Taring and Feathering.

TO
Capt. AYRES,

Of the SHIP *POLLY*, on a Voyage from *London* to *Philadelphia.*

SIR,

WE are informed that you have, imprudently, taken Charge of a Quantity of Tea; which has been sent out by the *India* Company, *under the Auspices of the Ministry*, as a Trial of *American* Virtue and Resolution,

Now, as your Cargo, on your Arrival here, will most assuredly bring you into hot water; and as you are perhaps a Stranger *to these Parts*, we have concluded to advise you of the present Situation of Affairs in *Philadelphia*---that, taking Time by the Forelock, you may stop short in your dangerous Errand----secure your Ship against the Rafts of combustible Matter which may be set on Fire, and turned loose against her; and more than all this, that you may preserve your own Person, from the Pitch and Feathers that are prepared for you.

In the first Place, we must tell you, that the *Pennsylvanians* are, *to a Man*, passionately fond of Freedom; the Birthright of *Americans*; and at all Events are determined to enjoy it.

That they sincerely believe, no Power on the Face of the Earth has a Right to tax them without their Consent.

That in their Opinion, the Tea in your Custody is designed by the Ministry to enforce such a Tax, which they will undoubtedly oppose; and in so doing, give you every possible Obstruction.

We are nominated to a very disagreeable, but necessary Service.---- To our Care are committed all Offenders against the Rights of *America*; and hapless is he, whose evil Destiny has doomed him to suffer at our Hands.

You are sent out on a diabolical Service; and if you are so foolish and obstinate as to compleat your Voyage; by bringing your Ship to Anchor in this Port; you may run such a Gauntlet, as will induce you, in your last Moments, most heartily to curse those who have made you the Dupe of their Avarice and Ambition.

What think you Captain, of a Halter around your Neck----ten Gallons of liquid Tar decanted on your Pate----with the Feathers of a dozen wild Geese laid over that to enliven your Appearance?

Only think seriously of this----and fly to the Place from whence you came----fly without Hesitation---- without the Formality of a Protest----and above all, Captain *Ayres* let us advise you to fly without the wild Geese Feathers.

Your Friends *to serve*

Philadelphia, Nov. 27, 1773

THE COMMITTEE *as before subscribed*

A group of Philadelphia patriots calling itself "the committee for Tarring and Feathering" warned Delaware River pilots of the consequences of guiding a British tea ship to port. Following threats of a violent mass meeting, this vessel eventually turned away. Courtesy, Historical Society of Delaware

ernment. The colony's attachment to the Penns provided a necessary legal shield against threatening land claims by the Lords Baltimore, who insisted that parts of the "Lower Counties" belonged to Maryland and made land grants accordingly. No wonder Delaware, at mid-century, seemed quite content to continue as a proprietary colony within the British Empire.

The political contentment of 1750 was not long lasting, however. Twenty-five years later Thomas Rodney, a Kent County planter of English ancestry, laconically summarized an extraordinary change in attitude by writing to his brother Caesar, "Let America be free." Delaware heeded Thomas Rodney's cry and joined with the twelve other colonies in cutting its ties to what had seemed, only a quarter of a century before, a benevolent, protective Empire. Why?

Great Britain's victory in the French and Indian War (1754-1763) drove the French from North America and ended the threat of French sea incursions. Consequently, Delawareans had far less need for the British fleet's

protection. Moreover, the final settlement of the boundary dispute between Maryland and Delaware, just prior to the American Revolution, ended the necessity of Delaware's attachment to the proprietary government of the Penns.

Although the majority of white Delawareans considered themselves Englishmen, by 1775 they were also third and fourth generation Americans who, for the most part, had never seen the mother country. Quite naturally their allegiance to England and its institutions was less intense than that of their ancestors. Of course the Scotch-Irish, from the beginning, felt little loyalty to either the King or Parliament.

While Delawareans began to drift away from some of their British ties, connections with Philadelphia became increasingly important. In addition to serving as a great commercial market for the products of Delaware's fields, woods, and streams, Philadelphia was a magnet for those in search of an education. Caesar Rodney attended Latin school in that city, George Read and

Thomas McKean, a New Castle lawyer, was the first of Delaware's Revolutionary-era statesmen to favor American independence from England. When he voted "for" and George Read "against" the Declaration of Independence, McKean summoned the like-minded Caesar Rodney from Dover to break the tie. Courtesy, Historical Society of Delaware

John Dickinson read law there, and James Tilton studied medicine at the College of Philadelphia. The Philadelphia connection was further strengthened by the
large number of Delawareans who had relatives living
in the Quaker city.

Most of the news that reached Delaware concerning
the outside world was first filtered through Philadelphia in such a way that many Delawareans perceived
Great Britain's relations with her American colonies
from the Philadelphia perspective.

After the French and Indian War, Parliament decided
to assert its taxing authority over the American colonies with the Stamp Act (1765) and the Townshend
Acts (1767). Philadelphians resented the British government's actions, and their growing discontent was soon
shared by Delawareans.

Despite living on this side of the Atlantic, most Delawareans joined Philadelphians in regarding themselves
as British. Both saw Parliament's new tax programs,
adopted without the approval of their respective colonial legislatures, as an open violation of the traditional
rights of Englishmen. John Dickinson, who alternately
resided in Delaware or Philadelphia, best expressed this
shared concern by writing that the issue was "whether
Parliament can legally take money out of our pockets
without our consent."

Delaware's opposition to British "oppression" generally lacked the zeal that surfaced in many of the other
colonies. Nevertheless, like a tiny pilot fish swimming
in the wake of a great shark, little Delaware joined her
much larger neighbors as they inexorably moved together towards military confrontation with the British
Empire.

In 1765 Delaware sent Kent County landowner
Caesar Rodney and New Castle County attorney
Thomas McKean to the conference held in New York
to protest the Stamp Act. From 1767 to 1770, following
the passage of the Townshend Acts, Delaware merchants joined with those from other colonies in boy-
cotting English imports. In late 1773, even before the
British government turned its wrath on Boston and
closed the port because of the Boston Tea Party, Delaware's assembly created a committee of correspon-
dence to maintain contact with the other colonies
about this potentially dangerous situation. Then, in
1774, Delaware sent Rodney, McKean, and George
Read, another New Castle County attorney, to the
meeting of the First Continental Congress in Philadelphia.

After fighting broke out at Lexington and Concord
in the spring of 1775, the same three men were again
dispatched to Philadelphia for the Second Continental

Congress. There they supported the creation of a continental army but also followed the instructions of the Delaware assembly to seek reconciliation with Great Britain. Indeed, the desire for reconciliation was just one example of the moderation—tempered by the need to keep in step with its powerful neighbors—that characterized Delaware during most of the American Revolution.

On June 7, 1776, the Second Continental Congress accepted a motion from Virginia's Richard Henry Lee for independence, although debate and a final vote were postponed for a few weeks. A week later, Scotch-Irish Thomas McKean presented to the Delaware assembly a recommendation from Congress that all colonies officially suppress "every kind of authority under the crown" and thus place each individual colonial government "under the authority of the people." Delaware's assembly complied with the request on the following day, and the state has subsequently celebrated June 15 as its Separation Day from the British Empire.

The debate in Congress over a collective declaration of American independence began on July 1 without the presence of Caesar Rodney, one of Delaware's three delegates. Rodney had just returned to his home southeast of Dover after leading a militia expedition into Sussex County to nip in the bud a threatened Tory uprising. Back in Philadelphia, the peripatetic John Dickinson, now a delegate from Pennsylvania, spoke out strongly against independence because he feared the effects of a long war and felt that reconciliation with Great Britain was still possible. The vote on independence found the Delaware delegation deadlocked with George Read, an old and trusted friend of John Dickinson, voting against and Thomas McKean voting for independence.

The need for a united front against Great Britain was obvious. Since only nine of the thirteen former colonies cast an affirmative ballot, the delegates decided to put off a final vote until the next day, July 2, so that unanimity might be achieved.

On July 2 only the abstention of New York marred a unanimous vote for independence. South Carolina and Pennsylvania had fallen into line rather easily, but it took an all night ride by Caesar Rodney to end the deadlock in the Delaware delegation. Although some of the details are unclear, an urgent message from Thomas McKean in Philadelphia reached Rodney at his Jones Neck plantation, southeast of Dover, sometime on July 1. Forty-eight years old and suffering from facial cancer and asthma, Rodney ignored a thunderstorm and travelled through the night—it isn't clear whether he rode all the way on horseback or used a

A resident of both Delaware and Pennsylvania, John Dickinson became known as "the penman of the Revolution" for his fervent pamphlets against British colonial policies. Although he always hoped for a reconciliation with England, and, as a delegate from Pennsylvania, refused to sign the Declaration of Independence, he fought bravely for American freedom during the Revolutionary War. Courtesy, Historical Society of Delaware

horse-drawn carriage for part of the trip—to arrive in Philadelphia on the afternoon of July 2. Though tired, dusty, and covered with mud, Rodney was in time to break the deadlock in his own delegation and put Delaware on record as favoring independence. On July 4, the day the delegates formally adopted Jefferson's written explanation of their action, Caesar Rodney laconically wrote of his ride to his brother Thomas: " . . . I arrived in Congress (tho detained by thunder and rain) time enough to give my voice to the matter of independence."

An indigenous and initially rev-
olutionary religion, Methodism
perhaps gained its largest follow-
ing in Delaware, due to the tire-
less efforts of Francis Asbury,
shown here being ordained in
Lovely Lane Methodist Church,
Baltimore. Courtesy, North Car-
olina Department of Archives
and History

CHAPTER IV

REVOLUTIONS OF DIFFERENT KINDS

On a hot, humid July morning in 1805 Dr. Jacob Wolf of Lewes, a leading Sussex County Federalist, made ready to leave home for a political meeting in Georgetown. As he mounted his horse, the Lewes physician told his wife that he expected to be murdered by Democrats before the day was out.

Hours later in Georgetown, Dr. Wolf and a number of other Federalists gathered in the jury room on the second floor of the Sussex County Courthouse. While Dr. Wolf was being nominated to chair the meeting, "the most awful flash of lightning and such a peel of thunder as made the whole town tremble" struck the cupola and "slivered the front of the Court House." Dr. Wolf was killed instantly and eleven other Federalists were knocked to the floor and presumed dead, only to be revived "by bleeding and other means."

William Morgan, a devout Methodist who lived

nearby, rushed to the courthouse to find the "most awful scene I ever witnessed." Later, after contemplating
what he had seen, Morgan decided that "it was a just
judgment from heaven." The victims of the lightning
bolt deserved Divine retribution, according to Morgan,
because they had abandoned more godly pursuits for
the excitement and rewards of the political arena where
such sinful practices as impugning the character and
motives of opponents were commonplace. Ironically,
both the increased interest and emotional commitment
by some Delawareans to political parties, and the con-
trasting desire of other Delawareans to avoid such involvement on religious grounds, can be traced directly
or indirectly to the American Revolution and to the
resulting destruction of English ties and institutions.

Delaware's declaration of independence from the
British Empire created an immediate need for a state
constitution. In the late summer of 1776, Delawareans
elected delegates to a state constitutional convention
which began meeting in New Castle on August 27 and
completed its work within a month. The convention
created a bicameral assembly and gave it most of the
governing power at the expense of the chief executive,
who was called the President of Delaware. It was in this
first constitution that the title "the Delaware State" was
officially adopted. (Delaware's second state constitution,
which went into effect in 1792, changed the titles of
president to governor and "the Delaware State" to "the
State of Delaware.")

During the Revolutionary War, the number of Delawareans who remained loyal to the British crown was
considerable. John Adams wrote in 1780 that more
Tories "in proportion" resided in Delaware than in any
other state. Often rumors from downstate spoke of
armed groups of Loyalists about to start an insurrec-
tion. But if there was any substance to the rumors, a
quick foray by Delaware militia generally caused the
Tories to disband without firing a shot.

Loyalists attracted the greatest support in Kent and
Sussex where most of the white population was of English descent. Although such wealthy landowners as
Thomas Robinson of Sussex led the downstate Tories,
they came from all classes of white society. Poor farmers in Sussex, for example, opposed independence because they resented the new state government's taxes,
recruitment laws, and ordered seizure of their weapons.
But despite opposition to independence, the tendency
of Delaware's Loyalists to fade away at the prospect of

*William Morgan, shown here at
age 67, was a Sussex County
farmer and physician whose autobiography chronicled Delaware
life before the Civil War. His di-
ary described political rallies,
camp meetings, agricultural
trends, and the impact of Methodism on everyday existence in
Sussex County. Courtesy, Historical Society of Delaware*

a military clash with rebel forces demonstrated that
most were, at best, only lukewarm Tories.

Perhaps the harsh nature of some of the punish-
ments decreed against insurrectionists caused many
Loyalists to have second thoughts about participating
in uprisings. Eight Tories in Sussex, for instance, were
sentenced to be hung "but not till . . . dead," at which
point their bowels were to be "taken out" and burned
in front of them. Finally, the unfortunate Tories were
to have their heads cut off and their bodies quartered.
But in a gesture that more accurately represented
Delaware's treatment of its Loyalists than such draconic
decrees, the assembly pardoned all eight. The willingness of rebels and Tories to treat each other with more
restraint than found in most of the other colonies
probably reflected the lack of strong commitment by
most Delawareans to either side. Indeed, during the
Revolutionary years most Delawareans simply went
about the business of making a living and hoping for
the best.

Delaware's comparative tranquility was abruptly shattered in early September of 1777 by the invasion of British regulars on their way from Cecil County, Maryland to the rebel capital of Philadelphia. General William Howe, the British commander in New York City, had decided to attack Philadelphia but felt that the direct overland passage through New Jersey or the water route up the Delaware Bay and River were too heavily fortified to augur military success. Instead, he chose to sail around Cape Charles and up the Chesapeake to land his 17,000 soldiers on the Elk Neck Peninsula in Cecil County, Maryland.

After debarking, Howe's army marched eastward into New Castle County where it was confronted by units of rebel light infantry. On September 3, as the British moved north along the road from Glasgow to Newark, the heavily outnumbered Americans held their ground just east of Iron Hill. Near Cooch's Bridge the two sides engaged in a brief fire fight in which forty rebels and an unknown number of British were killed or wounded.

Marching from Head of Elk in Maryland toward Philadelphia, Lord Howe's army encountered a small band of colonial troops at Cooch's Bridge near Newark on September 3, 1777. After skirmishing for several hours with heavy casualties, the Americans withdrew. Lord Cornwallis, the expedition commander, made his headquarters here in the home of Thomas Cooch, a miller. Courtesy, Historical Society of Delaware

The Americans then slipped away to join George Washington's 11,000 soldiers camped at Wilmington, astride the usual route to Philadelphia.

After resting his forces for a few days, Howe surprised the Americans by marching north from Newark to Pennsylvania. Intent on halting the British advance

By His EXCELLENCY

CÆSAR RODNEY, Eſq;

Preſident, Captain-General and Commander in Chief of the

DELAWARE STATE,

A

PROCLAMATION.

WHEREAS by an Act of the GENERAL ASSEMBLY of the ſaid State, intitled, "An Act to prohibit the Exportation of Proviſion from this State beyond "the Seas, for a limited Time," the Exportation of Wheat, Flour or other Proviſions is prohibited until the firſt Day of *September* next, unleſs the ſame Act be ſuſpended, or revoked as is therein mentioned. AND WHEREAS it hath been recommended by CONGRESS to permit the Exportation of ſuch Flour and Grain as have been, or may be purchaſed, within this State, under the Direction of the Board-of-War of the State of *Maſſachuſett's-Bay*, for the Uſe of the Inhabitants thereof; I DO THEREFORE, by and with the Advice of the Privy-Council, and in Virtue of the Powers and Authorities veſted in me by the ſaid recited Act, hereby ſuſpend the Operation of the ſame, ſo far as to permit the Exportation of ſuch Flour and Grain as have been, or may be purchaſed as aforeſaid, for the Uſe of the Inhabitants of the State of *Maſſachuſett's-Bay*: Whereof all Perſons concerned are to take Notice, and govern themſelves accordingly.

Given under my Hand and the Great-Seal of the State, at Dover, *the third Day of* May, *in the Year of our Lord One Thouſand Seven Hundred and Seventy-nine.*

CÆSAR RODNEY.

By his Excellency's Command,

JAMES BOOTH, *Secretary.*

WILMINGTON, PRINTED BY JAMES ADAMS.

Left
Supplies of food and grain were low as a result of the British occupation of Delaware from 1777 to 1778. Caesar Rodney, president of the Delaware State, restricted the exportation of wheat and flour as a means of preserving rations. Courtesy, Historical Society of Delaware

Facing page
Fearing that New Castle might come under attack by the British during their march to Philadelphia, Delaware legislators moved the capital from New Castle to Dover in 1777. This photo is of the state capital as it looked in the early twentieth century. Courtesy, Delaware State Archives

on Philadelphia, an alarmed Washington calculated that Howe intended to cross the Brandywine River north of the Delaware line, in the vicinity of Chadds Ford. Washington rushed his forces to the Chadds Ford area only to have Howe unexpectedly cross the river just to the north of the newly established rebel positions. The resulting Battle of the Brandywine ended with the outflanked Americans in retreat and the roads to Philadelphia and Wilmington wide open to Howe's conquering army.

While the main British army pushed on to Philadelphia, a smaller force was dispatched to the Wilmington area where it captured John McKinly, the president of Delaware. After occupying Wilmington for approximately one month, the British marched northeast to join up with Howe's main force in Philadelphia. The state was now free of a conquering army, but His Majesty's fleet still controlled the lower Delaware River and the Delaware Bay, and that caused considerable anxiety.

In June 1778, the British finally evacuated Philadelphia and, except for sporadic forays by small boats, their fleet withdrew from the Delaware River and Bay. Despite occasional raids by small British or Loyalist bands against individual farms along Delaware's coast and creeks, the military phase of the American Revolution had ended in Delaware by the early summer of 1778.

Elsewhere fighting continued and some Delawareans—the number is unclear—volunteered for the Delaware regiment or other units of the Continental Army. The soldiers of the Delaware regiment acquitted themselves so well in the Carolina campaigns that, according to tradition, they were called "Blue Hens Chickens" after some highly prized fighting cocks.

The British presence in and around Delaware during part of 1777 and 1778 interfered with voting procedures. Because of the brief occupation and the subsequent military threats to the town of New Castle by the British fleet, New Castle County's voting site for the fall elections was moved to Newark. But even before the ominous presence of British guns, strong political pressure from Kent and Sussex counties led to the decision to move the state capital from the town of New Castle. From 1777 to 1780 the Delaware assembly met at different sites around the state before finally settling, in 1781, on Dover as its permanent home.

Besides having found a permanent capital, Delaware was ahead of the national government in one other respect: it had a constitution. To remedy this shortcoming, the Second Continental Congress drew up the Articles of Confederation in 1777 and sent them to each of the thirteen states for ratification. The Articles would go into effect only after the approval of every state. Because it was unhappy about the claims of some of the larger states to land west of the Appalachians, Delaware joined Maryland and New Jersey in refusing ratification. The three small states made no claims on the territory beyond the Appalachians and, quite naturally, felt that the unsettled sections of the West should belong to the entire nation. Finally, after making their point, Delaware and New Jersey ratified in 1779. Maryland lent its approval two years later, establishing the Articles as our first written national constitution. Evidently some of the other states got the message and, in subsequent years, surrendered their western land claims to the national government.

The Articles of Confederation provided the United States with a weak central government, unable to either raise money by taxation or control international and interstate commerce. Individual states were even free to impose tariffs on all goods that crossed their boundaries.

Because much of Delaware's import trade with other states and foreign nations was unloaded at the port of Philadelphia, a considerable segment of Delaware's commerce was subject to the taxing whims of the Pennsylvania legislature. Moreover, because the national government could not levy direct taxes, it had to issue increasing amounts of paper money to meet its obligations. The almost worthless national tender produced a disastrous ripple effect, causing a sharp decline in the value of Delaware's state currency.

The chaotic currency situation and growing concern over Pennsylvania's ability to tax—and therefore control—so much of its commerce compelled Delaware to join with other states in supporting amendments to the Articles. But because amendments needed the unanimous approval of all the states, no amendment was ever adopted.

In 1786 Virginia requested that all of the states send delegates to Annapolis, Maryland to address the regulation of interstate commerce. Only Delaware and four other states sent representatives, but their meeting led

New Castle is one of the oldest towns in Delaware. It was first settled by the Swedes in the 1650s and later ruled by the Dutch and English. As the state's colonial capital and an important port, New Castle flourished during the eighteenth century. Courtesy, Historical Society of Delaware

to an agreement that a stronger national government was desirable. The Annapolis convention called for delegates from all of the states to meet in Philadelphia in 1787 to explore ways of expanding the national government's role.

The Constitutional Convention, as it has been subsequently called, met in May and continued its proceedings through the hot, sweltering Philadelphia summer of 1787. Only Rhode Island was absent as the delegates quickly decided to scrap the Articles of Confederation and write another constitution. Next, the delegates debated the nature and shape of the new central government. Predictably, Virginia proposed a legislature in which each state was represented according to population.

Delaware's delegation of John Dickinson—who had moved back to Delaware in 1785—George Read, Richard Bassett, Gunning Bedford, Jr., and Jacob Broom had been instructed to be wary of just such a move and to insist that Delaware's representation in the new government be equal to that of the larger states. George Read pointed out to the other delegations that ignoring the idea of equal representation might cause his state to leave the convention. Dickinson bluntly told James Madison of Virginia that Delaware "would sooner submit to a foreign power than be . . . under the domination of the large states."

Due, in part, to Delaware's stubborn insistence on the rights of the small states, the "Great Compromise" was reached. It followed Virginia's plan of proportional representation in the House of Representatives while upholding in the Senate the demands of Delaware and the other small states for equal representation. Satisfied with the Great Compromise, the Delaware delegation subsequently supported almost every measure adopted by the Constitutional Convention to strengthen the national government.

The newly drafted U.S. Constitution was to go into effect after ratification by special conventions in two-

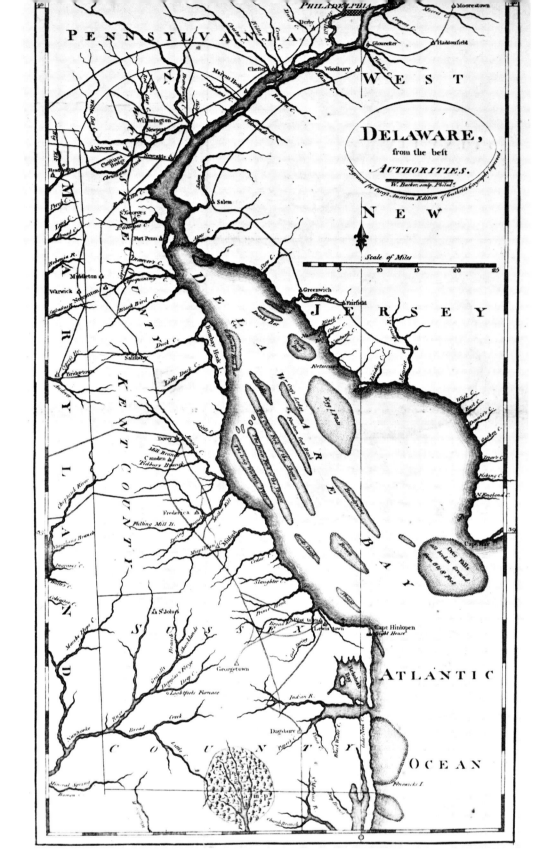

thirds (nine) of the states. Considerable political disagreement existed in Delaware about a number of issues, and elections were hotly contested. But on the need to ratify the new national constitution, there was an amazing unanimity. Meeting in Dover on Monday, December 3, 1787, the delegates elected to Delaware's special convention spent only four days in discussion before unanimously approving the new U.S. Constitution on December 7. This speedy response distinguished Delaware as the first state to ratify the U.S. Constitution. Subsequently, it has been called the

"First State" and December 7 is marked by the annual Delaware Day celebration.

Resolution of major political concerns did not put an end to revolution, however. Less than five months after Washington led his forces north out of Delaware to face the British at the Battle of the Brandywine, a second rebel on horseback rode into the First State. He stood a slender 5 feet 9 inches with piercing blue eyes, a prominent forehead, and long, blond hair. His name was Francis Asbury and he seemed to possess inexhaustible energy and a single-mindedness that gave

Above
The Wilmington Whaling Company was a short-lived business venture. One of their ships, the Lucy Ann, *is pictured here trying to capture a harpooned whale. The crew of one rowboat is capsized while another comes to their aid. Courtesy, Historical Society of Delaware*

Right
John Martin, a sailor on board the whaleship Lucy Ann, *kept a journal of a two-year voyage to South America. He recorded the ship's bearings, weather conditions, and the crew's attempts to bring in whales. Courtesy, Historical Society of Delaware*

Facing page
Robert E. Goodier depicts eight state convention delegates pondering the contents of the U.S. Constitution. Assembled at Battell's Tavern on December 7, 1787, Delaware delegates unanimously voted for ratification, reaching this decision before the twelve other states. Hence, Delaware became the "First State." The delegates, from left, are: Alan McLane, Gunning Bedford, James Latimer, Richard Bassett, Nicholas Ridgely and Gunning Bedford, Sr. (near fireplace), and James Sikes and Kensey Johns (in foreground). Courtesy, Bank of Delaware

Left
Joseph Newlin, a Wilmington cabinetmaker, built this high-style desk and bookcase during the late eighteenth century. He may have copied the design from more elaborate examples of desks built by Philadelphia cabinetmakers. Many Delaware artisans were trained in Philadelphia, and followed designs popular in that city. Courtesy, Historical Society of Delaware

Facing page
Delaware's State House is a Georgian-style brick structure facing The Green in Dover. Erected about 1792 to hold a court room, legislative chambers, and Kent County offices, it remains the second oldest government building in continuous use in the United States. Courtesy, Delaware State Archives

Right
Colonel John Haslet's regiment joined the fight for American independence in 1776. The regiment distinguished itself for bravery and came to be known as the "Blue Hens Chickens" after game hens known for their fighting abilities. The regiment's motto, later adopted by the state of Delaware, was "liberty and independence." Courtesy, Historical Society of Delaware

When President Washington
toured the country in 1791, he
stopped in Wilmington to thank
Joseph Tatnall for his Revolutionary War support. Tatnall
had defied British military orders to shut down his mill, and
at great personal risk, continued
to grind flour—food for Washington's armies. Courtesy, Bank
of Delaware

Left
Immanuel Episcopal Church, a New Castle landmark, overlooks the town's green. Founded in 1689, it was the first Anglican parish in the colony of Delaware. The church building, erected in 1703, was severely damaged by a fire in 1980, but has been restored. Courtesy, Historical Society of Delaware

Below
Old Swedes Church, built in 1698, has served the spiritual needs of Wilmington under four national flags—Swedish, Dutch, English, and the United States. Courtesy, Historical Society of Delaware

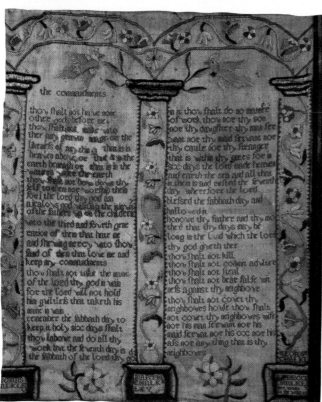

Left
Rebecca Chalkley worked this sampler of Bible verses in 1734 as a combined theological and needlework lesson. Her father, Reverend Thomas Chalkley, was an itinerant Quaker preacher who landed in Delaware in 1731 when his ship was wrecked on Reedy Island. Courtesy, Historical Society of Delaware

New Castle 3 M.

little thought to anything else but the spread of Methodism. While the American Revolution offered Delawareans freedom from the fetters of the British Empire, Asbury's Methodist revolution promised them liberation from the twin bonds of sin and death.

The first Methodist to actually appear in Delaware was Captain Thomas Webb, a retired British army officer who preached in New Castle County in 1769. Other Methodist itinerants pushed further south in subsequent years, until by 1780 almost all of Delaware had been exposed to the new religious message.

Methodist preachers were unordained laymen who felt moved by the Holy Spirit to saddle up their horses and travel through the countryside, spreading a faith far more evangelical than those found in contemporary houses of worship. Under the direction of Francis Asbury, they particularly criticized the Anglican Church's lack of religious fire, but perceived themselves as merely a reform movement within the Church of England. In fact, Methodist itinerants were careful that their preaching time not conflict with Anglican services, and they encouraged their audiences to attend those services and receive the sacraments from Anglican clergy.

Methodist support of the colonial Anglican Church ended with the collapse of the latter during the American Revolution. Because American rebels viewed the Church of England as just one more institutional example of British imperialism, they suspected Anglican clergy of being Loyalists and often badgered them into returning to Great Britain. Although Delaware seemed less hostile than some states, by 1780 only three Anglican priests remained in the state and at least one, Sydenham Thorne of Milford, was seriously restricted in his clerical duties by the government in Dover. Indeed, four years later a frustrated layman lamented, probably with some exaggeration, that in the entire Delmarva Peninsula there were but two Anglican clergymen, "and one of these is a drunkard."

Although the American Protestant Episcopal Church emerged from the ashes of the colonial Anglican Church, it lacked a clergy either numerous or energetic enough to meet the spiritual needs of most citizens of the First State. Increasingly, a large number of Delawareans and other Americans turned to the unordained Methodist itinerants, demanding that they administer the sacraments. From Britain John Wesley, the Anglican priest who founded Methodism, opposed such an initiative because it would surely cut the umbilical cord that bound the new movement to the Church of England. Wesley's American lieutenant,

Francis Asbury, agreed with his mentor.

From February 1778 to April 1780, Asbury lived in the friendly boundaries of Delaware, primarily at Judge Thomas White's home near Whiteleysburg, southwest of Dover. He used the house as a headquarters to evangelize Delaware and to fight against those Methodists who wished to sever the Anglican connection. However, the colonial Anglican Church's obvious demise and increasing pressure from American laymen to receive the sacraments caused Wesley to take further action. He requested that the Anglican bishop of London ordain American-bound Methodist missionaries. His request was refused. Seeing no other choice, Wesley ordained two of his Methodist preachers, Thomas Veasey and Richard Whatcoat, as elders. Anglican cleric Thomas Coke, who was also a Methodist preacher, became superintendent with the power to ordain. The three missionaries sailed for New York in the fall of 1784 with instructions from Wesley to set up an independent Methodist Church in America.

After debarking, the group split up. Coke and Whatcoat stayed together, making their way into the heart of Delaware. On Sunday morning, November 14, they arrived at Barratt's Chapel, approximately ten miles southeast of Dover, and Coke began to preach. At the end of his sermon, he tells us, "a plain robust man came up to me in the pulpit and kissed me. I thought it could be no other than Mr. Asbury, and I was not deceived." Then, for the historic first time, an ordained Methodist preacher, Richard Whatcoat, joined Thomas Coke in administering bread and wine to about five or six hundred Delawareans—with the approval of Wesley. This symbolic act cut the ties with the colonial Anglican Church and marked Barratt's Chapel as the Independence Hall of American Methodism.

Although the new religion quickly spread into every state, its greatest success during the early years of the Republic was in Delaware and in the rest of the Delmarva Peninsula. In 1778 Francis Asbury expressed the hope that Delaware would "become the Garden of the Lord," and by the end of the American Revolution, Methodists outnumbered the combined totals of all of the state's other faiths. So rapid was the growth of Methodism that in 1808 a euphoric Asbury noted: "In Delaware the millenium has certainly begun."

Methodism was most attractive to residents of Kent and Sussex where it was viewed by the heavily Anglo-Saxon population as the new "English" faith which would fill the void created by the collapse of Anglicanism. In 1810 one out of five adults in the lower two counties was a Methodist, which was extraordinary in view of the low percentage of Americans who officially belonged to any church during this period. By contrast, Scotch-Irish New Castle County had little use for "English" institutions of any nature and remained strongly Presbyterian. It was only after the migration of many Delawareans from Kent and Sussex to Wilmington in the mid-nineteenth century that Methodists became numerous in New Castle County.

The impact of Methodism on the residents of central and southern Delaware was greater than the American Revolution. On becoming Methodists, most slave holders freed their servants; some even joined abolitionist

Barratt's Chapel, a small brick structure in Kent County, Delaware, is the Independence Hall of American Methodism. It was there that Francis Asbury and Thomas Coke met to plan the organization of the Methodist Episcopal Church. Courtesy, Historical Society of Delaware

societies. Led by Richard Bassett, a Dover Methodist and a future governor of Delaware, the state legislature in 1787 made illegal the sale of Delaware slaves beyond the state's boundaries and, in 1803, came very close to outlawing the institution of bondage in Delaware. The Methodist message also encouraged abstinence and hard work. It condemned as self-indulgent, and therefore sinful, such practices as gambling, fox hunting, horse racing, card playing, dancing, unnecessary conversation, "revelings", and all other activity that distracted men and women from the serious business of serving God.

To maintain their Christian purity, Delaware's Methodists often remained aloof from the contaminating world of politics. As William Morgan pointed out after the tragedy in Georgetown's courthouse, political activity could cause men to abandon some of their Methodist principles. And yet other Methodists did turn out to vote and some, such as Richard Bassett, even ran for office, usually on the Federalist ticket.

Elections in Delaware during the colonial era were often contested by loosely organized factions that pitted rival ethnic and religious groups against each other. Independence from Great Britain and the subsequent adoption of the United States Constitution dramatically increased the number and importance of government officials to be directly or indirectly elected. Thanks to the Delaware Constitution of 1792, the property qualification for suffrage was removed, giving all white males over twenty-one who paid taxes the right to vote.

With considerably more at stake than in colonial times, two well organized political parties—the Federalists and the Democratic-Republicans—appeared in Delaware and across most of the rest of the nation during the 1790s to contest state and national elections. In general, the Federalist Party appealed to the conservative-leaning, downstate Delawareans of English ancestry. The Democratic-Republicans, on the other hand, were usually supported by the more radical, Scotch-Irish Presbyterians residing in New Castle County. Questions that divided the two parties tended to focus on national issues: How much power did the Constitution give to the U.S. government? In what manner should the nation react to the French Revolution and to France's arch foe, Great Britain?

Generally speaking, Delaware's Federalists hewed closely to their national party line, favoring a strong central government, restrictions on the constitutional rights of those sympathizing with the French Revolution, and friendly relations with Great Britain. But in other matters Delaware's Federalists demonstrated a greater ability than Federalists elsewhere to bend with the times and to adopt some of the democratic practices introduced by their Democratic-Republican opponents.

Initially, Delaware's Federalists continued political practices inherited from colonial times, when a few gentry dictated who would run on the party ticket and when all voters were required to travel to their respective county seats to cast a ballot in county and state elections. But as one Democratic-Republican asked: Didn't the former practice assure that political "offices run in the blood of families and descend from father to son?" Moreover, wasn't the latter practice also undemocratic because it restricted voter turnout? Sensing the necessity of change in order to maintain the support of downstate yeoman farmers, Delaware's Federalists switched to the Democratic-Republican practice of a state nominating convention. In 1811 they also joined with their political opponents to enact legislation which set up polling places in each hundred (subdivisions of Delaware's counties).

During the late eighteenth and early nineteenth century, the Federalist Party won most statewide elections. The few Democratic-Republican victories resulted from a strategy of running a downstate candidate who would attract some normally Federalist votes to augment predictable support from New Castle County. David Hall and Joseph Haslet of Sussex, for example, were two Democratic-Republicans elected by this strategy to the governorship in 1801 and in 1810, respectively.

When the United States declared war on Great Britain in 1812, Delaware's Federalist Party faced a particular challenge. Its traditional pro-British stance was well known. Moreover, the national Federalist leadership, now concentrated in New England, made no bones about opposition to the war and in subsequent years, would even talk of secession. Delaware's Federalists also initially resisted what they called "Mr. Madison's war." But unlike their New England brethren, they strongly supported the war effort once hostilities broke out, thus escaping the charge of disloyalty. In fact, at the end of the War of 1812, President Madison chose leading Delaware Federalist and U.S. Senator James A. Bayard as one of the American peace negotiators.

During the war some Delawareans made a name for themselves. Thomas Macdonough directed the key American naval victory on Lake Champlain, while Dr. James Tilton was appointed surgeon general of the U.S. Army. Very little actual fighting occurred on Delaware soil but the presence of English warships in nearby waters, and the constant threat of British landing parties, kept residents in a state of anxiety. Of particular

Above
Commodore Thomas Macdonough, a Delaware native, gained fame as a naval hero when he led the American fleet to victory over the British in Lake Champlain during the War of 1812. Courtesy, Historical Society of Delaware

Right
In April 1813, the village of Lewes was bombarded by British warships demanding provisions. The townspeople held firm, and the English finally gave up their attempt. The cannons used in defense of Lewes remained in place when this photograph was taken sometime during the 1890s. Courtesy, Historical Society of Delaware

concern were British raids in Cecil County, Maryland in 1813, which brought enemy forces within sixteen miles of the town of New Castle.

The only military event to have taken place in Delaware, however, was the British attack on Lewes. In early 1813 a British squadron appeared at the mouth of the Delaware Bay and bottled up regional shipping. The British commander threatened to destroy Lewes that April if its townspeople didn't supply his ships with provisions. Under the command of native son Colonel Samuel B. Davis, the small Delaware town refused and three British vessels began a twenty-two-hour bombardment. Seeing that the shelling was ineffective, the British experienced further frustration when a landing party of marines was driven off by militia. The British fleet then gave up the attack, leaving the townsmen to survey the results of the bombardment. A few houses were slightly damaged and a few domestic animals had been hit, giving rise to a bit of Lewes doggerel: "The Commodore and all his men, shot a dog and killed a hen."

The Nanticoke River linked Sea-
ford with the Chesapeake Bay.
During the nineteenth century,
schooners carried oysters to this
town for packing and shipping.
Courtesy, Historical Society of
Delaware

CHAPTER V

DELAWARE IN THE NINETEENTH CENTURY

igh on a hill to the west of Wilmington stood the blue granite mansion and farm of Dr. James Tilton, former surgeon general of the United States Army. It was Christmas, 1815, but inside his home the tall, spare, bachelor of seventy-one could be excused for not getting into the festive spirit of the season. Less than three weeks earlier the discovery of a large tumor had led to the amputation of one of his legs.

Confined to his home, Tilton followed from his window the courses of the Brandywine and Christina rivers as they twisted their way to Union just to the east of Wilmington. What a contrast they were and how they complemented each other and the town. The fast flowing Brandywine was ideal for mill sites. Only a decade earlier Tilton had written that the grain mills along the Brandywine, just below the bridge connecting Wilmington with the road to Philadelphia, "were the largest and most perfect {for the} manufacture of flour within a like space of ground in the world." By contrast, the meandering Christina proved unsuitable for mill sites but ideal as a highway for the river traffic which connected Wilmington with the rest of the Delaware Valley and ports beyond. Between the two rivers lay a growing commercial center of approximately 5,000 inhabitants. And yet, despite Wilmington's obvious vitality, the panorama before Dr. Tilton remained fundamentally bucolic. Indeed, most of the mills on the Brandywine, most of the river traffic on the Christina, and much of the commercial activity in Wilmington were tied to the agricultural economy of the surrounding area.

Dr. Tilton died in 1822, too soon to observe from his window the remarkable changes about to occur between the valleys of the Brandywine and the Christina. Perhaps that was for the best because Dr. Tilton believed in the virtues of the agrarian way of life which had characterized Delaware's past. The rapid population growth and industrialization of the Wilmington

Above
Dr. James Tilton, surgeon, abolitionist, and agriculturalist, witnessed many political and economic changes in his native state. He was born during the colonial era, watched Delaware achieve statehood, but died before Wilmington became a manufacturing center. Courtesy, Historical Society of Delaware

Right
The Chesapeake and Delaware Canal became a national waterway in 1919, when purchased by the federal government. Besides being deepened and enlarged, the canal subsequently underwent another major change: its locks were removed to facilitate transoceanic shipping. Courtesy, Delaware State Archives

area during the mid- and late-nineteenth century would have been very difficult to accept.

In 1810 only one of fifteen Delawareans lived in Wilmington; ninety years later it was six of fifteen. By 1900 Wilmington's population had grown to more than 76,000 and had dramatically altered Delaware's traditional population pattern. In 1810 New Castle County had been slightly larger than Kent, but slightly smaller than Sussex. Thanks to Wilmington's remarkable growth, by the turn of the century New Castle County's population was approximately 35,000 larger than the combined total of Kent and Sussex. The key to this extraordinary demographic change was concentrated industrial development along the Christina and, to a lesser extent, the Brandywine.

During the early nineteenth century, the growth and prosperity of an American city was largely dependent on the size and nature of its hinterland. The larger and more bountiful the geographic area serviced by the city, the greater the demand for urban businesses to market the products of the countryside and to provide commercial services and consumer goods for residents of the hinterland.

Philadelphia recognized the importance of expanding its own hinterland—even if it was at the expense of nearby cities—and commenced building canals and railroads into regions economically tied to Wilmington,

Baltimore, and other nearby urban centers. One example was the Chesapeake and Delaware Canal, completed in 1829 and primarily financed by Philadelphia's business community. Crossing the Delmarva Peninsula approximately fifteen miles south of Wilmington, the canal diverted much of the commerce of the Susquehanna Valley from Baltimore to the Quaker City. Although it reduced Baltimore's hinterland, the Chesapeake and Delaware Canal had little impact on Wilmington.

A few years later it was Wilmington's turn to lose much of its hinterland to Philadelphia. The fertile grain lands of southeastern Pennsylvania, which had been economically tied to Wilmington, became part of Philadelphia's economic empire with the completion of a railroad line from the Quaker City to Columbia on the lower Susquehanna in the early 1830s. Toward the end of the decade, the newly constructed Philadelphia, Wilmington and Baltimore Railroad further diminished Wilmington's commercial hinterland and, by 1840, not only New Castle County but most of the rest of Delaware lay under the commercial domination of the Quaker City.

But history is full of ironies. The same transportation innovations that allowed Philadelphia to curtail Wilmington's future as a trading and commercial center, paradoxically made possible the latter's remarkable development as an industrial city. By the mid-nineteenth century a network of railroads and canals was bringing large supplies of coal and iron to Philadelphia which,

The Wilmington and Western Railroad first chugged through the hilly terrain of northern New Castle County in the 1870s. Company directors, local farmers, and industrialists hoped to connect Wilmington to new western markets, but the line only expanded twenty miles to nearby Landenberg, Pennsylvania. Courtesy, Historical Society of Delaware

in turn, could be easily transported to Wilmington via rail and barge connections. In addition to the availability of coal and iron, Wilmington already possessed a skilled work force that had built and serviced the Brandywine mills, plus considerable venture capital gained through mill profits and the shipping operations of earlier years. All three of these factors combined to transform the city's economic base. According to historian Carol Hoffecker, so rapid was the industrializing process that "in the thirty years following 1840, Wilmington became the first city in the United States in the manufacture of railroad cars and iron ships."

Most of Wilmington's factories were built on the city's east and south sides, along the narrow corridor of land between the Philadelphia, Wilmington and Balti-

more Railroad and the north bank of the Christina River (see map of Delaware). Besides the availability of transportation facilities, this area attracted manufacturers because the decline in Wilmington's maritime commerce kept real estate prices along the river at reasonable levels.

The once clean air of the lower Christina Valley was now smudged by the plumes of black smoke belching from the factories of railroad equipment producers and iron shipbuilders such as Harlan and Hollingsworth, Pusey and Jones, the Lobdell Car Wheel Company, and Jackson and Sharp. Along the Brandywine a secondary industrial concentration of paper, cotton, and gunpowder mills poured pollutants into the river.

But fouling the air and water seemed a small price to

pay for the new jobs created and the new fortunes amassed. By 1853 railroad car manufacturing employed 675 workers. As 1880 approached, a thousand men labored at Jackson and Sharp's railroad car plant alone and approximately 45 percent of Wilmington's employed residents worked in factories. Employment possibilities in new and expanding plants caused the local population to register enormous gains as shown in the chart on page 126.

Because of rapid industrialization, Wilmington took on many of the social characteristics of a typical American factory town. Recalling his boyhood as a business executive's son during the 1890s, Henry S. Canby remembered the city as a very class conscious society. "There were Negroes, and the working people, the plain people and us."

In the 1700s Wilmington's "Negroes" lived in scattered clusters on the least valuable land, a pattern that continued into the nineteenth century. Although a few black residents owned shops or served as ship's carpenters, trade union discrimination during the nineteenth century seriously diminished opportunities for blacks to become skilled workers.

By the late 1800s, blacks represented between 10 and 15 percent of Wilmington's population. Although a very modest figure by modern urban standards, their presence created tensions that erupted in a race riot in 1880, when seventeen whites and six blacks were injured by flying stones and gunfire. Wilmington's white politicians often took advantage of racial tensions by launching verbal attacks on blacks as a means of diverting attention from controversial local issues.

Henry Canby's "working people" were Wilmington's blue-collar labor force. They and their families lived on the city's crowded east side near the factories and shops where they regularly put in sixty-hour weeks. Their numbers were constantly augmented during the mid- and late-nineteenth century by a steady influx of farm boys from Delaware and nearby Pennsylvania and Maryland, as well as immigrants from Ireland, Germany, and later, southern and eastern Europe. Although 19 percent of Wilmington's population was foreign born by 1860, the immigrant population never reached the proportions found in most other northern American cities. As a result, friction between European immigrant and native born was less in Wilmington than in other urban centers.

Canby's "plain people" represented the city's lower middle class, including clerks, most of the other white-collar business and industrial employees, and owners of small establishments such as grocery and clothing stores. They lived in identical brick houses which covered the lower slopes of Wilmington's hills, overlooking the congested tenements of the factory workers.

Above
Moving pictures and vaudeville shows at theaters like Wilmington's Majestic delighted thousands of city dwellers. Courtesy, Historical Society of Delaware

Right
The Kickapoo Indian Medicine Company, a traveling patent medicine troup, camped at Tower Road and West Nineteenth Street in Wilmington in 1892. Hucksters offered both entertainment and cure-all remedies. Courtesy, Historical Society of Delaware

The growing number of white-collar workers, employed as clerks or managers, kept some distance from the poorer neighborhoods. This unidentified family furnished their home with the "artistic" styles popular after the turn of the century. Courtesy, Historical Society of Delaware

Wilmington's working class and immigrants endured the crowded east side, where public playgrounds and settlement houses provided recreation and educational opportunities. Both children and adults turned out to watch this marbles contest circa 1910. Courtesy, Historical Society of Delaware

Above the "plain people" on the crest of hills that stretched to the west were the spacious homes of Wilmington's wealthy—Canby's "us"—who owned or managed the factories and large business operations. Clearly, by the late nineteenth century, class affiliation dictated where most of Wilmington's citizens resided.

Although the city's housing patterns generally echoed those of other American factory towns, in one significant way Wilmington was different. In many industrial centers such as Lowell and Chicopee, Massachusetts, the owners of local factories often lived elsewhere, and were correspondingly insensitive to the social, educational, and health needs of the community. By contrast, Wilmington's leading entrepreneurs continued to dwell in or near the city, and this made them sensitive to many of the problems created by the city's rapid industrial and population growth. As a result, the factory owners and business executives stood at the forefront of reform movements to improve Wilmington's water supply, sanitation facilities, schools, religious and charitable institutions, and cultural life.

Positive steps to meet Wilmington's specific needs included the establishment, in 1871, of the city's first public high school, complementing thirteen elementary

schools already in service; and municipal sewerage construction and repavement of city streets in the 1890s. By the end of the century, nearly 11,000 students were enrolled in Wilmington's public schools and the city's death rate had significantly declined.

The wives and daughters of Wilmington's upper middle class spearheaded many of these reforms. Freed from the drudgery of domestic labor by house servants, some women found an outlet for their energies and talents in establishing organizations and institutions which would improve the quality of local life. One example was Emalea Pusey Warner, daughter of a Quaker manufacturer and wife of a shipping executive. She founded the city's Associated Charities in 1884 to coordinate the rapidly growing number of private welfare agencies. Martha Gause joined her husband, the railroad car manufacturer J. Taylor Gause, in organizing the Homeopathic Hospital, later Memorial Hospital, which, in 1888, admitted its first patients. The wife of a prominent Wilmington lawyer and politician, Mary H. Harrington played a major role in the founding of the Delaware Hospital which opened in 1890.

The transformation of Wilmington from commercial town to industrial city forced its residents to confront, at an early date, some of the same problems that would one day tax the resourcefulness of the entire state. Because they had already taken positive steps in dealing with health and educational needs, as well as unemployment, Wilmingtonians possessed the necessary experience and insight to lead long overdue state-wide efforts to cope with these and many other issues dur-

Right
Founded by followers of Henry
George in 1900, the northern
Delaware village of Arden flourished as a haven for artists, writers, and craftsmen who shared
utopian ideals. Courtesy, Historical Society of Delaware

Far right
This interesting octagonal structure in Hockessin was one of
many schools built after the 1829
passage of the Delaware School
Law which first established public education in the state. Courtesy, Delaware State Archives

ing the nineteenth and twentieth centuries.

Education in Delaware was haphazardly organized and questionably effective throughout the late 1700s and early 1800s. Privately run elementary schools and, subsequently, Sunday schools (until the mid-nineteenth century the latter concentrated on basic education rather than religious instruction) could be found in most towns and villages. More advanced education was offered through private academies which first appeared during the 1760s in Newark and Wilmington and later, in many other Delaware communities.

Newark Academy became Newark College in 1833, only to change its name to Delaware College in 1843. It closed within sixteen years because of a financial crisis. The resultant image problem was exacerbated by a murder stemming from a student fracas. In 1870 Delaware College reopened to an assured future as the state land grant institution. It eventually evolved into the University of Delaware.

Despite these private and church related educational efforts, probably a majority of Delawareans were either illiterate or only semi-literate well into the nineteenth century. Moreover, because so few finished high school or had the money to go on, attendance at Delaware College or an out-of-state college was a possibility open to only a tiny minority of young people during the nineteenth century.

In 1803 Willard Hall, a Massachusetts native and Harvard graduate, arrived in Dover to practice law. Accustomed to relatively good schools in New England, he was shocked by the private schools he found in central Delaware and particularly by the teachers, whose primary qualifications seemed to be the "inability to earn anything in any other way," and who were sometimes drunk on the job. After a distinguished political career, Hall was appointed a federal district judge. He moved to Wilmington in 1823 where he viewed first-hand the educational concerns and opportunities facing Delaware's largest community. Convinced that not only Wilmington but the entire state desperately needed a public school system, Hall drew up and then persuaded the legislature to pass the School Law of 1829. This bill divided each of the three counties into a number of school districts, promising state matching funds up to $300 of what the local school distict could raise. Because local districts were free to collect any amount they wished, a considerable disparity developed between them; some districts completely failed to provide public education because they did not wish to levy a local tax. And yet, despite its imperfections, Judge Willard Hall's School Law of 1829 committed Delaware's state government to meet at least part of the expenses of a statewide public school system.

Only two years before the passage of the school law, a special congressional election led to the demise of Delaware's two political parties. In 1827 neither the dominant Federalists nor their Democratic-Republican opponents could unite behind one congressional candidate. Indeed, the election caused so much internal discord that both parties ceased to exist in the state. Louis McLane of Wilmington then led some erstwhile Delaware Federalists and many former Democratic-Republicans into the Democratic party of Andrew Jackson. However, a majority of Federalists and the remaining Democratic-Republicans became anti-Jackson Whigs.

The leader of Delaware's Whigs was John M. Clayton who, according to historian John Munroe, became "the most successful politician in Delaware's history." Clayton was so well known and liked by his fellow Delawareans, that on occasion it would take him an hour just to cross the Dover Green. Dagsboro-born and Milford-raised, he held a number of important state offices, served three terms in the U.S. Senate, and accepted a cabinet seat as U.S. Secretary of State from 1849-1851. The famous Clayton-Bulwer Treaty of 1850, providing for the neutralization of a future canal across Central America, and Buena Vista, Clayton's home, now preserved by the state on the west side of Route 13 in New Castle County, are just part of this remarkable politician's legacy.

One of Delaware's most popular and successful politicians, John M. Clayton, was born in Dagsboro in 1796. He attended Yale, trained in law, and began his long political career in his twenties. Clayton served as U.S. senator, secretary of state, and chief justice of Delaware. Courtesy, Historical Society of Delaware

Like the Federalists before them, the Whigs proved strongest in Kent and Sussex, but also received support from the factory and mill owners of New Castle County who agreed with the Whig program of protective tariffs, internal improvements, and a national bank. This coalition of downstate farmers and upstate manufacturers made the Whigs the dominant political party in the state until 1850. Shortly after mid-century, however, a combination of divisive issues and poor leadership led to the collapse of the Whig Party in Delaware and across the United States.

The most divisive political issue was slavery. Although Delaware never did have the number of slaves found in states to the south, the question of abolition produced heated debates and roiled political waters for decades.

Delaware's slave population declined from a high point of 8,887 in 1790 to 1,798 in 1860. By the latter date, 75 percent of the remaining slaves were concentrated in Sussex County. The anemic condition of slavery in Delaware reflected certain economic realities, plus the early abolitionist efforts of Methodists and Quakers. Another significant inhibiting factor was the absence of one-crop agriculture—such as cotton, sugar, or tobacco—to which slavery seemed particularly well suited. In addition, the profitable Virginia practice of selling slaves to the plantations of the rapidly expanding cotton lands of Alabama, Mississippi, and Texas was difficult to emulate in Delaware because a 1787 law prohibited the sale of slaves beyond the state's boundaries.

As practiced in Delaware, slavery was probably less repugnant than elsewhere in America. With the most liberal slave code, the state also claimed the lowest average of slaves per master. By 1860 only eight of Delaware's 587 slave masters owned more than fifteen blacks. Indeed, the twenty-eight bonded to Benjamin Burton of Indian River Hundred, Sussex County, made him the largest slave owner in the entire state. The low number of slaves per master insured that master-slave relationships in the First State were more personal and, therefore, more humane than found on the large plantations of the deep South.

But there were some examples of Delaware's slave owners physically abusing their servants. One extreme case involved Theophilus, a slave in the Lewes area, who ignored his master's injunction against attending church by going to a Sunday evening service in 1858. The next morning Theophilus was called into the master's home where he paid the price for disobedience: he was beaten so harshly by a whip, iron tongs, gun, and shovel that the last two instruments were broken in the process. Terrified and severely battered, Theophilus told his master that he was determined "to come out of that room." His master then drew a pocket knife and proceeded to lay open the unfortunate slave's stomach and stab him in the head. Somehow the desperate Theophilus broke free and headed for Georgetown, "carrying a part of my entrails in my hands for the whole journey, sixteen miles." Although not expected to live, Theophilus did recover thanks to the ministrations of an old black woman and some white physicians. Subsequently he made his way north via the underground railroad to Pennsylvania and freedom.

For Theophilus and the other slaves fleeing north through the Delmarva Peninsula, the last underground railroad station before the Pennsylvania line and freedom was the Wilmington home of Thomas Garrett, a Quaker iron merchant. In 1820 Garrett decided to devote his life to abolitionism and over the next four de-

Thomas Garrett, a Quaker iron merchant, is credited with helping over 2,000 slaves escape to freedom on the underground railroad. Courtesy, Historical Society of Delaware

cades, he helped more than 2,000 blacks reach freedom. Garrett was repeatedly threatened with physical violence by irate slaveholders and their sympathizers in the process. Moreover, because his actions were illegal, a U.S. circuit court fined him so heavily that he lost all of his property. Undeterred by this decision, Garrett turned defiantly to Presiding Judge Roger B. Taney, who was also Chief Justice of the U.S. Supreme Court. The Quaker abolitionist promised that although "thou has left me without a dollar, ... I say to thee and to all in this court room, that if anyone knows a fugitive who wants shelter ... send him to Thomas Garrett and he will befriend him." Thanks to business loans, the abolitionist made an economic recovery while simultaneously keeping his promise of continued aid to runaway slaves. After the Civil War Wilmington's blacks honored Garrett with a parade which included a banner proclaiming him "Our Moses."

As slavery declined, the number of free blacks dramatically rose from 3,899 in 1790 to nearly 20,000 in 1860. By the latter date, free blacks represented nearly one out of five Delawareans. Uneasiness among whites over the presence of so many free blacks reached new heights after Nat Turner's rebellion resulted in sixty white deaths in Virginia in 1831. Petitions demanding increasingly oppressive measures to curtail the liberty of free blacks were received by the Delaware legislature, and some became law. By 1837 a visiting representative of the American Anti-Slavery Society found that the state's free blacks enjoyed "a mere mock freedom."

Despite the 1847 abolition bill which came very close to passage in the Delaware legislature, white racial fears continued to be well pronounced, particularly in rural areas. With the collapse of the dominant Whig Party in the early 1850s, the Democrats seized the opportunity to capture the allegiance of white Kent and Sussex countians by opposing both equal rights for free blacks and the emancipation of Delaware's remaining slaves. Although the anti-Catholic American Party, made up of former Whigs, won the state election of 1854, the Democratic Party's willingness to pander to white racism brought victory at the polls in 1856.

Across the nation the increasing acrimony over race and slavery dramatically intensified regional differences, eventually leading to war between the North and the South. Just as with the American Revolution, Delaware's small size and geographic location limited its options during the Civil War. The First State's traditional loyalty to the Union and the decision of its much larger neighbors, Pennsylvania and Maryland, to oppose secession caused Delaware to cast its lot with the North and to reject overtures made by several representatives of the Confederacy.

Loyalty to the Union, however, didn't necessarily translate into statewide support for President Lincoln and his policies. This attitude was reflected in the election of 1860 when Lincoln captured only 24 percent of Delaware's vote and in 1864 when he won merely 48 percent of the ballots cast. During the latter contest, Delaware earned the distinction of being one of three northern states to support Lincoln's Democratic opponent, George McClellan. Indeed, suspicion of the Republican president and his policies probably led to the rejection of Lincoln's November 1861 proposal calling for the liberation of Delaware slaves. If the state legislature had approved this measure, all slaves would have been freed and their owners compensated from federal funds at approximately $500 per slave. As Lincoln told Sussex County slaveholder Benjamin Burton, he envisioned the Delaware initiative as a trial balloon. "If I can get Delaware to undertake this plan, I'm sure the other border states will accept it. This is the cheapest and most humane way of ending this war and saving lives." But Lincoln's hopes were dashed when the Delaware legislature failed to bring his emancipation plan to a vote.

In its reaction to this measure and to the president's prosecution of the war, the First State split along predictable geographic lines. Kent and, more particularly, Sussex were very vocal in their opposition to Lincoln's actions. U.S. Senator Willard Saulsbury, a Democrat from Georgetown, even rose on the floor of the U.S. Senate to call the president "a despot." A number of southern Delawareans—perhaps a few hundred—went so far as to join the Confederate army. Conversely, New Castle County supported Lincoln and gave him 53 percent of its vote in the 1864 election.

Despite the political tensions that divided the First State, Delaware provided thousands of recruits for the Union army, at first through voluntary enlistment and later by way of a lottery draft. Irish immigrants, attracted by enlistment bounties, were particularly numerous among the Delaware regiments. Although no battles took place on the state's soil, casualties to its servicemen—over one-third of the seven hundred members of the First Delaware Regiment were killed or wounded at Antietam—and rumor of Confederate invasion brought home at least some of the realities of the Civil War. Moreover, the festering prisoner of war camp at Fort Delaware, on Pea Patch Island, was yet another reminder of the terrible struggle between the Union and the Confederacy.

Although the Republican Party was founded in 1854, it didn't take root in Delaware and provide opposition to the dominant Democrats until the war years. The party of Lincoln particularly attracted New Castle County manufacturers because it stood for the same high tariffs and internal transportation improvements supported by the old Whigs. But it was the Republican Party's willingness to support the rights of blacks and the Democratic Party's sympathy for the South during the Civil War that set the tone and content for postwar political invective. Unabashedly proclaiming themselves "The White Man's Party," Delaware Democrats called Republicans "nigger lovers." Delaware Republicans countered that during the Civil War, their political opponents had clearly shown themselves to be "The Party of Treason."

Of particular concern to the state's Democrats was the projected impact of the Republican supported Fifteenth Amendment, ratified in March 1870, which guaranteed the right of black males to vote. Hitherto denied suffrage, approximately forty-five hundred Delaware blacks were now eligible to cast their ballots; and that would ensure a Republican victory because most blacks would definitely vote for the party of the Great Emancipator, Abraham Lincoln.

But Delaware's Democrats weren't willing to surrender their political power without a fight. Back in the Civil War years, Lincoln's government had sent troops into Delaware to police elections, preventing Democrats from intimidating voters. The Democrats claimed, however, that the actual bullying came from the soldiers who kept some voters away from the polls and caused others to flee for their lives to the swamps of Sussex. Effectively using this example of federal interference to build up resentment against the Republican Party, the Democrats gained popularity during and right after the Civil War. But in 1870 they needed new tactics to win election contests. They consequently turned to voter intimidation and to an old state law which restricted suffrage to those males who paid either property or a capitation tax. Since the state's tax collectors were all Democrats, they prevented some blacks from paying taxes and refused to give receipts to others who were taxpayers. In addition, election day shenanigans by Democrats kept black voter participation to a minimum. At the request of irate Republicans, federal marshalls were positioned at polling places

Fort Delaware was called the "Andersonville of the North" because of a high disease death rate. Courtesy, Historical Society of Delaware

to assure black voting rights, but they proved ineffective and were even driven from the polls in Smyrna and Odessa. Needless to say, the Democrats won the election.

Because of the rough treatment of some of his federal marshalls in 1870, President Ulysses S. Grant sent troops into Delaware to police the election of 1872. Their presence at polling places, combined with a general dissatisfaction among Democrats with their own party's ticket, made some Republican candidates victorious. But the Democrats remained in control of the state legislature, and subsequently passed two measures that further restricted black voter participation and guaranteed Democratic domination of Delaware politics until the election of 1888.

The long-term success of the Democratic Party rested on its ability to attract the vote of the conservative,

The Bayard family dominated Democratic politics in Delaware for over a century. The son of Senator James A. Bayard, Thomas F. Bayard later occupied his father's seat, then became secretary of state and ambassador to Great Britain. His son, Thomas, followed the family political tradition, also rising to the U.S. Senate. Courtesy, Historical Society of Delaware

race-conscious, downstate farmers and, to a lesser degree the growing number of Wilmington's Irish immigrants who competed with blacks for unskilled jobs. Continually capturing both voting blocs through its image as "The White Man's Party," the Democrats pointed to success at halting Delaware's ratification of the Thirteenth (abolition of slavery), Fourteenth (equal rights for blacks), and Fifteenth Amendments (suffrage for black males). Indeed, thanks to Democratic intransigence, slavery persisted longer in the First State than anywhere else but Kentucky. It was only when the Thirteenth Amendment was approved by the requisite

number of states and took effect across the nation in December 1865, that both Delaware and Kentucky abandoned slavery.

Exercising power over the Democratic Party like medieval barons were the Bayards of Wilmington and the downstate Saulsbury family. Thomas Francis Bayard, scion of three generations of U.S. senators, was the most successful of these political power brokers. He served in the Senate (1869-85), then as U.S. Secretary of State, and Ambassador to Great Britain. In 1876, 1880, and 1884 Bayard was runner-up for his party's presidential nomination, a distinction that no other Delawarean has come close to sharing.

Three brothers who closed ranks when fighting with the Bayards for control of the Democratic Party, Eli, Gove, and Willard Saulsbury, also competed against each other for political office. Willard held a U.S. Senate seat from 1859 until 1871 when his serious drinking problem sparked senatorial ambitions in his two brothers. Just having completed a gubernatorial term, Gove narrowly lost the contest in the state legislature for Willard's seat to Eli, who went on to serve in the U.S. Senate for eighteen years. (U.S. senators were elected by Delaware's state legislature until the election of 1916).

The dynastic nature of the Democratic Party's leadership in the mid- and late-nineteenth century partly explains the Democrats' desire to maintain the old order and their reluctance to break new ground. But there were remarkable economic changes afoot that extended far beyond the booming industrial city of Wilmington, and these changes would one day set the stage for the defeat of the Democratic Party.

Initially, however, economic change came slowly to Delaware. Despite the rapid industrialization taking place along the Christina and Brandywine valleys, on the eve of the Civil War Delaware was still an overwhelmingly rural state with approximately seven times as many farmers and farmhands as factory workers. Although New Castle County farmers shared in the economic good times of nearby Wilmington, the rural economy farther south was in bad shape. Downstate agricultural lands had became unproductive after years of use and misuse. In Kent County alone, the wheat yield per acre was only one-third of what it had been in earlier years, and in Sussex many farmers simply ignored their played-out fields and turned to cutting timber. In 1850 New Castle County, containing less than one-third the combined land area of Kent and Sussex, produced twice as much wheat. No wonder so many young people from downstate Delaware recognized that better economic opportunities lay elsewhere and de-

WOODLAND BEACH.

HOTEL, PAVILION AND PARK
BOMBAY HOOK, DELAWARE BAY.

THE TERMINUS OF THE DAILY MORNING
EXCURSION STEAMER "THOMAS CLYDE"

Above
Like other resorts on the Dela-
ware Bay, Woodland Beach
boomed during the era of steam-
boat travel. Swift ships such as
the Thomas Clyde encouraged
day trips from Wilmington and
Philadelphia. Courtesy, Delaware
State Archives

Left
Blacksmiths like Glenn Truitt
provided a variety of goods and
services in the rural economy.
They shod horses and repaired
or built farm equipment, house-
hold tools, hinges, and hardware.
Courtesy, Delaware State Ar-
chives

87

Above
"Alberta McNadd on Chester Truitt's farm. Alberta is 5 years old and has been picking berries since she was 3. Her mother volunteered the information that she picks from sun-up to sun-down." Reformer and documentary journalist Lewis Hine wrote these descriptions and took this picture in Cannon, Sussex County, on May 28, 1910. Courtesy, National Archives

Right
"James Loqulla, a newsboy, 12 years old. Selling papers for 3 years. Average earnings 50 cents a week. Sellings not needed at home. Don't smoke, visits saloons, works 7 hours a day." Wilmington, May 1910. Courtesy, National Archives

Above
"Group of girl workers at the gate of the American Tobacco Co. Young girls obviously under 14 years of age, who work about 10 hours every day except Saturday." Wilmington, May 1910. Courtesy, National Archives

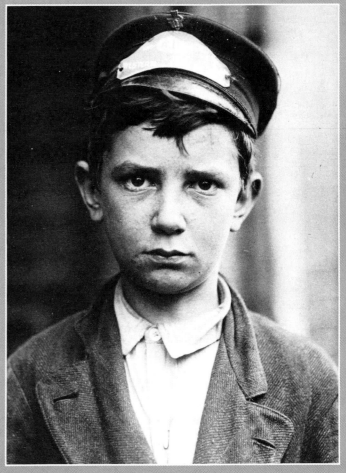

Above
Reformer and documentary photographer Lewis Hine described his subject: "Richard Pierce, Western Union Telegraph Co. Messenger No. 2. 14 years of age, 9 months in service, works from 7 A.M. to 6 P.M. Smokes, and visits houses of prostitution." Wilmington, May 1910. Courtesy, National Archives

Left
"Daisy Langford, 8 years old, works on Ross's Canneries, Seaford, Del. She helps at the capping machine, but is not yet able to keep up. She places caps on cans at the rate of about 40 per minute working full time. This is her first season in the cannery." June 1, 1910. Courtesy, National Archives

Left
Documentary photographer Lewis Hine wrote, "Michael Mero, bootblack, 12 years of age, working one year of own volition. Don't smoke. Out after 11 P.M. on May 21. Ordinarily works 6 hours per day." Wilmington, May 1910. Courtesy, National Archives

Top, facing page
"Mother and children hulling strawberries at Johnson's Hulling Station. Cyral (in baby cart) is two years old this May and works steadily hulling berries. And Cyral would rest his little head on his arm and fall asleep for a few minutes and wake up again commencing all over to hull berries. This is an extreme case by no means typical and while it was found in this investigation that children of 3, 4, 5 years are accustomed to start out before sun-up to pick berries, we have not found cases like this." Seaford, May 26, 1910. Courtesy, National Archives

Right
"3 year old and 2 boys hulling
berries at Johnson's Canning
Camp." Seaford, May 26, 1910.
Courtesy, National Archives

91

parted in very substantial numbers for the West or
such urban centers as Baltimore, Wilmington, and Philadelphia. This large out-migration caused the combined
population of Kent and Sussex to remain approximately the same from 1810 to 1850. For those who stayed,
the only hope rested in the use of fertilizers to replen-
ish the mineral-depleted soil and in the development
of a transportation system that would provide quick
and cheap delivery of perishable farm produce to the

rapidly growing urban centers stretching from Baltimore to New York City.

The spreading of horse, cow, and sheep manure;
guano (excrement of sea birds); and lime on the fields
of northern Delaware was commonplace by the 1830s.
The resulting increase in fertility of the area's farmland
caused the *Baltimore Sun* in 1846 to call New Castle
County "the paradise, the garden spot of Delaware,"
comparing it with the nation's most productive agricul-

much more remains to be done, particularly in the lower two counties."

Prior to the early nineteenth century, most of Delaware's bulk goods were moved slowly and erratically by sail on creeks and rivers. Transporting bulky cargoes over sometimes impassible roads via wagon was much costlier and neither faster nor markedly more dependable.

To improve land transportation, a number of turnpike companies were chartered in Delaware beginning in 1808. All of the toll roads subsequently built however, radiated out from Wilmington to service only northern New Castle County. In any event, water continued to be cheaper than turnpikes for moving most bulk cargoes. Water transport became more dependable when steamboats with fixed schedules connected many downstate Delaware towns with Philadelphia after the War of 1812. In addition to the usual corn and wheat, downstate farmers near steamboat landings could now think seriously about raising a perishable cash crop for shipment to northern urban centers.

Peaches had been grown in colonial times, but it wasn't until 1832 that Delaware's first commercial orchard was planted near Delaware City. By 1840 half of the surrounding land was covered with peach orchards. Philip Reybold quickly established himself as Delaware's peach king by growing 117,720 trees in the Delaware City area and sending 125,000 baskets via steamer to Philadelphia and New York markets in 1848. Two years later, one observer said: "There probably is not another place in the United States that supplies so

tural areas. From New Castle County, the new methods for restoring the soil spread southward, and in 1846 one observer found them being employed in Kent, "but not yet extended into Sussex." By 1851 a native of the Seaford area noticed that more Sussex farmers were using fertilizers. However, he also admitted that poor farming practices continued. Governor William Burton of Milford praised Delaware's recent agricultural advances in his 1859 inaugural address, but added "that many peaches for market as Delaware City."

Peach orchards were slow to spread to Kent and Sussex because most downstate farmers were some distance from steamboat landings, and the connecting wagon ride over poor roads bruised the fruit before it could be loaded aboard a steamer. An extension southward of the already existing railroad in New Castle County was the obvious solution to the problem.

In 1859 the Delaware Railroad, which had been pushing south from Wilmington for more than a decade, finally reached Delmar on the Maryland border. Once south of Dover the line had cut through southwestern Kent and western Sussex, opening up for agricultural development some of the most isolated and neglected sections of Delaware. Economic life quickened all along the train route. New towns such as Clayton, Wyoming, Felton, and Harrington appeared, and older communities such as Middletown, Dover,

and Seaford grew more rapidly than the old port towns along the Delaware River and Bay.

A blight decimated the peach trees around Delaware City in the decade before the Civil War, but within proximity of the railroad in Sussex, and particularly in Kent, peach orchards dominated the landscape. During

The crew of the oyster schooner Doris *posed for this portrait in 1924 near the Delaware or Chesapeake Bay. Oyster boats might be at sea for a week or more before returning to harbor, where the catch was shipped—fresh or canned—to distant markets. Courtesy, Delaware State Archives*

the post-Civil War years, the rail network pushed into almost every corner of the state and touched almost every community, causing peach orchards to spread all over the southern portions of Delaware. By 1875, five million baskets of the fruit were annually shipped north by the Delaware Railroad.

The peach era was shortlived. Having decimated the orchards in the Delaware City area in the 1850s, the blight reached downstate Delaware three decades later. Due to this epidemic, the total number of Delaware peach trees was almost cut in half from 1890 to 1900, and by 1911 the apple had replaced the peach as the state's primary orchard fruit. Other perishable cash crops such as tomatoes, peas, beans, melons, and particularly strawberries helped fill the void. According to the census of 1900, more strawberries were produced in Sussex than any other county in the nation. As for northern Delaware, easy access to Wilmington's growing population caused many New Castle County farmers to turn to the production of milk.

A widespread rail network and a growing demand from nearby urban centers for fruits, vegetables, and milk, had caused a marked change in the economy of rural Delaware by the early twentieth century. Although farming continued to be the occupation of the overwhelming majority of downstate citizens, the increasingly volatile urban marketplace reshaped its nature.

And yet the pace and rhythm of daily life in the countryside remained virtually uninterrupted. Field work continued to follow the predictable patterns of an earlier era, dictated by the changing seasons and the closely tied cycle of clearing, plowing, planting, cultivating, and harvesting. As in the past, the mules and horses which did the pulling and hauling demanded daily attention. Although cash income rose over earlier years, farm life continued to offer little material reward. In fact, one-half of Delaware's farms in 1890 were worked by tenants, causing the state to rank sixth nationally in this category.

Conservative attitudes maintained their hold over the countryside as they had since time out of mind. The only real challenge to the status quo had come from the radical principles espoused by early Methodism; but that challenge largely ended in the early 1800s when Methodism began to modify some of its most revolutionary ideas. So uncomfortable was the typical Delaware farmer with new ways and attitudes that he could best be described as reluctantly and uneasily sliding his front foot forward into the twentieth century while keeping his back foot firmly planted in the eighteenth century.

Spring in Delaware traditionally meant the return of shad to the Delaware River. Fishing fleets at Bowers brought back boatloads at a time. Although pollution caused a decline in the catch by the 1950s, the shad population is now making a comeback. Courtesy, Delaware State Archives

The junction of Fourth and
Market streets was Wilmington's
busiest intersection in 1928.
Businessmen, factory workers,
and shoppers hastily shuffled
about the sidewalks, and trolley
lines converged from all points.
Courtesy, Historical Society of
Delaware

CHAPTER VI

THE AGE OF DU PONT

On February 14, 1902, Pierre S. du Pont of Lorain, Ohio received a long distance phone call from Wilmington, Delaware. On the other end, cousin T. Coleman du Pont's booming voice related some interesting news: the family-owned powder-making firm was for sale and he and cousin Alfred I. du Pont intended to purchase it. Wouldn't Pierre join them? Pierre, who had some premonition of the offer, took only three minutes before saying yes. He then made ready to return to Delaware. That three-minute phone call marked a turning point in the history of the Du Pont Company, the city of Wilmington, and the state of Delaware.

Pierre du Pont had been born in 1870 at Nemours, his family's home on the Brandywine, a few miles from downtown Wilmington. When he was eleven his family moved to Philadelphia where Pierre attended private school. Three years later his father was killed at work by a nitroglycerin explosion leav-

Pictured here is Alfred I. du Pont, who with his cousins, Coleman and Pierre S., kept the Du Pont Company in family hands and greatly diversified its operations. Courtesy, Delaware State Archives

modernize its archaic business practices, he moved to Ohio in 1899 where he became a successful financier. When Coleman's important phone call reached him three years later, Pierre was confident that his two cousins shared his own feeling; the Du Pont Company needed a drastic overhaul if it was to meet the challenges of the twentieth century.

Cousins Coleman and Alfred each played a significant role in the modernization of first the company and then the state. But it was Pierre who cast the largest shadow and who ultimately proved to have the greatest impact on the lives of his fellow Delawareans. Indeed, more than any other person, Pierre S. du Pont shaped the development of twentieth century Delaware.

In the thirty-five years that followed the Civil War, the First State underwent a remarkable economic transformation. By 1900 more Delawareans were employed in manufacturing than in farming. Even downstaters felt the impact of the Industrial Revolution. Soon after Kent and Sussex turned to the growing of perishable farm produce, factories began to appear along train sidings to process food and build baskets, crates, and boxes in which local fruits and vegetables could be shipped to distant markets. In Georgetown during the

ing Pierre, as the oldest son, with considerable responsibility for nine brothers and sisters.

Like his two older cousins, Coleman and Alfred, Pierre attended Massachusetts Institute of Technology. But unlike his two Delaware cousins, he stayed long enough to graduate. A painfully shy child, Pierre was never totally comfortable with public speaking. Although he always regarded this personal trait as a handicap, it made him a particularly sensitive listener, and that proved to be an invaluable asset in later life.

Pierre returned to Delaware after graduating from M.I.T. and spent nine frustrating years working for the family's powder-making firm. Thoroughly disgusted with the unwillingness of the Du Pont Company to

late 1880s, for example, several hundred workers were
employed by local canning and basket-making firms.

The owners and managers of these new, downstate
industries, such as Henry Richardson of Dover and
Charles H. Treat of Georgetown, found the pro-
business stance of the Republican Party far more to
their liking than the ultra-conservative position of the
Democrats. Under the leadership of this new class of
entrepreneurs, the Republican Party experienced remarkable growth in Kent and Sussex.

The Republican Party's new appeal to downstate
whites combined with traditional Republican strength
in New Castle County and among Delaware blacks to
produce some election victories in the last twelve years
of the nineteenth century. Indeed, so rapidly did this
strength increase that during the first three decades of
the twentieth century, Republican candidates won most
statewide elections from their Democratic opponents.
But before Republican dominance could be firmly
established, a serious split in party ranks had to be
mended.

Shortly after 1:00 a.m. on January 1, 1889, John
Edward Charles O'Sullivan Addicks, sartorially elegant
in sealskin coat and tall silk hat, startled a group of
celebrating Republican legislators at Dover's Hotel
Richardson by suddenly announcing that he would be
available if the U.S. senatorial contest became deadlocked. The legislators asked each other: "Who is this

Above
John Edward O'Sullivan Addicks is best known for his unsuccessful and shady attempts to become a U.S. senator. Having earned his fortune by investing in gas company stocks, the maverick spent about three million dollars trying to buy votes in the Delaware Republican party. He went bankrupt by 1906 and died a pauper in New York thirteen years later. Courtesy, Historical Society of Delaware

Left
Milton was noted for tomato growing and canning. At one time the town boasted four tomato canneries, though most of these factories only operated during a six-week canning season and closed down the rest of the year. Courtesy, Delaware State Archives

mystery man?"

The son of a Philadelphia Republican politician, Addicks had become an extremely wealthy manipulator of gas company stocks. In 1887, at the age of thirty-six, he established his official residence in Claymont, Delaware. Initially unfamiliar with the state and its boundaries, Addicks was convinced that Claymont was in Delaware County, Pennsylvania. In 1888, a division in the leadership of Delaware's Democratic Party helped the Republicans win a surprise victory and control of the state legislature. On reading about the political upset in a New York City newspaper, Addicks suddenly remembered that he was a Delaware resident and subsequently made his surprise New Year's offer to the victorious Republicans.

Although the Republican-controlled legislature elected Anthony Higgins to the U.S. Senate, Addicks was not discouraged. Over the next fifteen years he spent perhaps three million dollars in a futile attempt to buy a U.S. Senate seat. In the process, Addicks created considerable turmoil and division within the Republican Party, paralyzing election procedures in the state legislature to such a great extent that Delaware had no U.S. senators from 1901-1903 and only one for the years 1895-1897, 1899-1901, and 1905-1906. A respected magazine of the day called the Addicks fiasco "a national scandal," and the general denunciation of events in Delaware eventually helped spark passage of

Built in 1881 to accommodate visitors to Delaware's capital city, the Hotel Richardson proclaimed itself to be the finest hotel in the state. It offered guests reading areas, parlors, and dining rooms and featured steam heat, gas lighting, and a bathroom on every floor—indeed, the most modern facilities of the day.

the Seventeenth Amendment in 1913, which provided for the direct election of U.S. senators.

Despite his offer to the Republicans in 1889, Addicks' initial concern was to get the Delaware legislature to charter the Bay State Gas Company, a Massachusetts venture that would become the lynch pin of his financial empire. (Delaware's very liberal General Incorporation Law, which has led to the chartering of many American corporations in Delaware and resulted in considerable tax income for the state, wasn't enacted until 1899. But even prior to 1899, Delaware had liberal chartering procedures which caused a number of out-of-state companies to apply to Delaware for incorporation.) Convinced that the Democrats would bounce back to win in 1890, Addicks donated $25,000 to their campaign coffers and, after the predicted victory, the state legislature chartered his Bay State Gas Company.

Since he no longer needed the Democratic Party, in 1892 Addicks officially registered as a Republican. By 1894 the Republicans were desperate for money to meet delinquent poll taxes so that many of their impoverished downstate supporters might vote. J. Frank Allee, a Dover Republican, brought this urgent issue before the party's leaders, who just happened to live in New Castle County. These upstate power brokers proved unsympathetic and an angry Allee turned to Addicks, an already established party contributor. Addicks met Allee in Philadelphia and promptly wrote out a check large enough to pay most of the delinquent Republican poll taxes in Kent and Sussex. In return, Allee may have promised to compensate Addicks with a U.S. Senate seat. Whatever the case, Addicks' financial support contributed to the 1894 Republican victory. Addicks then began his unscrupulous drive for a U.S. Senate seat, only to fall short because of courageous opposition by principled Republican leaders—or so the story goes. Actually, the Addicks' phenomenon was a bit more complicated than that.

As the nineteenth century drew to a close, the increasing demands of Kent and Sussex Republicans for a stronger voice in party affairs were largely ignored by the New Castle County leadership. Frustration led many downstaters to join the Addicks faction, which was called the Union Republican Party. Those remaining loyal to the New Castle County leadership referred to themselves as Regular Republicans, and portrayed Addicks' followers as venal opportunists who played right into the hands of the Democrats. In truth, both Republican factions as well as the Democrats so freely engaged in the buying and selling of votes that the Addicks era was the most corrupt period in the state's political history.

By 1907 financial reversals and the subsequent desertion by J. Frank Allee and other supporters drove Addicks from Delaware's political stage and finally, in 1919, to a pauper's death in a cheap Brooklyn flat. But even after Addicks' political demise, the same corrupt practices continued, causing the *New York Evening Post* to characterize Delaware in 1910 as a "degraded and debased little rotten borough with a polluted and debauched electorate."

With Addicks gone, Republican unity was restored—but not before downstate Republicans had made their point. Amidst tremendous intrigue and corruption, the willingness of Kent and Sussex Republicans to align themselves with Addicks and against the "old guard" sent a warning message that state party leaders could not ignore. Henceforth, Delaware's Republican Party became increasingly sensitive to the needs of Kent and Sussex.

While corruption permeated the political system, optimism loomed elsewhere. Wilmington during the first decade of the twentieth century seemed to be a vibrant, growing city with a marvelous future. Its population increased from 76,508 to 87,411, and activity filled its newly paved streets. But developments along the north bank of the Christina, Wilmington's industrial heartland, were cause for considerable concern and cast a dark shadow over the years ahead. Some of the factories between the railroad tracks and the river lay idle. In the first five years of the twentieth century, Wilmington lost fifteen manufacturing establishments and almost 1,000 industrial jobs.

The reason for their city's industrial decline puzzled Wilmingtonians, but efforts to reverse the trend seemed futile. Shipbuilding and railroad car manufacturing, the key Wilmington industries, no longer represented economic growth areas and were particularly hard hit. In retrospect, Wilmington was heading down the dismal road to urban decay. At this juncture, however, the Du Pont Company entered the picture, redirecting and revitalizing the economic life of the city.

Having left behind the dangerous uncertainties of revolutionary France in early October 1799, Pierre Samuel du Pont and his two sons, Éleuthère Irénée (referred to as simply Irénée) and Victor, arrived with their families in Newport, Rhode Island on New Year's Day, 1800. The du Ponts fruitlessly looked up and down the eastern seaboard for a profit-making business venture in which to invest their money. In the fall of 1800 Irénée visited a friend who had also emigrated from France and was presently living just northwest of Wilmington along the road to Lancaster, Pennsylvania. The two men went hunting and stopped at a country

Above
The Wilmington Marine Terminal was constructed in 1923 at the junction of the Christina and Delaware rivers. International cargo—anything from automobiles to bananas—passed through these facilities, and some goods went into storage here. Courtesy, National Archives

Right
Horsedrawn wagons hauled the Du Pont Company's gunpowder, though this proved to be a dangerous method of transportation. In 1854 three such wagons exploded while rolling through the heart of Wilmington. Courtesy, Historical Society of Delaware

store for ammunition. Having been involved in the manufacture of gunpowder in France, Irénée was surprised at the high cost and inferior quality of the American-made gunpowder that he purchased. His friend assured him that all American-made gunpowder proved inferior to its European counterpart.

After touring an inefficient Pennsylvania gunpowder plant, Irénée convinced his father to back him in the establishment of a powder works along the west bank of the Brandywine several miles upstream from Wilmington. The site was chosen for its utilization of water power and access to the navigable waters of the Christina and the Delaware. But the considerable distance from Wilmington was also an important factor in site location: after the Du Pont powder works began operation in 1802, accidental gunpowder explosions often rocked the tranquility of the Brandywine Valley. One 1818 blast caused ground tremors as far away as Lancaster, Pennsylvania, and cost forty lives. By mid-century, the Du Pont Company averaged one accidental explosion and three deaths every fourteen months.

In order to make dangerous powder mill jobs more attractive, Du Pont paid good wages and took a paternal interest in its employees. Many men kept their jobs for forty or fifty years, and many of their children came to work for the company. Courtesy, Historical Society of Delaware

Generally Wilmington was far enough away to escape destruction. In 1854, however, three Du Pont wagons, loaded with powder, suddenly blew up while rolling through the heart of Wilmington. Three teamsters, two bystanders, and eighteen mules were killed; buildings were destroyed and a huge hole was left in the street.

To attract and keep workers under such hazardous conditions, the Du Pont Company paid good wages and took a paternal interest in their employees and their families. By the 1820s, approximately 140 men

THE AGE OF DU PONT

were employed in the powder works along the Brandy-wine, and by 1900 the figure had climbed to approximately 400. As early as the late 1830s, all but a handful of these workers were Irish. They lived with their families in company-owned stone houses along the Brandywine in such tiny hamlets as Henry Clay Village, Hagely, and Squirrel Run.

Under the leadership of the shy and often despondent Irénée, the Du Pont powder works became the leader in an industry that was very vital to a young nation intent on blasting away tree trunks and rocks to clear farm fields, roads, canal and railroad beds, and mine tunnels. But it was the demand for ammunition—created by war—that yielded the highest Du Pont profits and eventually led critics to label both the company and the family "merchants of death."

Although Irénée died in 1834, the company that he founded continued to grow under the ownership and direction of other family members. By the late nineteenth century well over one hundred direct descendents of Irénée and his brother Victor lived in the vicinity of the Brandywine, and thanks to shares in the Du Pont Company, many had become quite wealthy.

And yet, more than wealth separated the du Ponts from other Delawareans. One characteristic was an intense sense of family loyalty which largely restricted social life to a circle of other du Ponts. Under those conditions it was not surprising that a number of du Ponts married first cousins, and that many seemed to lack social skills in meeting other Delawareans. This semi-isolation and clannishness caused at least one late nineteenth-century Wilmington observer to speak of the du Ponts as "a race apart."

To assure stable profits in the chaotic and generally depressed explosives market following the Civil War, the Du Pont Company took the lead and exercised direction over a powder trust that controlled more than 90 percent of the nation's production by 1889. Further steps to insure increased profits and company stability included membership in an international cartel in 1897 and the 1899 incorporation as E.I. du Pont de Nemours. (Delawareans, however, continue to call it the Du Pont Company.)

Despite considerable growth and demonstrated leadership in the gunpowder and explosives industry, Du Pont was not one of the industrial giants of the international or national scene at the beginning of the twentieth century. Indeed, it was not even Delaware's leading industrial employer.

In 1902 company president Eugene du Pont died, leaving no suitable successor within the family. Du Pont elders were about to sell the business to a competitor when the three young cousins—Alfred I. and T. Coleman (both thirty-eight) and Pierre (then thirty-two)—stepped in and acquired controlling shares. Not only did these three keep the Du Pont Company in the family, but they also directed the firm through a period of unprecedented growth.

The cousins quickly discarded the antiquated business practices of their ancestors, thoroughly revamped company procedures, and simultaneously bought out competitors all over the United States. By 1906, only John D. Rockefeller's Standard Oil Trust was as well organized. Six years later, however, an anti-trust suit caused the breakup of part of the family-owned corporation into the Hercules Powder Company and the Atlas Powder Company, now a part of Imperial Chemical Industries Americas. But Du Pont's earning capacity remained largely unimpaired.

World War I produced an insatiable demand for explosives which meant enormous profits for the Du Pont Company. Realizing, nevertheless, that the end of hostilities in Europe would cause the bottom to drop out of the munitions market, the Du Pont Company used most of its World War I profits to make itself the world's largest chemical company. In 1917, as part of its planned diversification, the firm also purchased more than one-fourth of the stock of the General Motors Corporation. To protect the Du Pont Company's investment, Pierre served as president of General Motors from 1920-23, and as chairman of the board for thirteen years. (In 1957 the federal government ruled that the Du Pont Company had to sell its General Motors stock.)

Even before assuming direction of General Motors, Pierre S. du Pont was familiar with the trappings and prerogatives of executive power. He had already taken control of his family's firm by working with T. Coleman to reduce Alfred's influence in 1911 and four years later, by buying some of Coleman's stock. Maneuvers to diminish Alfred's role in the company produced such lasting mutual bitterness that Pierre's presence, brief though it was, at his cousin's funeral in 1935 surprised many Delawareans. (Coleman had died five years earlier).

The growth of the Du Pont Company dictated that headquarters be moved from the vicinity of the Brandywine powder yards to an urban center which could provide some of the amenities needed by a modern corporate giant. By the early twentieth century, the company's holdings spread across the nation, making New York or some other large metropolitan area a logical choice. The three cousins, however, decided on Wilmington. By the outbreak of World War I, a massive headquarters building, which included the splendid 100-bed Hotel Du Pont, dominated the city's skyline. Wilmington was becoming a corporate and banking center and, in the process, lost its image as a blue-collar, factory city. Indeed, by 1936 the *Sunday Star* agreed that Wilmington was "well on its way to becoming a white collar town."

In hindsight, the decision to locate the Du Pont Company's offices in Wilmington proved of enormous

Above
A new Hagley yard machine shop, shown here in 1905, was used to build and repair equipment in the powder mills. Sixteen years later, Du Pont abandoned its century-old factories on the Brandywine in favor of more efficient western manufacturing sites. Courtesy, Historical Society of Delaware

Left
Employees at Green and Wilson's Shop, a keg mill that supplied containers for Du Pont black powder, posed outside their plant in the 1880s. Courtesy, Historical Society of Delaware

economic consequence to both city and state. Another accidental explosion ripped through the Brandywine powder works in 1920. Sensitive of the danger to increasing numbers of people who were building homes in the region as Wilmington expanded westward, the company decided to shut down the Brandywine powder works in 1921. Except for pigments plants at Edge Moor and Newport, and the Seaford nylon center built in 1939, almost all Du Pont production sites henceforth would be located outside Delaware. But the continued presence of the Du Pont headquarters in Wilmington acted as a magnet, attracting most of the company's research, experimental, and marketing facilities to northern Delaware. As it has in the recent past, Du Pont continues to be the single most dominant economic force in the First State. In 1984 it employed approximately 26,000 people or about 10 percent of Delaware's full-time work force.

In addition to being the major force behind the remarkable growth and diversification of his family's firm, Pierre S. Du Pont was also the founder of Delaware's modern school system. His efforts to revolutionize public education in the First State met with strong support from John G. Townsend, a Selbyville entrepreneur who had amassed a considerable economic empire of downstate farms, timberlands, and a bank. In contrast to Pierre's shyness, upper middle-class heritage, and lukewarm Episcopalianism, Townsend was an extrovert, a farm boy, and a deeply devout Methodist. Where du Pont possessed a degree from M.I.T., Town-

The Du Pont Company expanded and diversified into the production of chemicals and dyes during the early years of the twentieth century. Their plant at Newport yielded pigments for paints. Courtesy, Historical Society of Delaware

send claimed only six or seven years of formal education in a one-room school house. Moreover, Townsend, like many downstate Republicans, had been a supporter of John Addicks while Pierre and his family despised the maverick. And yet John G. Townsend and Pierre S. du Pont saw eye to eye on the need for a number of dramatic changes in Delaware, including a revamping of the state's public school system.

At the end of World War I, Delaware counted 425 local school districts and they weren't doing the job. Rather than the strong commitment to public education that typified New England, school districts in Delaware seemed apathetic and indifferent to their mission. One 1918 study ranked Delaware's educational system thirty-eighth among the states, and Pierre S. du Pont wrote a friend that "the schools of Delaware are a state and national scandal."

During World War I, Pierre organized and headed the Service Citizens of Delaware, a reform group urging significant changes in such areas as the state governmental structure and public health practices. But it was in public education that du Pont and his citizens' committee demanded the most drastic reforms and achieved the most stunning success.

In 1917 Republican John G. Townsend began his re-

Above
Selbyville entrepreneur John G. Townsend lacked Pierre S. du Pont's college training and distinguished lineage, but the two shared a strong commitment to advancing Delaware's public school system. Courtesy, Delaware State Archives

Right
Pierre S. du Pont, the soft-spoken president of the Du Pont Company, shaped the modernization of both his family's firm and his home state. Among Delaware's most generous philanthropists, he funded the rebuilding of the state's schools, and took an interest in libraries, public health, and the education of immigrants. Courtesy, Historical Society of Delaware

Facing page
These students at Delaware College (University of Delaware), among them several young World War I veterans, lounge in their dorm rooms. Except for the upper classes, post-secondary educational opportunities were limited until after the Second World War. Courtesy, Historical Society of Delaware

Above
Erected as a tribute to Delaware's patron of education, the Pierre S. du Pont High School in Wilmington boasted the most modern facilities, including a chemistry laboratory to train students for the state's leading industry. Courtesy, Historical Society of Delaware

Right
Black students at the Georgetown Colored School stand beside their one-room building in the 1920s. They received woefully inadequate education until Pierre S. du Pont enacted an ambitious program of reform in 1918. After the philanthropist paid for the construction of eighty-seven new schools for blacks, the state raised funds to build white schools. Courtesy, Delaware State Archives

markably active, four-year gubernatorial term. Thanks to the Delaware Constitution of 1897 (the state's present constitution), the powers of the governor had been considerably increased. Townsend used that new leverage to push through the state legislature a series of reform bills which included, at the urging of the Service Citizens, the reorganization of the public school system. By 1921 a more centralized state school system had been established. It featured the reduction of one-room school districts through merger, compulsory attendance rules, higher salaries and certification requirements for teachers, and the construction of new schools.

The major responsibility for financing the public schools was taken on by the state, and Pierre S. du Pont was appointed State School Tax Commissioner in 1925. By 1927-28 Delaware's government provided 85.5 percent of school tax revenue, a higher percentage than in any other state. Pierre S. du Pont also contributed approximately six million dollars from his own pocket to help build new facilities representing an estimated 30 percent of the total expenditures on school buildings in Delaware from 1920 to 1935.

In the process of reforming public education, Delawareans lost some control over their local schools to a group of professional educators in Dover, who dictated both curriculum and policy. But in return, per pupil average attendance climbed from 90 days in 1918 to 148 days in 1924; and the same study that ranked Delaware's school system thirty-eighth in 1918, ranked it tenth in 1930.

Some years before Pierre led the school reform movement, his cousin Coleman offered to give Delaware a modern highway that would connect Selbyville and Delmar to Wilmington. The state's transportation routes certainly warranted such action. Downstate roads were unpaved and generally impassible much of the year. Moreover, the railroad took advantage of its downstate monopoly by routinely overcharging Kent and Sussex county farmers and manufacturers. And yet, downstate Delawareans greeted Coleman's offer with suspicion. After all, there were only a few automobiles south of the canal to make use of a modern highway, and downstate Delawareans distrusted Coleman's motives. Hadn't President William Howard Taft described him as "slippery as an eel and crooked as a ram's horn"?

But Coleman found a firm ally in Selbyville's John G. Townsend who resented the railroad's high freight rates and sensed that a modern highway would allow trucks to break this monopoly. Drawing on his considerable prestige in business and political circles, Townsend helped persuade downstate Delaware to be more receptive to Coleman's gift. When the road was finally completed in 1924, it cost Coleman four million dollars and, like the educational reforms, did much to alter the provincialism of downstate Delaware.

Despite the educational reforms and highway innovations which brought New Castle County and downstate Delaware closer together, traditional economic, ethnic, cultural, and religious differences still divided the First State along geographic lines. During the first half of the twentieth century, Kent and Sussex primarily continued to be inhabited by the descendents of Anglo-Saxon farmers and their slaves who had moved into Delaware from Maryland's Eastern Shore one or two hundred years earlier. By contrast, New Castle County's growing population resembled a potpourri of old, established families and newcomers, including European immigrants, Southern blacks, and whites from Kent, Sussex, and out of state. The latter group of whites was increasingly drawn to research and managerial positions offered by Du Pont and the Wilmington area's other large firms.

While most downstate whites continued to share the same Anglo-Saxon blood lines, commitments to traditional rural values, and a strong attachment to Methodism, New Castle County's white population represented a variegated patchwork of different ethnic groups, value systems, and religious faiths.

Irish immigrants (not to be confused with the Presbyterian Scotch-Irish) began arriving in Delaware during the eighteenth century, but were particularly attracted to the First State in the early nineteenth century, when they obtained positions as Du Pont mill hands, Chesapeake and Delaware Canal laborers, and workers on the New Castle to Frenchtown (Cecil County, Maryland) Railroad.

In the 1840s the Irish potato famine greatly accelerated immigration to America. Although earlier Irish newcomers had often lived in work camps and hamlets some distance from Wilmington, those who arrived after 1840 tended to locate in the city, finding employment as unskilled or semi-skilled factory laborers, construction workers, or domestic servants in the homes of Wilmington's upper middle class. Throughout the 1800s the Irish were Delaware's most numerous immigrant group. They and their children also became a very significant force in Wilmington's Democratic party and probably represented a majority of the state's rapidly growing Roman Catholic population by the turn of the century.

Italians began arriving in the Wilmington area in substantial numbers after 1880. Like the Irish, they were Roman Catholic and worked at low paying jobs. Some Italians were familiar with stone masonry, a skill

Right
T. Coleman du Pont (top, far right) stands with his family celebrating the state's 1924 completion of the Du Pont Highway from Wilmington to Selbyville. Du Pont financed this transportation improvement himself at a cost of four million dollars. Courtesy, Delaware State Archives

Below
Automobiles quickly gained popularity, replacing carriages and trolleys for local transportation. The construction of the Du Pont Highway created new links between upstate and downstate Delaware. Courtesy, Historical Society of Delaware

which drew them to the construction industry. Unlike the Irish, however, Wilmington's Italians didn't speak English and consequently had a greater tendency to congregate. They formed a large ghetto on the west side which was quickly dubbed "Little Italy," as well as some smaller pockets of settlement in other sections of the city.

When the Italians first came to Wilmington, they found that its Roman Catholic churches and parochial schools mainly responded to the needs of Irish and German Catholics. Unable to worship in their own language, these Southern European newcomers drifted away from Catholicism until 1924, when the dynamic J. Francis Tucker, a Wilmington-born priest of Irish ancestry, was assigned to serve the city's Italian population. Because Father Tucker had studied in Rome, he was fluent in Italian and familiar with Italian customs. He quickly marshalled the energies, skills, and resources of most of Wilmington's 4,500 Italians. Together, they completed St. Anthony's Church by Palm Sunday, 1926, and then made it the heart of "Little Italy's" social, cultural, and religious life.

Poles also began arriving in Wilmington during the late nineteenth century and generally worked at low paying jobs. They were particularly attracted to Wil-

Above
Many Italian immigrants who labored as stonemasons and in the construction trades volunteered their time and skills to build St. Anthony's, Wilmington's first church for Italians. Father John Francis Tucker, the energetic leader of the parish, is shown here with a worker and some neighborhood children. Courtesy, Historical Society of Delaware

Right
St. Anthony's Roman Catholic Church was dedicated on June 13, 1926, and became a source of pride and hope for Wilmington's Italian community. Courtesy, Historical Society of Delaware

mington's important leather industry, and like the Irish and Italians, were predominantly Roman Catholic. Most Poles settled in "Little Poland," located in southwestern Wilmington in what was known as Browntown. A much smaller group chose Wilmington's east side as their place of residence.

At first the Poles lacked their own church. Those who understood German attended Sacred Heart Roman Catholic Church, built in Wilmington's west side. In 1890 a Polish priest, Father John S. Gulcz, settled in Wilmington to begin fifty years of pastoral service to his countrymen. Under Gulcz's leadership, St. Hedwig's was completed in Browntown during the early 1890s, ministering to Wilmington's Poles in much the same manner that St. Anthony's served "Little Italy." Today, to the west of I-95, the gothic spires of St. Hedwig's and the Italian-style architecture of St. Anthony's offer mute testimony to the Roman Catholic Church's role in guiding so many immigrants through the initially difficult adjustment to a new life in the state of Delaware.

Although the Italians and Poles would soon outnumber them, at the turn of the century the Germans were second only to the Irish as the leading nationality among Delaware's immigrant population. Having entered the First State in considerable numbers since the mid-1800s, they organized German clubs and churches. Unlike the Irish, Italians, and Poles, however, some

Germans settled in downstate Delaware and attended Protestant as well as Catholic churches. Indeed, Germans founded Zion Lutheran Church on Wilmington's east side in 1848, the first Lutheran congregation in Delaware since Old Swedes became Episcopalian in the late eighteenth century. Many Germans were relatively unskilled and could find only low paying jobs, but others were well educated or highly skilled and quickly filled responsible positions in Wilmington's factories and businesses.

By 1900 Delaware counted approximately twelve hundred Jewish residents, most of whom lived in Wilmington. Split between the traditional eastern European refugees from the pogroms of czarist Russia and the more liberal, German-born Jews, these newcomers generally rejected factory work and turned, instead, to starting up small wholesale and retail businesses. Because Jews tended to live near their businesses, they maintained no large ghetto in the sense of a "Little Italy" or a "Little Poland."

In 1920 Delaware's foreign-born population reached an all time high of approximately 9 percent. Perhaps no one better exemplified their struggles and triumphs than Mary Feret. She left her native Poland in 1910 and, at the age of seventeen, sailed alone to America. Heading for Wilmington where a cousin lived, she departed from New York City by train wearing a tag with her destination plainly printed; Mary Feret knew

Skilled German craftsmen came to Delaware with the experience necessary to work in the woodworking and leather tanning trades. Others, like Jacob Swinger, started grocery stores, saloons, breweries, and similar businesses. Courtesy, Historical Society of Delaware

no English. She arrived safely in Wilmington, found her cousin, and then, like many other Poles, went to work in a leather tannery. Subsequently she married Stanley Babiarz, who had immigrated from Mary's section of Poland, and together they raised six children. Because Mary and Stanley lived in east Wilmington, which was somewhat distant from "Little Poland" and St. Hedwig's, they joined with Polish neighbors in building St. Stanislaus Roman Catholic Church (1913) to serve as the heart of their east side ethnic community. In 1961 a proud Mary Feret Babiarz looked on while her son John was sworn in as mayor of Wilmington.

Four years after Mary Feret left her native Poland, World War I engulfed Europe. In 1917 the United States entered the conflict and by 1918 a large contingent of Americans was fighting on the Western Front. Of the approximately 10,000 Delawareans who served in the armed forces, 270 lost their lives. While some Delawareans fought in Europe to "make the world safe for democracy," others at home engaged in the struggle to extend the right to vote to women.

After the Civil War a few men, such as the former abolitionist Thomas Garrett of Wilmington, joined Delaware's feminists in demanding equal rights for women. Perhaps the most colorful of the early feminists was Mary A. Stuart of Greenwood, Sussex County, who was described in 1881 by a Wilmington newspaper as dressed "in black, weighs 250 pounds, is good natured and can talk 10 hours a day at the rate of 200 words per minute." During the 1870s this formidable woman annually lobbied Delaware's state legislature for the extension of women's rights. Although she met with some success in expanding female property rights, she made no progress on the suffrage issue.

In general, the strongest support for female voting rights in Delaware came from the Women's Christian Temperance Union; Methodist church leaders; some of the women most actively involved in civic, philanthropic, and charity organizations; and many of the Republican Party power brokers, such as T. Coleman, Pierre S., and Alfred I. du Pont and Governor John G. Townsend. Downstate Democrats and, surprisingly, blue bloods like Mary Wilson Thompson, the leader of Wilmington society, offered the stiffest opposition.

Despite a number of appeals to the legislature and a petition presented to the 1897 state constitutional convention, Delaware's women were still without the right to vote at the end of World War I. In 1918 the U.S. Congress went on record as favoring women's suffrage by approving the Nineteenth Amendment which then needed ratification by thirty-six states for adoption. Two years later, Delaware's legislature began to consider the amendment, and suffragettes and their supporters had high hopes that Delaware would make history by becoming the decisive thirty-sixth state to cast an affirmative vote.

Both sides sponsored rallies all over the state. On March 25 a hearing on the Nineteenth Amendment was held before the General Assembly. Partisan Delawareans poured into Dover, and stores, hotel lobbies, and streets were filled with people heatedly arguing the merits of women's suffrage. Opponents sported a red rose, while supporters wore a yellow jonquil. Regardless of the fact that the rose only symbolized one viewpoint, the struggle in Delaware over women's suffrage has been subsequently labelled "The War of the Roses."

Despite optimism from suffragist quarters, opposition forces succeeded at blocking ratification. Disapproval by the powerful railroad lobby; the fear that so many more blacks would now be enfranchised; and the general linking, in the minds of many, of women's suffrage with other revolutionary changes—school reform, prohibition, and new highway construction—sweeping the First State, caused Delaware's very conservative Democratic Party to close ranks in opposition to the Nineteenth Amendment. Even a last minute telegram from President Woodrow Wilson asking three fellow Democrats in Delaware's lower house to support the amendment because "it would be the greatest service to the party" was of no avail. Joined by a few dissident Republicans, the Democrats prevented a vote on ratification in the lower house. Yet, despite the intransigence of the First State, the Nineteenth Amendment officially passed in August 1920 when Tennessee became the thirty-sixth state to ratify. Delaware was now forced to extend the franchise to women in the same manner that it previously had been forced to grant voting rights to black males.

The emerging "Roaring Twenties" found many Delawareans adopting the era's frenzied cultural fads. Young women—particularly in the Wilmington area—who rejected traditional dress and moral codes, were known as "flappers." They danced the Charleston with young men who wore long fur coats and owned automobiles with rumble seats. The flappers and their escorts used new expressions like "bee's knees" (superb), "hep" (wise), and "lounge-lizard" (ladies man).

But above all else, the 1920s was the era of Prohibition when bootleggers waited for moonless nights along Delaware's coast to smuggle in their contraband whiskey, and when even in the highest circles it became fashionable to flout the law. A waiter at the exclusive Wilmington Country Club recalled that at 12:45 p.m. daily, he was directed to provide a meeting room

with ice, glasses, ginger ale, and a mixing spoon. He had "strict orders not to reenter until all of the participating members left the room." Later, when the waiter cleaned up, he always noticed the strong smell of whiskey. "This was my first actual observation of the disregard in which Prohibition was held by the upper crust of Society."

South of the Chesapeake and Delaware Canal, the zany behavior patterns and outlandish dress codes of the 1920s seemed far less evident. Also far less evident was the prosperity that had marked the decade in New Castle County. Depressed prices for agricultural commodities caused downstate farmers to join with those from across America in experiencing a severe economic crisis. As one Kent County man pointed out, "though this period was the 'roaring' and supposedly ... affluent twenties, for us times were hard and money almost nonexistent."

Understandably, when the Depression hit Delaware in the 1930s, many downstaters regarded it as just more of the same. By contrast, the economic collapse was a very traumatic experience for residents in urban and suburban northern Delaware. By 1934 approximately 11,000 Delaware families lacked working breadwinners. Of the families asking for relief, more than 90 percent lived in New Castle County.

Even before the onset of Depression-caused unemployment, Alfred I. du Pont came to the aid of one group of unfortunate citizens. In 1929 he urged the

General Assembly to make Delaware the second state in the Union to pass a pension bill for impoverished elderly people. When the legislators refused, Alfred I. personally financed his own statewide pension program. On November 1, 1929, 800 checks were sent out and by July 1931, the number of monthly recipients had climbed to 1,600. Because the ravages of the Depression emphasized the critical economic needs of increasing numbers of senior citizens, Delaware finally instituted its own pension program in August 1931: it was based on a model conceived by an old age commission. Not surprisingly, Alfred I. du Pont had chaired this group.

The Depression wreaked such economic havoc among northern Delawareans of all ages that emergency church and private charity funds were soon exhausted. In 1932 Republican Governor C. Douglas Buck, a collateral descendent of John M. Clayton, pushed an important bill through the General Assembly to create the Temporary Emergency Relief Commission, with two million dollars to distribute. Three years later, New Castle County levied a special income tax for poverty relief.

These actions, plus a series of federally-funded programs, helped the First State muddle through the Depression years—but with a certain lack of grace. Although it was rated fourth in per capita income, Delaware's welfare payments to victims of the Depression ranked forty-second among the states. Part of the fault lay with the traditional antagonism between upstate and downstate. Kent and Sussex countians simply did not want to increase their taxes for unemployment relief, especially since most would-be recipients lived north of the Chesapeake and Delaware Canal. Indeed, a legislative committee reported that "it was almost the unanimous opinion of the people of Sussex County that each county should take care of its own."

Although upstaters and downstaters opposed each other on virtually every issue, by 1933 they did agree that Prohibition was a mistake. Thanks to the right of local option, the entire state (except Wilmington) had voted itself dry before the Eighteenth Amendment went into effect on January 16, 1920. But the corruption and disregard for the law which accompanied Prohibition soon changed the minds of most Delawareans. In 1933 Delaware became the seventh state to ratify the Twenty-first Amendment repealing national Prohibi-

tion. The next year every section of Delaware—Sussex, Kent, rural New Castle, and Wilmington—individually rejected the local option to ban alcoholic beverage sales.

The Depression years also marked the end of political domination by Delaware's Republicans. During the early 1930s, the First State's Democratic Party decided to reverse past practices in order to broaden its support base among voters. Subsequently, it abandoned its racist image as "the white man's party" and moved away from traditional opposition to women's rights. During the presidential election years of the 1930s, the shifting political allegiance of some blacks and many white females, combined with the presence of the widely popular Franklin Delano Roosevelt at the top of the ticket, produced Democratic victories in most state and local contests. Off-year elections, however, continued to give the previously dominant Republicans an edge.

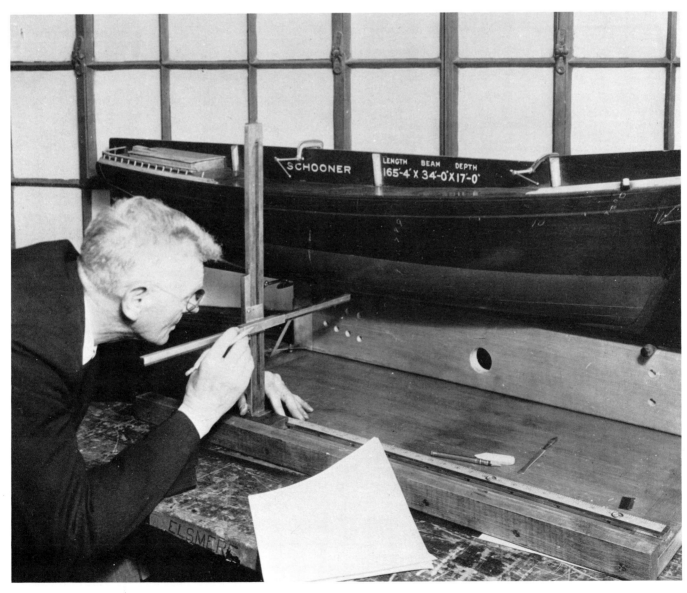

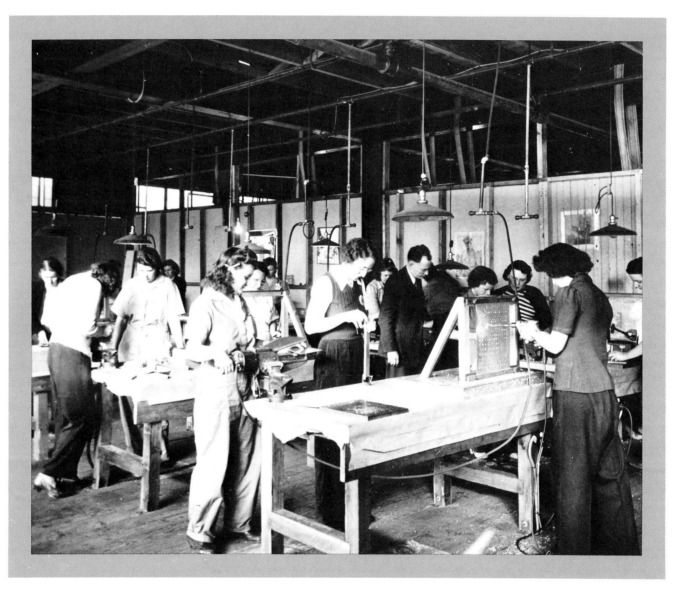

As white males engaged in World War II combat duties, civilian women and blacks gained access to the job market. It was several decades, however, before equal opportunity laws actually began to alter the nature and composition of the work force. Courtesy, Delaware State Archives

CHAPTER VII

TOWARDS A MORE DEMOCRATIC SOCIETY

On an early September morning in 1952 an anxious Shirley Bulah watched through a window in her home for a glimpse of the school bus which would take her to the opening day of third grade at Hockessin's elementary school No. 29. Later, when she entered her classroom, Shirley was very grateful to her teacher for "being kind and thoughtful and not singling me out as different." But Shirley was different—she was black.

About fifteen miles to the northeast, fifteen-year-old Ethel Belton, who was also black, attended her first day at all-white Claymont High School. The two girls were important, not only because they were among the first blacks to break the racial barriers that had existed in Delaware's public school system since its inception in 1829, but also because their presence in previously all-white schools marked the beginning of a number of historic changes which would sweep through the First State and make Dela-

ware a more democratic society.

World War II brought an end to the economic stagnation and unemployment that marked the Depression years. More than 30,000 Delawareans served in the armed forces and 903 were listed as killed or missing in action.

On the home front, shipbuilding quickly became Delaware's largest industry. Defense contracts caused the Dravo Corporation of Wilmington to expand its work force along the Christina from 400 in 1940 to approximately 11,000 three years later. Other Wilmington shipyards, as well as those in Milford and Seaford, produced naval craft for war use. In order to further meet

Above
German prisoners of war incarcerated at Fort Miles near Lewes were put to work on Delaware farms and factories because of a critical shortage of wartime labor. Courtesy, Delaware State Archives

Left
The New Castle Army Air Base served as home to the Air Transport Command, a group that ferried important military shipments to U.S. stations here and abroad. Courtesy, Delaware State Archives

Facing page
The General Motors Boxwood plant, located outside of Wilmington, provided jobs to returning World War II veterans. Courtesy, Delaware State Archives

American defense needs, Du Pont, Hercules, and Atlas also hired additional employees, and many Delaware industries converted or altered their production procedures.

Although thousands of veterans returned at the end of World War II, Delaware's revived economy was able to provide most of them with jobs while simultaneously turning to peace-time production. The First State experienced an economic boom during the post-war era and, for a number of years, it ranked first nationally in per capita income. (The large number of resident millionaires helped skew the per capita income figures in Delaware's favor.)

While some traditional industries such as shipbuild-

ing and leather manufacturing faced hard times, the changing skyline of downtown Wilmington and the newly constructed laboratories and office buildings in the surrounding countryside testified to the dynamic expansion of Delaware's chemical industry. The postwar economic boom was also fueled by the decision of several industrial giants to locate plants in the state. A new General Motors facility on Boxwood Road near Elsmere turned out its first car in 1947 and employed more than 1,000 Delawareans. In 1950 Chrysler constructed a parts division in Newark which was subsequently converted into an assembly plant. General Motors and Chrysler together employed approximately 3 percent of Delaware's full-time work force by 1983.

Other companies to build in Delaware during the postwar years included International Latex and General Foods in Dover, and Getty Oil, which constructed a refinery outside Delaware City in 1957.

Delaware's farmers also experienced better times. Declining farm prices at the end of World War I and the resulting two decades of economic hardship were ended by World War II demands for agricultural goods. After the Second World War, the New Castle County farms which survived suburban homebuilding encroachments, continued to sell milk and the same field crops grown there since 1900. Downstate, however, a remarkable agricultural transformation had taken place.

By the end of World War I, Kent and Sussex farms raised increasing numbers of chickens and distributed their eggs to nearby urban markets. Young roosters, not required for breeding, were often culled out of the flock, then sold to satisfy an increasing culinary demand which first centered in Philadelphia and later, in the large, New York City Jewish community. In 1923

Cecile A. Steele of Ocean View (southeastern Sussex) decided to raise a flock of 500 chickens with the sole purpose of selling them as "broilers." When the birds weighed approximately two pounds, they were shipped off to market where they brought sixty-two cents per pound. Cecile and husband Wilmer doubled the size of their broiler flock the following year. So successful was this new enterprise that Wilmer left his job at the Bethany Beach coast guard station to devote full time to poultry raising. By 1927 the Steele farm reached a 25,000-bird capacity and was being duplicated throughout Sussex, in parts of Kent, and other locations throughout the United States. Delaware's annual poultry production skyrocketed from two million broilers (1928) to sixty million (1944) to 182 million (1983). By the latter year, Delaware ranked fifth among the states and Sussex, first among the nation's counties, in the number of chickens sold. In the 1980s, over half of Delaware's agricultural income came from boiler production.

Thanks to the rapidly increasing demand for chickens, relatively poor farmers could grow rich overnight. As historian Richard Carter points out, more millionaires were created during the 1930s and 1940s in Sussex when "the poultry business was at its prime than in all of the rest of the county's history." Some of these quick fortunes were amassed through illegal, black market sale of chickens during World War II.

Ironically, the enjoyment of this new-found prosperity ended the lives of Cecile and Wilmer Steele. In the fall of 1940, the two broiler industry pioneers were fishing a few miles off Ocean City, Maryland when an explosion ripped through their thirty-nine-foot cabin cruiser, killing both of them.

The industry which the Steeles helped to create had a ripple effect on Delaware agriculture. Increasing demands for chicken feed caused downstate farmers to expand corn acreage and begin growing soybeans. Today, a late summer drive through the flat, downstate farmland confirms the primacy of corn and drought-resistant soybeans as the First State's leading cash crops. The driver would also notice, on occasion, the vertical storage towers built by agribusinessmen to process corn and soybeans into mash for chickens.

With the move from truck crops to broilers, many of the canneries which once thrived in Sussex disappeared. Taking their place were chicken processing plants owned by Perdue, Townsends, Cargill and a number of others. From these processing facilities poultry was shipped to markets in Baltimore, Philadelphia, Boston,

and, particularly, New York. Initially it was the dietary needs of New York City's large Jewish community that created a growing demand for Delaware's chickens. By the 1960s, Delaware's broilers had also become very popular with New York's gentile population. Although the broiler was king in Sussex, truck farming survived, most notably in Kent County, where lima beans and green peas became important crops.

Clearly, agriculture and agribusiness generate enormous amounts of money in the First State. Yet, the percentage of working Delawareans actually dependent on full-time farming or farm labor for a living declined dramatically from a majority in the mid-nineteenth century to approximately 3 percent in 1984.

The development of the seashore from Lewes south to the Maryland line has also had a considerable economic impact on eastern Sussex County. At the center of this development lies Rehoboth Beach, originally rescued from the obscurity of a sandy, scrub pine wasteland by the decision of Methodists in 1872 to turn it into a camp-meeting site. Although camp meetings had ended by World War I, the completion of a railroad to Rehoboth Beach in 1878 assured a constant stream of summer vacationers from nearby urban centers. By the 1920s highways further opened up the Rehoboth area, but mosquitoes proved such a nuisance that local women often wrapped newspapers around their ankles for protection while doing yard and garden work. The Civilian Conservation Corps drained many of the marshes during the 1930s, largely controlling the insect problem. From then on it was almost

Mrs. Wilmer Steele, a Sussex County farm wife, first introduced the modern poultry industry to the Delmarva Peninsula. By the 1940s, broilers were raised on large farms, then processed and packaged on assembly lines. The Swift Company's plant, pictured here, handled thousands of broilers at a time. Courtesy, Delaware State Archives

Left
Students of Georgetown High School learned tree planting and soil conservation techniques on the Tunnell farm in 1948. Such progressive methods made the most of Sussex County land. Courtesy, National Archives

Below
Many New Castle County farms were sold to housing developers when property values in suburban Wilmington skyrocketed after World War II. Farmers north of the canal mainly raised dairy cattle, while those in Kent and Sussex counties utilized their larger acreage for corn, soybeans, and poultry. Courtesy, National Archives

uninterrupted boom, as vacationers vied with each other to bid up building lots and summer rental prices. After World War II, development spread southward to include Dewey Beach, Bethany Beach, and Fenwick Island.

It took the most destructive coastal storm in Delaware's history to force a brief pause in shore construction. On Monday night, March 5, 1962, the weather report out of Salisbury, Maryland assured Rehoboth television viewers that Tuesday would be cold and cloudy, but that the overcast sky would partially clear during the day. However, on Tuesday the confluence of two storms produced a northeast wind with gusts of up to 80 miles per hour. Combined with unusually high tides, huge waves destroyed or badly damaged Rehoboth's boardwalk, many of its oceanside hotels, and other buildings. For three disastrous days the storm pounded coastal Delaware, causing seven deaths and twenty-two million dollars in property damage.

Despite the fact that the storm of 1962 came close to wiping out their town, Rehoboth residents demonstrated resilience and confidence about the future. July 4 found the boardwalk completely rebuilt, and subsequent development of the coastal area has been spectacular. On a given summer weekend, sixty-five thousand sun worshippers—most from out-of-state—jam into the "nation's summer capital," and thousands

of others flock to the beaches that stretch from Lewes to Fenwick Island. Their free spending habits provide Delawareans with an increasing number of investment and employment opportunities.

There are, however, a few citizens who remember 1962 and consequently warn of the far more terrible destruction that a similar storm would cause along today's highly developed ocean front. Still others feel un-

Right
Sand dunes along the coastline support a wide variety of plant and animal life, including wild bayberry, dune grass, and migrating shorebirds. The phenomenal growth of beach resort communities threatens this fragile ecology. Courtesy, National Archives

Above
Bethany Beach was a small resort with boarding houses and seaside cottages in 1926. Founded by the Christian Church Disciples, the town forbade drinking, gambling, and amusement rides. Although some of those restrictions have long passed out of existence, the area retains much of its quiet nature. Courtesy, Delaware State Archives

Facing page
The Massey family of Wilmington enjoyed fishing and swimming excursions to Delaware's beaches. Still wet from the surf when this snapshot was taken at an unidentified beach, Bes and her sister Liz sport wool bathing suits. Courtesy, Historical Society of Delaware

easy about the extraordinary construction boom and the heavy seasonal population concentrations, viewing these factors as a threat to Delaware's entire coastal ecology.

Other parts of the state also experienced dramatic population growth. Until 1930, Delaware's growth rate had been significantly lower than in the rest of the country. From 1930 to 1970, however, it far exceeded the national average. But Wilmington didn't reflect this statewide pattern. After reaching 110,000 in 1920, the city's population held at approximately the same level until the 1950s, when it began a noticeable decline. By 1980 Delaware's largest urban center had only 70,000 residents.

Conversely, the population growth of the rest of New Castle County was spectacular, increasing from approximately 54,000 in 1930 to almost 330,000 in 1980. Indeed, as early as 1960 the majority of Delawareans lived in the suburban sprawl that lay within a fifteen mile radius of Wilmington.

Delaware's suburbanization began in earnest in the years just prior to World War I. By 1912 trolley tracks had pushed out from Wilmington to the north, west, and south, allowing workers to commute into the city from such communities as Elsmere, Richardson Park, and Montrose (Bellefonte). But it was increasingly common automobile ownership after World War I and, particularly, after World War II that made possible the remarkable demographic revolution which has turned the typical Delawarean into a suburbanite. New housing tracts almost immediately filled up with families who sought refuge from the noise, smoke, crime, and declining quality of public schools that seemed to characterize Wilmington. White flight to the suburbs was particularly spurred, after 1950, by Wilmington's rapidly growing black population. Only about 13 percent of the city's residents in 1940, blacks represented 44 percent by 1970.

White racial fears were particularly fueled by black unrest in Wilmington during the summer of 1967 and by more serious disturbances in April 1968, following the assassination of Martin Luther King, Jr. On April 9, 1968, black rioters set fire to a number of abandoned buildings on the city's near west side. Forty people sustained injuries and police arrested 154 others. That afternoon, terrified commuters, frantically trying to

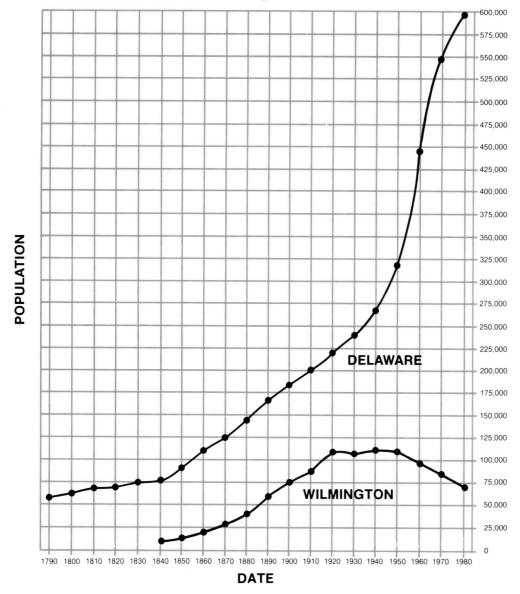

**Population of Delaware from 1790-1980
and the
Population of Wilmington from 1840-1980**

DELAWARE

WILMINGTON

POPULATION

1790 1800 1810 1820 1830 1840 1850 1860 1870 1880 1890 1900 1910 1920 1930 1940 1950 1960 1970 1980

DATE

*Facing page
A deep sense of pride and dignity appears on the faces of the members of the Bethel A.M.E. Church in Wilmington. Independent churches were a vital part of black life in Delaware from the early years of the nineteenth century when Peter Spencer founded the African Union Church, the first independent church for blacks in America. Courtesy, Historical Society of Delaware*

Chart by Graphics, Etc., Newark, Delaware

escape to the security of their all-white suburban developments, caused massive traffic jams along some of the city's major arteries. The clouds of smoke which hung over Wilmington that day marked another chapter in the troubled history of race relations in the First State.

Although 92 percent of Delaware's blacks were no longer slaves on the eve of the Civil War, they were treated as third class citizens by the dominant white community. The racial mores of a deeply segregated society dictated virtually every aspect of black life from education and job opportunities to church going. Indeed, it was not until the post-World War II years that

blacks could actually see dramatic progress in the lowering of racial barriers in the First State.

A series of early nineteenth-century incidents indicate that Delaware's blacks didn't always meekly accept discrimination. Although black Wilmingtonians had been systematically excluded from most economic, educational, and social opportunities, they were invited to join Asbury Methodist Episcopal Church, located at Third and Walnut. But resentment over segregated seating caused them to leave the congregation in 1805 and, under the leadership of Peter Spencer, to build Ezion Methodist Episcopal Church at Ninth and

French. Now self-governing, Ezion's black worshippers thought they "could refuse any that were not thought proper persons to preach to us."

Eight years later, however, their assigned white pastor refused to recognize his black congregation's claim to self government. After the minister dismissed most of Ezion's lay leaders, Peter Spencer led thirty-one angry black families out of the congregation to build the African Union Church, or Old Union as it was called, almost directly opposite Ezion. Old Union's congregation completely severed ties with the white-dominated Methodist Episcopal Church, becoming the first independent black congregation to be established in the

United States. The Ezion and Old Union story illustrates that at an early date, Delaware's blacks found at least one way to maintain personal dignity in the face of white segregation policies: developing and centering their lives around a voluntary black organization.

Ironically, subsequently organized black churches and fraternal clubs further accentuated racial separatism. Throughout most of the First State's history there have been two Delawares: white Delaware which controlled all, or nearly all, the economic and political power; and black Delaware which worked hard to maintain some sense of self respect while carefully avoiding actions which would trigger the retaliatory

Right
Buttonwood School in New Castle was built by Pierre S. du Pont during the 1920s. Despite improvements in black education, Delaware's schools remained segregated for another three decades. Courtesy, Historical Society of Delaware

Below
The movement of middle class white families from the city to the suburbs, the decline in blue-collar jobs, and the influx of poor blacks from the south all contributed to the formation of slums. The northeast section of Wilmington, once a working-class neighborhood of neat row houses, became one of the city's most depressed areas. This block of Fourteenth Street between Claymont and Heald is shown in 1949. Courtesy, Delaware State Archives

wrath of the dominant white community.

Traditionally, schooling has offered Delawareans an alternative to a lifetime of poverty and menial labor. Prior to the Civil War, however, the overwhelming majority of blacks were denied formal educational opportunities. Indeed, the school law of 1829 specifically prohibited black children from entering Delaware's public education system. To partially remedy the situation, a group of white businessmen and clergy met in Wilmington in 1866 to form the Delaware Association for the Moral Improvement and Education of Colored People. Combining private donations with grants from the U.S. Freedmen's Bureau, this organization built thirty-two primary schools and imported black teachers who had been trained in the North.

Although the black community responded enthusiastically, some downstate whites used violence to halt the schooling of minority children. In Georgetown in 1867, for example, a black female teacher was chased out of town by a rock-throwing mob. Despite such interruptions, the efforts of the association continued. But at best they were regarded as only stop-gap measures until the state legislature could be persuaded to provide for the funding of black schools.

Initially, Delaware's lawmakers expressed little interest in supporting black education. After becoming very concerned about interference from Washington, however, in 1875 the state legislature granted local government officials the power to tax black residents for the support of black schools. (Although the other former slave states had dual educational systems based on race, none had such a dual tax structure). Delaware's black schools, subsequently dependent on a very low tax base, proved very inferior to even the poorly regarded white schools.

Dramatic changes sweeping through Delaware during and after World War I ended the dual tax system. Although a racially unified tax would now support both black and white schools, the terrible physical condition of the former desperately urged an expensive, statewide school construction program. And because the costs of the new black schools would primarily fall on white taxpayers, Pierre S. du Pont decided to head off potential opposition by paying for the new black schools out of his own pocket.

Delaware's black schools continued to be the impoverished step-children of the state public education system despite a substantial improvement in funding and physical facilities. Equipment, textbooks, and other supplies were often, as a black from Lewes remembered, "hand-me-downs" from the white schools. Even more alarming was Delaware's reluctance to provide a high school education for most of its black teenagers. The black schools set up after the Civil War by the Delaware Association and subsequently taken over by the state, offered only a grade school education.

Towards the end of the nineteenth century, Wilmington's Howard High School and Dover's Delaware State College, which offered high school courses for much of its existence, provided a secondary curriculum for blacks. But those who desired a diploma and lived some distance away were compelled to find boarding in those two cities during the school year. For the black teenagers who chose to leave home, the stay in Dover or Wilmington often proved very traumatic. In 1932, for example, a young girl arrived at Dover from Lincoln in northern Sussex. After two years she gave up and returned. "I lost a lot of weight and cried, because I wanted to be at home. I was only fourteen and that was a very bad experience for me."

Even more difficult was the situation faced by the Nanticoke Indian community located in the Oak Orchard area of Sussex County. Categorized as "colored," their children could not attend white schools. Furthermore, most Nanticoke parents refused to send their offspring to nearby black schools because it was seen as a surrender of Indian identity and an acceptance of bur-

densome racial stigmas. In response to pressure from the Nanticokes, the state legislature as early as 1881 recognized the right of the Indians to erect and maintain their own educational system. During the 1930s and 1940s, the Nanticokes maintained a one-room school which served students through the eighth grade. The lone teacher's salary was paid by the state beginning in 1935.

Few options existed for those Indian students who wanted a high school diploma but did not wish to attend one of Delaware's two black high schools. If they were lucky enough to have family in a state north of Delaware, they might board there and attend an integrated high school. The other alternative was to head for the Haskell Indian Institute in Lawrence, Kansas. Only the most self-confident and venturesome of fourteen-year-olds could follow either path. Although small in number, the peculiar plight of Nanticoke teenagers offers yet another perspective on life in racially segregated Delaware.

Wilmington's black community began to assert itself at the turn of the century, despite numerous obstacles. In 1901 Thomas Postles became the first in a continuous line of blacks to be elected to the Wilmington City Council. The first Delaware chapter of the NAACP also was organized in Wilmington just prior to World War I, and in 1915 it convinced the City Council to

ban a public showing of the pro-Ku Klux Klan movie, "Birth of a Nation." Moreover, the local NAACP led a successful effort to defeat U.S. Representative Caleb Layton's 1922 reelection bid, after the legislator refused to support an anti-lynching bill in Congress. Nevertheless, Wilmington's NAACP chapter and the rest of the black community were unable to prevent the Ku Klux Klan from marching through city streets in the 1920s.

Outside Wilmington, Delaware's black population exercised very little political power. As late as 1947, no black held a significant position in the state government. It wasn't until 1948 that the first black state legislator, Republican William J. Winchester, was sent to the House of Representatives and he hailed from Wilmington.

It was on education rather than on politics that Delaware's blacks focused most of their energies to bring about racial equality. By the early 1950s a small black high school in lower New Castle County joined with Howard in serving northern Delaware. Partly fearing federal intervention if black educational opportunities were not improved, the downstate white community also finally supported the construction of two black high schools, one in Kent and the other in Sussex. Despite some physical improvements, however, Delaware's black schools continued to lag behind their white counterparts.

Louis L. Redding of Wilmington, a Harvard Law School graduate and the first black admitted to the Delaware Bar (1929), led the legal assault against the state's segregated school system. He was convinced that only through integration could racially-based educational disparities come to an end.

In 1952 two black girls, Shirley Bulah and Ethel Belton, desired to attend white schools in their neighborhoods. Chancellor Collins J. Seitz of Delaware's court of chancery, who had already ordered the University of Delaware to integrate, ruled that "the cold hand of fact is that the state in this situation discriminates against negro children." He then ordered Shirley's admission to Hockessin's elementary school No. 29 and Ethel's to Claymont High School. In spite of this legal breakthrough and the U.S. Supreme Court's famous *Brown vs. Board of Education* decision in 1954, massive integration of public schools didn't occur in Delaware until a decade later, when mandated by the Federal Civil Rights Act of 1964. In 1967 the state's last all black school was finally closed. The federal government then informed Delaware that it was the first former slave state to eradicate a dual public school system based on race.

In the years after Shirley Bulah and Ethel Belton began attending white schools, opposition to integration led to a few ugly incidents such as the 1954 demonstrations which briefly shut down Milford High School. But on the whole, most Delawareans followed the example of such public figures as Republican U.S. Senator John J. Williams (1947-71) of Millsboro, who opposed integration but even more vehemently rejected disobedience of the law as laid down by the federal courts. In nearby Virginia, where U.S. Senator Harry F. Byrd called for "massive resistance," public opposition to school integration was far more demonstrative.

The other shoe dropped for northern Delaware in 1978. Integration provided a racial mix in individual Kent and Sussex schools, roughly reflecting each county's demographic composition. In New Castle County, however, the disappearance of the dual public school system quickly led to white flight from Wilmington's increasingly black public schools. By the mid 1970s, almost 90 percent of Wilmington's public school students were non-white. Conversely, public schools in the rest of the county claimed a minority population of only 10 percent. De facto had replaced de jure segregation in New Castle County.

Although originally opposed to integration, U.S. Senator John J. Williams (1947-1971) encouraged Delawareans to accept and execute the Supreme Court's plan as outlined in Brown vs. Board of Education *and enforced by the Civil Rights Act of 1964. Courtesy, Delaware State Archives*

For reasons not entirely based on the educational needs of black children, both the city of Wilmington and some of its residents sought a judicial injunction to reverse the racial imbalance in the city's public schools. A federal court ruled that an approximate racial equilibrium should exist in each of New Castle County's public school systems. To achieve this goal, court-ordered, large-scale busing began in 1978. Only the Appoquinimink District, covering southern New Castle County, was exempt.

No contemporary issue has so roiled the waters in northern Delaware, nor caused so much perverse pleasure in southern Delaware. Because of the reluctance of Kent and Sussex to integrate their schools during the 1950s and 1960s, downstaters had long been the targets of self-righteous attacks from north of the canal. Now,

downstaters pointed out, the shoe was on the other foot.

White suburban parents vigorously protested the transportation of their children to inner city schools, while many inner city blacks were not so sure that an integrated education was worth the cost. Despite assuring words from administrators and the publication of test scores purporting to show that an integrated education justified its cost, many parents complained of school violence and of lower educational standards. Some frustrated suburban families moved out of northern Delaware; others turned to private and parochial schools for their children's education. This reaction to federally ordered busing combined with a steady decline since 1971 in the number of white school-age children in New Castle County to cause a dramatic drop in white public school enrollment north of the Appoquinimink District over the next 13 years. By contrast, the number of non-white students grew slightly, causing the non-white portion of the public school population in northern New Castle County to increase from approximately one out of five in 1971 to almost one out of three in 1984.

About the same time that Delaware's public schools were integrated, other racial barriers began to fall. Although libraries, trains, and buses had not practiced racial separation, colleges, restaurants, and theatres remained segregated. In 1948 the University of Delaware admitted its first black student. Two years later the facilities of the Hotel Dupont were opened to blacks, and most of Wilmington's movie theatres ended their discriminatory practices in the following year. Thanks to new federal guidelines and the infusion of federal funds during the 1960s, Delaware's blacks were being considered for jobs previously closed to non-whites. Urban renewal, which began in a black slum area of Wilmington's east side in 1963, proved to be another positive step.

Despite progress on many fronts, deep frustrations lingered throughout Delaware's black community, but particularly in Wilmington. New agricultural technology and machinery had increasingly rendered traditional farm labor obsolete during the 20th century. Needing jobs, large numbers of rural blacks from downstate Delaware and the farther South migrated to Wilmington and other northern cities. Except for the war years, however, Wilmington's new residents found that their adopted city offered few jobs because it was phasing out heavy industry and becoming more of a white-collar town. Although some white-collar positions were now open to blacks, most blacks possessed neither the educational background nor the requisite skills to take advantage of these opportunities. In 1960, for example, 80 percent of Wilmington's black adults had not finished high school.

With few blue-collar jobs available, unemployment among Wilmington's black males reached 13 percent by 1960; it was considerably higher among the city's black male teenagers. Adding to this frustration was the repeated refusal of the Delaware legislature to enact open housing legislation. Such a bill was approved by the House of Representatives in 1967, but the Delaware Senate blocked passage, while a tearful Herman Holloway, Sr., a black state senator from Wilmington, looked on.

Compared to the destruction and violence experienced by Washington, D.C. and many other northern cities, Wilmington's 1967 disturbances and the more serious 1968 riots did relatively little damage. But Demo-

cratic Governor Charles L. Terry, Jr., refused to take any chances. When, in April 1968 Mayor John Babiarz asked for 1,000 national guardsmen to stop the chaos, Terry sent in 800 and then insisted that some remain long after Babiarz requested their withdrawal. The occupation of Wilmington didn't end until newly-elected Republican Governor Russell Peterson, who had just defeated Terry, finally recalled the troops in January 1969. The guards' long stay drew the attention of the national media-no other American city spent so long a period under military occupation during the urban riot year of 1968-and further polarized Wilmington's black and white communities.

Yet, in spite of racial tension, a "back to Wilmington" movement began in the late 1960s during the Babiarz administration and was particularly encouraged by the succeeding mayors, Harry Haskell and Thomas Maloney. A city wage tax was levied in 1969, relieving some of the burden from overtaxed city real estate. To attract shoppers and concert-goers, part of Market Street was converted into a pedestrian mall and the Grand Opera House was restored.

With the election of Democrat Jimmy Carter to the White House in 1976, increased federal aid to the nation's troubled cities became available. Much of this new funding arrived in the form of Urban Development Action Grants, low interest loans to businesses willing to locate in inner cities. The federal program proved particularly timely for Wilmington because new construction in its struggling downtown area had become prohibitively expensive.

By 1984 businesses locating in downtown Wilmington had obtained almost $40 million in Urban Development Action Grants, with the building of the Raddison Hotel as the first example of the local impact of this federal loan program. Indeed, during Democratic Mayor William T. McLaughlin's administration (1977-85), Wilmington received a higher per capita percentage of Urban Development Action Grants than any municipality in the United States.

A second stimulant to Wilmington's economic renaissance was the General Assembly's passage, at the request of Republican Governor Pierre S. du Pont IV (1977-85), of the Financial Center Development Act in 1981. Aimed at attracting out-of-state banks to Delaware by offering tax incentives and unlimited interest rates, the Act enticed branch offices and operations of 13 lending houses (six in Wilmington) by the end of 1984. To make room for such financial giants as Chase Manhattan, more high-rise office buildings were designed and constructed in the downtown Wilmington-area. Indeed, Delaware's largest

Above
National guardsmen were called to Wilmington to quiet rioting and arson following the assassination of Martin Luther King, Jr. on April 4, 1968. The Guard remained in the city until January 1969, despite the black community's growing resentment and the request of Mayor Babiarz that they leave.

Right
Martin Luther King, Jr.'s assassination sparked violence in many American cities, including Wilmington. On April 9, 1968, thirty fires were set in abandoned buildings on the city's near west side.

134

Above
Modern homes, open spaces, new schools, and low-interest federal mortgage programs attracted urban dwellers to suburban housing developments north and west of Wilmington during the late 1930s and 1940s. Located north of the city near the Delaware River, Belleview witnessed a residential housing boom during this time. Courtesy, Historical Society of Delaware

Left
Republican Governor Pierre S. du Pont IV (1977-1985) sponsored a number of economic development measures and helped the state avert a likely financial crisis. Courtesy, Delaware State Archives

135

city was in the process of establishing itself as an important regional banking center while continuing to proclaim itself "the chemical capital of the world."

Particularly important to Wilmington's new vitality was the change in the city school taxes that accompanied court ordered busing in 1978. Prior to that date, a larger property tax base per pupil enabled the suburbs to support first rate schools through real estate assessments which were only a fraction of the rates paid in Wilmington. But along with busing, the federal court established a unified school tax rate for Wilmington and the surrounding New Castle County areas. The suburbs subsequently lost the dual advantage of better public schools and lower tax rates. As historian Carol Hoffecker points out, the court-ordered desegregation plan of 1978 "has been the single most important step toward restoring the city's ability to compete successfully with its own suburbs."

Another struggle with the suburbs, however, did not bode so well for Wilmington. As of 1965, all of northern Delaware's general hospitals were located in the city. Seeking to avoid expensive duplication of services and to keep abreast of the newest advances in medical care and technology, Delaware's three largest hospitals—Memorial, Delaware, and Wilmington General—then merged to become the Wilmington Medical Center. Implicit in the merger was the recognition that a new medical facility, or facilities, needed to be built. Moreover, the site of the new facility, or facilities, should be chosen with New Castle County's rapidly growing suburban population in mind.

One option considered by the medical center in 1968—and endorsed by the city of Wilmington—was the construction of a large addition to the Delaware Division on the grounds of adjacent Brandywine Cemetery Association. But despite the pleas of such civic and political leaders as Mayor Harry Haskell, whose own parents were buried on the proposed construction site, the cemetery association refused to sell.·

In 1969 Henry Belin du Pont's welfare foundation donated to the medical facility a 200-acre tract of former farmland near Stanton, southwest of Wilmington. The Medical Center then announced that "a major health complex" would be built on the suburban site. But it wasn't until 1975 that the center's board adopted Plan Omega which called for the construction of a major general hospital on the Stanton site, the closing of two Wilmington facilities, and the conversion of the Delaware division at Fourteenth and Washington streets to an emergency and routine care unit.

Plan Omega was strongly opposed by Wilmington's political leaders because its implementation meant the

loss of medical services and jobs that were important to the city. The subsequent struggle between the suburbs and the city over the medical center's future site ended only after four years of litigation and the promise of a free shuttle service between Wilmington and Stanton. In addition, a pledge was made that the Delaware Division, the facility's only city hospital scheduled to remain open, would not become a racially identifiable unit. Despite concessions pleasing to Wilmington, the suburbs clearly had won the battle over Plan Omega. In January 1985 the new 780-bed Christiana Hospital, costing approximately 140 million dollars, opened for business on the Stanton site. Meanwhile, in Wilmington, the General and Wilmington divisions closed, while the Delaware Division was reduced to only 250 beds and renamed Wilmington Hospital. To add to the city's chagrin, the Wilmington Medical Center changed its name to the Medical Center of Delaware.

Before winning its fight over the location of the new medical facility, suburban New Castle claimed an even more significant victory. But this time the loser was rural Delaware.

By 1960 more than one half of the state's population lived in the New Castle County suburbs and, on the whole, were Delaware's best educated and wealthiest citizens. And yet, because of the antiquated election district lines drawn by the Delaware Constitution of 1897, the suburbs were scandalously underrepresented in the General Assembly. A case in point was the Brandywine Hundred Representative District north of Wilmington, which had thirty-nine times the population of the rural Blackbird District in southern New Castle County. Because of the extraordinary population growth in suburban northern Delaware, old election district boundaries increasingly ignored the concept of equal representation and gave disproportionate political power to rural and downstate residents.

In 1962 seven suburban Republicans went to court to challenge Delaware's antiquated election district lines. By doing so, they also contested downstate Delaware's traditional control of the General Assembly. After litigation reached all the way to the United States Supreme Court, the General Assembly was directed to reapportion election districts according to population. A statewide reapportionment, which went through several steps, was finally completed by the election of 1972, giving suburban New Castle control of a majority of seats in both houses of the General Assembly. As historian John Munroe points out, Delaware's politics—like housing, shopping, and even industry—had become "suburbanized."

In the late 1960s suburban New Castle began flexing

Atlantic Ocean beach near Indian River Inlet. Courtesy, Delaware Tourism Office

Right
In 1828 Jonathon Fell, a Phila-
delphia spice merchant, pur-
chased this old mill on Mill
Creek in the village of Faulk-
land, Delaware. The Fell family
gained a worldwide reputation
for their spices and they stayed
in business until 1874. Courtesy,
Hagley Museum and Library

During the eighteenth and nineteenth centuries, the Brandywine River in northern Delaware supported a variety of water-powered industries. Gilpin's Paper Mill operated until destroyed by a flood in 1822. Courtesy, Hagley Museum and Library

Right
A race between two rival Wilmington fire companies was depicted by artist J.A. Morgan in 1880. The pumper of the Water Witch Steam Fire Company, pulled by a pair of white horses, tries to edge out the Delaware Fire Company engine. Courtesy, Historical Society of Delaware

Below
Camp meetings converted thousands to Methodism in a wave of religious enthusiasm. The Red Lion Camp Meeting was like many others on the Delmarva Peninsula. Tents remained secluded in woods, while wagons and carts surrounded the cleared preaching area. Courtesy, Historical Society of Delaware

Above
The Republic, *a paddlewheel steamboat built by Harlan and Hollingsworth of Wilmington in 1878, could carry up to 4,000 passengers at a time on the Delaware-to-Philadelphia route. Courtesy, Historical Society of Delaware*

Left
Each spring, fishermen spread wide nets across the Delaware River in an effort to trap shad swimming upstream to spawn. Commercial plants salted and cured the meat, then packed it in barrels for winter use. Fresh shad and their roe, however, remained a seasonal delicacy. Courtesy, Historical Society of Delaware

141

James A. Bayard, U.S. senator from Delaware, greets Albert Gallatin, secretary of the treasury, and his son, James, as they arrive in New Castle. The three men boarded the ship Neptune on May 9, 1813, as part of a U.S. delegation which sought to end the War of 1812. Robert E. Goodier's painting looks east on Delaware Street, showing the stables and terminus of the New Castle and Frenchtown Stage Coach Lines. Courtesy, Bank of Delaware

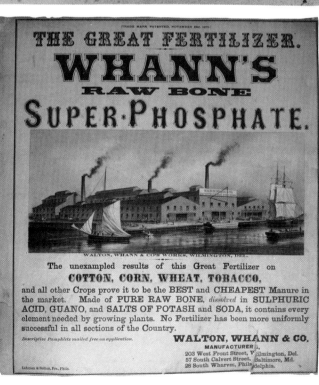

Above
A tin advertising sign used by the Du Pont Company during the nineteenth century associated gunpowder with the opening of the West. Courtesy, Hagley Museum and Library

Right
Fertilizers and improved farming techniques helped to revitalize Delaware acreage exhausted by centuries of cultivation. Whann's Raw Bone Super-Phosphate works in Wilmington, like downstate companies, produced fertilizers from agricultural by-products. Courtesy, Delaware State Archives

Facing page
Nineteenth-century advertisers used commercially-produced trade cards as prizes to attract shoppers to particular stores or products. Courtesy, Historical Society of Delaware

The Great Wilmington Fair,

Come, doggie, come, and go
with me,
To see the grand new fair,
Prick up your ears, your nose
keep clean,
For others will be there.

Tuesday, Wednesday, Thursday, Friday and Saturday.
OCTOBER, 9, 10, 11, 12, and 13 1888.

PRESENTED BY **HENRY PIKE,**
304 Market Street, WILMINGTON, DEL.

EDWIN C. BURT, FINE SHOES.

Oh John I am so glad you brought that Cooked Corned Beef. We have had Company come and I did not know what I should give them to eat

always keep on hand

LIBBY M°NEILL & LIBBY'S COOKED CORNED BEEF

*Facing page, top, and left
These colorful cards were used
as advertisements by Delaware
retailers from the 1860s to the
1890s. Courtesy, Historical Society of Delaware*

147

FRESH TOMATOES

PUT UP BY
SAMUEL TOWNSEND,
TOWNS END, DEL.

Above
The most important Delaware crops during the nineteenth century were peaches and tomatoes. After blight destroyed many peach orchards in the 1890s, farmers switched to the succulent red vegetable. Samuel Townsend's cannery, a small factory similar to many others throughout the state, placed decorative labels on its products. *Courtesy, Delaware State Archives*

Right
Peter Sigfredus Alrichs, a Dutch settler, built a small frame house on the south bank of the Christina River near Old Swedes Church in the 1600s. The Alrichs family owned the house for over two hundred years. Over time, two brick sections were added to the house, leaving the original frame building as the rear wing. *Painting by Robert Shaw. Courtesy, Historical Society of Delaware*

Above
Robert Shaw (1859-1912) was one of Delaware's most talented artists. A resident of Penny Hill, he won fame for his many etchings, as well as book and magazine illustrations. This exacting work led to temporary blindness. Upon regaining sight, Shaw took up watercolors, capturing some fine landscape scenery. Courtesy, Historical Society of Delaware

Above
Cape Henlopen and the light-
house, on the inner breakwater, in
winter. Photo by Eric Crossan.

Facing page
Return Day in Georgetown is more
than simply the announcement of
election results. It is also an
opportunity for voters to meet the
candidates, and for the candidates
to "mend fences" and to gather
support. Courtesy, John Purnell

Facing page bottom
Improvements along the banks of the
Mispillion River in Milford attract
strollers. Milford's new public library
is the brick building on the right.
Photo by Eric Crossan

Left
A celebrant at Dover's 1998
African-American Festival.
Courtesy, Delaware Tourism Office.

Following page
Encouraged by the movement for
historic preservation, urban
professionals have renovated
Victorian row houses once owned
by factory workers. These homes on
Sixteenth Street in Wilmington are
a short walk from the Hercules
Corporation headquarters. Courtesy,
Lyn Stallings

its newfound political muscle by supporting the Republican Party. Since the Depression, neither Democrats nor Republicans had been able to dominate Delaware's elections for any extended period of time. In 1968, however, suburban New Castle helped elect one of its own, Du Pont Company scientist and executive Russell Peterson, as Republican governor. Suburbanites were also partially responsible for Republican majorities in both houses of the General Assembly.

Governor Peterson reflected the priorities of many of his constituents when, for the sake of efficiency, he decided to reorganize the executive branch of Delaware's state government. He also pushed legislation to protect the state's coastal ecology. In 1970 Peterson replaced approximately 140 commissions and agencies with a ten-agency cabinet. The next year, he signed the Coastal Zone Act, prohibiting oil refineries and certain other types of industrial development from locating along Delaware's shoreline. Responding to Shell Oil's plans for a refinery in southeastern New Castle County, the governor's "To hell with Shell" remark made him a hero to ecologists across the nation.

But Republican domination was brief, in part because the party couldn't consistently depend on overwhelming support from suburban New Castle. Many blue-collar workers and unionized clerks now lived outside of Wilmington and, more often than not, supported the Democrats. By the 1950s most black Wilmingtonians had turned against the party of Lincoln in local elections. With few exceptions they could also be counted on to pull the Democratic lever during statewide contests. Adding to Republican woes, downstate Delawareans became increasingly resentful of the new political power exercised by suburban New Castle and personified in the active governorship of Russell Peterson. After turning back a primary challenge that

The introduction of electric trolley cars in the 1880s originally expanded the bounds of Wilmington. Distinct "streetcar suburbs" were developed along these transportation lines. Courtesy, Historical Society of Delaware

First elected to the U.S. Senate in 1972 at age thirty, Delaware Democrat Joseph R. Biden, Jr., is seen as one of his party's up and coming leaders.

split the Republican Party, Peterson was defeated in his 1972 re-election bid by Democrat Sherman Tribitt of Odessa. Two years later the Democrats won control of both houses of the General Assembly.

But Democratic control in Dover was just as short-lived as Republican political domination. With the state government facing a financial crisis, Delaware's voters turned to Republican gubernatorial candidate Pierre S. du Pont IV, grandnephew of education reformer Pierre S. du Pont, to lead the state government to solvency in 1976. Belt tightening and a recovering economy worked so well that within eight years, near the end of du Pont's second term, his administration announced a very sizeable surplus for the fiscal year ending June 30, 1985. By the time du Pont turned the governor's office over to Republican Michael Castle in January 1985, he was assured the same respect that Delawareans accorded two other former governors, Democrat

Elbert N. Carvel (1949-53, 1961-65) and Republican J. Caleb Boggs (1953-60).

Since 1940 the First State has sent a number of capable men to Washington, D.C., but with the exception of U.S. Senator John J. Williams (1947-1971), no Delawareans in recent memory have exercised more national influence than the tandem of Democrat Joseph Biden (1973-) and Republican William Roth (1971). At the 1984 Return Day celebration in Georgetown, Delaware's Democratic Congressman Thomas Carper (1981-1993) paid tribute to the growing national reputations of Senator Biden and Governor du Pont by predicting that in 1987 the two would be slogging their way through the snows of New Hampshire, wearing Delaware "Small Wonder" buttons and campaigning for votes in the first of a long series of presidential primaries.

Since World War II the state of Delaware has considerably increased its commitment to public education. Of particular importance was the General Assembly's 1968 decision to institute kindergartens throughout the state. That same year, legislators passed the Educational Advancement Act, which forced many of Delaware's smaller school districts to consolidate and established an equalization formula which provided increased funding for the state's poorer districts.

Consolidation didn't sit well with many downstate Delawareans. To some communities, it meant the loss of the local high school and necessitated busing local children to other towns. A poll taken in Georgetown in 1968, for example, showed that a clear majority of the local school district's residents opposed any form of consolidation. Educational authorities in Dover countered this opposition by arguing that the enlarged districts would offer a greater variety of courses, provide specialized services to meet the peculiar needs of a heterogeneous student body, and do it all in a cost-efficient manner. Moreover, they pointed out, consolidation merged many poorer districts with wealthier ones, thus reducing the disparity in educational opportunities throughout the state.

During the next two decades, falling test scores and reports alleging lack of discipline and serious purpose evoked considerable criticism of public education in Delaware and across the nation. Amidst the recriminations, however, there was a growing realization that positive action, legislative and otherwise, was immediately necessary. Recommendations by a state education task force, for example, led to a 1984 hike in teachers' salaries, which improved Delaware's 1983 national ranking of 22nd among states.

Despite widespread criticism of their schools,

Delaware's students generally scored well on standardized examinations. Their 1984 performance ranked Delaware fifth out of the 21 states emphasizing the Scholastic Aptitude Test. Dr. William B. Keene, superintendent of Delaware's Department of Public Instruction, reflected a new optimism about the future of the state's elementary and secondary schools here when, in late 1984, he confidently predicted that Delaware "will emerge as one of the significant education leaders in the country."

Extraordinary growth by the University of Delaware and the founding of Delaware Technical and Community College highlighted developments in post-secondary education. Undergraduates at the University of Delaware's Newark campus increased dramatically from less than 1,000 prior to World War II to approximately 13,000 in 1984. By the latter year, the school employed 800 full-time faculty and a total of 2,400 full-time employees -almost one percent of the First State's work force. Graduate programs also began to proliferate in the '60s, and the university offered 41 different doctoral degrees by 1984. Over the same period the school demonstrated an increased willingness to cater to the needs of the market place, adding new colleges in nursing, business and economics, urban affairs, and marine studies. Much of this recent growth was made possible by the University of Delaware's large endowment which, in the early 1980s, ranked among the top 30 of all higher educational institutions across the nation.

Even more sensitive to the needs of the market place than the University of Delaware has been Delaware Technical and Community College. The school opened its first campus at Georgetown in 1967 under the aegis of Democratic Governor Charles L. Terry, Jr. Offering two-year vocational degrees, Delaware Technical and Community College's 1984 enrollment numbered 2,940 full-time and 3,699 part-time students on four campuses.

Many museums and restored historic buildings have also expanded educational opportunities to Delawareans. Founded in 1951 by Henry Francis du Pont and located on his estate northwest of Wilmington, the Winterthur Museum opened to the public a world famous collection of early American furniture and decorative art. The Hagley Museum and the Museum of Natural History are two other educational institutions recently spawned by du Pont money and located just northwest of Wilmington. In Wilmington, the Delaware Art Museum (1938) exhibited Delaware illustrator Howard Pyle's works, plus a marvelous Pre-Raphaelite collection once the property of Wilmington textile manufac-

turer Samuel Bancroft, Jr. Other museums, restored homes, and public buildings open to the public were found throughout the state, but especially in New Castle, Odessa, Dover, and Lewes.

Women were particular beneficiaries of the expansion of educational opportunities in the First State. It wasn't until the 20th century that the barriers restricting women to domestic duties and to a lesser extent, factory jobs, secretarial work, nursing, and public school teaching, began to disappear. A crucial first step in breaking the shackles of tradition was for Delaware women to acquire a post-secondary education.

Contrary to the mores of his day, President William Purnell of Delaware College (University of Delaware) initiated coeducation on the Newark campus in 1872, only to have the experiment abandoned 14 years later, after his resignation. When opening its doors in 1892, all-black, Dover-based Delaware State College introduced the first permanent coeducational program in the state. For white women seeking a college education, however, it was necessary to go outside of Delaware. Those few who did leave generally attended two-year normal schools which prepared them to become public school teachers. Prior to World War I, the Delaware General Assembly annually appropriated $4,500 in scholarship aid to help defray the costs of tuition at out-of-state normal schools.

Led by Emalea Pusey Warner, the Delaware State Federation of Women's Clubs and other women's organizations convinced legislators in 1911 to direct the State Board of Education "to evolve a feasible plan for the higher education of women in Delaware." Three years later, under the leadership of Dean Winifred Robinson, formerly an assistant professor of botany at Vassar, the Women's College of Delaware admitted its first students. This fledgling female college was built on grounds adjacent to all-male Delaware College in Newark and shared the older institution's administrative staff. Although the men's and women's colleges merged to become the University of Delaware in 1921, it wasn't until after World War II that the classroom integration of male and female students established itself as a permanent policy on the Newark campus.

Since the 1950s, there has been a remarkable increase in the number of women pursuing college degrees in Delaware and across the nation. Consequently, the percentage of female undergraduates at the University of Delaware climbed from 33 percent in 1950 to 57 percent in 1984. As older, stereotyped images of a woman's proper place in society gave way to new perceptions, larger numbers entered Delaware's graduate and professional schools. At the University of Dela-

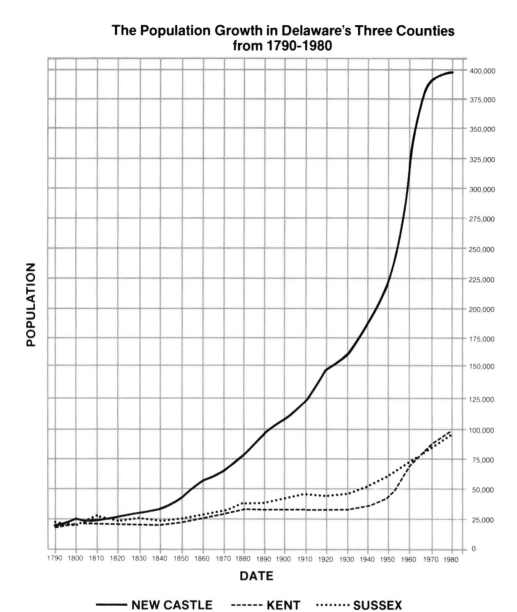

The Population Growth in Delaware's Three Counties from 1790-1980

—— **NEW CASTLE**   ------ **KENT**   ········ **SUSSEX**

ware, female graduate students increased from 26 percent of the total in 1960 to 46 percent in 1984. Delaware Law School also experienced an impressive rise in its full and part-time female students from 6 percent in 1974 to 33 percent in 1984.

Well-educated, capable, and aided by federal affirmative action guidelines, Delaware women moved quickly into responsible positions that were all but closed to them only a few decades earlier. From 1960-64, for example, women accounted for less than one percent of newly admitted attorneys to the Delaware Bar and 13 percent of newly licensed Delaware physicians. By contrast, in the years 1980-84 almost 30 percent of newly admitted attorneys and 19 percent of newly licensed physicians were females. Women have also been making remarkable employment advances in the First

State's large corporations. For example, only a few women were found among the DuPont Company's managerial and professional staff in 1964. In 1984, however, DuPont reported that women occupied 23 percent of its Delaware-based managerial and professional positions. Recent gains in the professional and business spheres have been most evident among white females.

Since 1920 Delaware women have exercised their right to vote, but few, prior to 1984, ran for elective office. In 1924 Republican Florence M. Hanby became the first female elected to the state's House of Representatives. But another 22 years elapsed before Republican Vera G. Davis pioneered her way to the Delaware Senate. After serving as Senate president pro tem and later as majority leader of the House of Representatives,

Davis claimed another distinction: the first Delaware woman to win a statewide position when she was elected Treasurer of Delaware in 1956. Within three decades, however, the number of Delaware women elected to public office had dramatically increased. Sixteen percent of the 1985 General Assembly was female, yet no Delaware woman had been elected to the U.S. Senate, U.S. House of Representatives, or served as governor.

The rolling hills of northern Delaware gradually give way to flat, open fields and marshlands in the southern and coastal regions. "A View Near Newark," painted by Kevin McLaughlin, depicts a tranquil New Castle County vista. Courtesy, Kevin McLaughlin

*Wilmington in 1998 looking north
from the Christina River. Photo by
Eric Crossan*

CHAPTER VIII

CLOSING OUT THE CENTURY

One day in 1994, a prominent Delaware businessman told Lieutenant Governor Ruth Ann Minner that a woman could certainly perform well enough as lieutenant governor because the job required ribbon cuttings and upbeat presentations to civic organizations. But a female couldn't be elected governor because women "weren't strong enough" to do the job. At that moment, what had previously been a vague notion about her future, suddenly crystallized in Ruth Ann Minner's mind. She decided that in 2000 she would seek the office of Governor of Delaware and, if elected, she would continue her long commitment to public service while demonstrating that women were "strong enough" to do the job.

Born Ruth Ann Coverdale and raised on a tenant farm 12 miles southeast of Milford on Slaughter Neck, Delaware's Lieutenant Governor had certainly come a long way. She loved school, but at age 16 she left Milford High to work on the tenant farm and at a local five-and-dime store to help support her family. In 1967 Ruth Ann's first husband died suddenly of a heart attack. "I'm 32, with no education, three children and nowhere to go," were her thoughts about the future. To add to her troubles, the Milford bank that held her home mortgage was now uneasy about its loan and called Ruth Ann in to review her financial situation. That, she recalls, was an example of the sexist treatment women had to deal with in those days.

Somehow she was able to find a job, raise her three boys, earn her high school equivalency certificate, and then launch a remarkable political career that led to 18 years in the Delaware General Assembly and to two terms as Delaware's first female Lieutenant Governor. She maintained that the key to a woman's success in a male-dominated world is quite simple: "work harder than everyone else." Ruth Ann Minner is just one example of the extraordinary change that swept through Delaware in the late 20th century as women moved into positions of power and prestige in unprecedented numbers.

In 1999 Delaware's economy—with one or two exceptions—was humming along like a fine-tuned engine. Since the recession of 1992, it had grown at the robust rate of about 5 percent annually, while inflation and unemployment remained at remarkably low levels. Although Delaware was the beneficiary of an expanding national economy, the vision and leadership of the state's government and its individual entrepreneurs were crucial to this sustained economic growth. Indeed, Delaware's success at constructing a friendly ambiance for corporate growth caused *Financial World*, in 1997, to rank Delaware second only to Texas in having the best business climate among the 50 states.

Delaware's economic good times were reflected in statistics. From 1982 to early 1999, unemployment in the First State dropped from 8.5 percent to slightly less than 4 percent, and was consistently below the national average for the period. Delaware's expanding economy caused it to move from sixth place, in 1990, to fifth among the states in per capita income, by 1997. Although the upper and middle classes benefited most by the state's economic miracle of the 1990s, there are indications that some material benefits trickled down to Delaware's working lower class.

Incomes continued to be higher in New Castle County, where two-thirds of Delaware's population and nine-tenths of its largest corporate employers were concentrated, than in Kent and Sussex. In 1997, for example, accountants earned $21.06 per hour in New Castle County compared to slightly more than $14.00 per hour further south. But in less skilled occupations, the gap between northern and southern Delaware narrowed considerably with typists in New Castle receiving $9.92 per hour while those in Sussex were paid $9.10.

Manufacturing continued to play an important, although relatively less significant role in Delaware's expanding economy. In 1997, for example, only 15

Lobby of First U.S.A. Riverfront Arts Center, Wilmington. The Riverfront Arts Center is just one example of the impact that corporate bank contributions are having on Delaware's cultural life. Courtesy, Delaware Tourism Office

Rodney Square, Wilmington, with MBNA's corporate headquarters in the center and the Daniel Herrmann Court House on the right. DuPont corporate headquarters building is to the left but is not shown in the photo. Photo by Eric Crossan

percent of Delaware's non-farm jobs were in manufacturing compared to 22 percent in 1987. Although cutbacks reduced its Delaware work force from 26,000 in 1984 to just over 13,000 in 1999, DuPont continued to be Delaware's largest corporate employer. But clearly, by the latter date, it was casting a considerably smaller shadow in Delaware than it had in times past.

Despite the continued presence of DuPont and some other traditional standbys such as Chrysler and General Motors, Delaware's manufacturing base has become increasingly diverse in recent years and features hundreds of smaller companies. The high-tech nature of many large and diminutive manufacturers was enhanced by the fact that, in the 1990s, Delaware had the highest per capita concentration of Ph.D. degrees in the sciences and engineering of any state. This extraordinary concentration of scientific brain power helped

explain why Delaware routinely led all other states in patents per capita.

Delaware's government worked hard to attract both manufacturing and non-manufacturing companies to the First State. In 1999, the newly merged pharmaceutical giant, AstraZeneca, decided to build its international headquarters just north of Wilmington in Fairfax, because of an attractive incentive package put together by the Delaware and the New Castle County governments. By 1999, AstraZeneca's Delaware operation had 2,600 employees and expected to add another 2,000 in the near future.

Even more impressive were the results produced by the Financial Center Development Act of 1981, which aimed at attracting out-of-state banks to Delaware. That year the state's banks employed only 5,000; in 1998 they employed more than 31,000 or 8 percent of Delaware's non-farm labor force. During those 17 years, bank franchise taxes paid to the state jumped from $2.5 million to approximately $120 million, with more than $84 million of the total from credit card companies. By 1998, corporate headquarters of five of the nation's 10 largest credit card banks were located in Delaware.

In 1998, one credit card company, MBNA, had a combined payroll of 11,000 people at four sites—downtown Wilmington, Newark, Greenville, and Dover—which ranked it a close second to the DuPont Company as Delaware's leading corporate employer. The growing influence of MBNA was reflected in its expanding physical presence in Wilmington's Rodney Square area, the traditional locus of Delaware corporate and institutional power. In addition to the already imposing presence of its headquarters building, MBNA planned to take over the Daniel Herrmann Court House that faces the DuPont corporate headquarters building directly across Rodney Square. All of this sends a clear visual message: now there are two corporate big boys in Delaware.

Not only has the construction of new bank buildings changed Wilmington's skyline, the economic clout exercised by such newcomers as Chase, First U.S.A., and MBNA has rippled through Delaware's political, cultural, and educational landscape. By the late 1990s, selective contributions from Delaware's most powerful banks were exercising an increasingly profound impact on the nature of Delaware's non-profit institutions and on the character of the state's public life. Art museums, historical societies, performing arts organizations, public and private schools and colleges, and political parties and candidates increasingly turned to Delaware's banking community for financial support.

But not every sector of Delaware's economy was prospering. Since the 1980s, most of Delaware's farmers found themselves hard pressed to meet rising operating expenses from the meager returns produced by their field crops and livestock. In 1999, Delaware farmer David W. Baker voiced this growing frustration when he complained that crop prices, when adjusted for inflation, were as low as during the Depression of the 1930s. "Why," he asked, "do we want to do this anymore?" By 1999 many Delaware farmers had long since decided that they *didn't* "want to do this anymore." Sensing that there was little future in farming, they sold their farms and retired or turned to more profitable employment outside of agriculture. Consequently, the number of Delaware farms declined from 4,401 in 1964 to only 2,400 in 1997. This caused the percentage of Delawareans living on farms to decline from approximately 3 percent in 1984 to less than 1 percent in 1999.

Because those who remained in farming believed that economic survival lay in the increased efficiency provided by larger farm units, they added to their own acreage by buying part or all of the many farms that were put up for sale. In 1964, for example, the average

Kent County farmland west of Dover in Amish country. Courtesy, Delaware Tourism Office

Delaware farm was only 163 acres; by 1999 it had climbed to 235 acres. The pattern of ever fewer but larger farms is, of course, a national phenomenon and will probably continue in Delaware and across the United States into the 21st century.

Pessimistic predictions about the future of agriculture in Delaware have been accompanied by an alarming decline in Delaware's farm acreage. From 1970 to 1999, Delaware lost almost 25 percent of its agricultural land, much of it to residential and commercial development. Since 1993, however, the rate of loss has slowed, perhaps due in part to the Agricultural Lands Preservation Program begun in 1991. This is a voluntary program that requires farmers to promise not to develop their land for a minimum of 10 years in return for a package of benefits provided by the state.

Most Delaware farmers have directly or indirectly benefited from the dramatic changes that have taken place since World War II in the nation's meat-eating habits. In 1940, broilers—chickens raised only for eating—represented 1.4 percent of the average American's annual consumption of meat; by 1996 the figure had skyrocketed to 34 percent, making chicken the nation's preferred source of protein.

The growing preference for chicken over beef, pork, and lamb, has fueled the expansion of southern Delaware's broiler industry well into the late 1990s. From 1982 to 1998, for example, Delaware growers doubled the pounds of broilers that they raised annually. This rise in production caused the percentage of the state's annual agricultural income represented by the production of live broilers, to climb from 63 percent in 1985 to 72 percent by 1998. By the latter date, corn and soybeans, the two field crops grown primarily to meet the local demand for chicken feed, combined for another 7 percent. Put another way, almost 80 percent of Delaware's agricultural income was directly or indirectly dependent on the raising of broilers.

In 1998, Sussex continued to lead all other counties in the nation in the production of meat-type chickens while Kent County ranked 54th. But because of even more rapid expansion of the broiler industry elsewhere,

Soybean harvesting in southern Delaware. Most of the soybeans will be used for chicken feed. Courtesy, Delaware Tourism Office

Delaware had slipped from first place in 1943 to seventh place in 1998 among states in the value of broilers produced. As in other areas of agriculture, modern technology and the economy of size have caused the number of Delaware broiler growers to decline from approximately 2,000 in 1967 to as few as 1,150 by 1999.

In the early days of the Delaware broiler industry, most growers owned the chickens that they raised. The volatile broiler market made it possible for a grower to sell one flock for a considerable profit, only to lose his shirt on a second flock three months later. In the 1950s and 1960s, however, growers surrendered the right to own the chickens they raised—and therefore their economic independence—to local poultry processing plants in return for a contractual relationship that considerably reduced the growers' financial risks.

By 1999, the Delmarva Peninsula's giant agribusiness corporations, sometimes called "integrators," exercised control over all facets of Delaware's broiler industry because they owned the chickens, the feed, the process-

ing plants, and the trucks that shipped the chickens to wholesale and retail markets. The growers were now individual contractors who simply grew the chickens on their farms under considerable direction from representatives of the integrated companies. These organizational changes, along with dramatic advances in avian nutrition, breeding, processing, and marketing, have transformed what was once the most expensive of meats into the cheapest of meats. Indeed, the modern broiler industry in Delaware and in other areas of the United States is often referred to as "the most advanced form of food production in the entire world."

However, recent trends towards consolidation and greater size by the integrators have raised significant concerns among many Delaware broiler growers. In 1985, there were nine fully integrated poultry companies offering contracts to Delaware growers; by 1999 there were only five left—Perdue, Townsends, Mountaire, Allen's, and Tyson—and this meant fewer contract choices for the growers. Georgetown chicken and grain farmer Jim Baxter voiced the concerns of

Left
Broilers in a chicken house in southern Delaware. Photo by Eric Crossan

Below
One of many Latinos working on a conveyor line in Mountaire's chicken processing plant in Selbyville. Courtesy, Mountaire Farms Inc.

many when he complained that the situation left the grower with "no options."

By contrast with declining numbers of growers, the demand for more laborers in southern Delaware's chicken processing plants increased in the 1990s. Despite the presence of state-of-the-art labor-saving poultry-rendering machinery, the public's accelerating demand for easy-to-cook chicken created an urgent need for more line workers. By 1999, the total number of employees in southern Delaware's five chicken processing plants had reached 6,000, and in some plants one half or more were Spanish-speaking immigrants.

Clearly, at the dawning of the 21st century, the broiler remained king of the roost in southern Delaware. But the rapid expansion in the production of meat-type chickens was not universally accepted. In the 1930s, it was observed that chicken manure produced by the expanding broiler industry had a remarkable impact on the fertility of southern Delaware's worn-out crop land. According to one Sussex farmer, the spreading of poultry manure caused corn fields to produce "about three times as much as before."

By the early 1980s, the liberal use of chicken manure enabled Kent and Sussex to produce most of the corn and soybeans necessary to feed their increasing flocks of chickens. In turn, the growing numbers of chickens produced more and more manure for fields which sprouted bumper crops of corn and soybeans. For a while, it all resembled one big closed, but nicely balanced circle. In the early 1990s, however, environmentalists began demanding government controls

because, they maintained, the increasing amounts of chicken manure on southern Delaware's fields created a nutrient rich run-off which posed a public health threat as it made its way into southern Delaware's waterways and drinking wells.

Poultry growers and integrated companies responded that it would be very costly for chicken farmers to substitute the more expensive chemical fertilizers and then pay for the proper disposal of excess chicken manure. Such government controls, they argued, would make the production of chickens, southern Delaware's most important year-round industry, so expensive that its growers and integrated companies couldn't compete with other broiler-growing areas across the nation where very few restrictions were applied to the use of chicken manure.

Historically, Delaware's state and local governments have been very sympathetic to the needs and concerns of farmers and other businessmen. Columnist Ralph Moyed refers to this pro-business stance as "Delaware's doctrine to do anything to save any and all the geese that lay golden eggs." To preserve the broiler industry goose, the General Assembly dragged its feet in responding to demands by both environmentalists and southern Delaware's tourist industry to enact strict controls on the use of poultry manure and chemical fertilizers on Delaware's corn, soybean, and wheat fields.

In 1999, partially in response to increasing pressure from the U.S. Environmental Protection Agency, the General Assembly created a Nutrient Management Commission—on which representatives of agricultural interests had a very powerful voice—to write, oversee, and enforce limits on the use of both chicken manure and chemical fertilizers. Some critics called this a halfway measure that put the interests of the broiler industry ahead of the need to halt the further ecological degradation of southern Delaware's well water, streams, rivers, and inland bays.

Along Delaware's seacoast, it has been the Sussex County Council that has been accused of protecting the goose that laid the golden egg. Since 1985, the dramatic increase in the number of people in Sussex has been even more visible than the rising number of chickens. Most of the population increase occurred in a swath of land that stretches southward from Lewes to Fenwick Island and extends approximately three to four miles inland. To attract both tourists and retirees, developers have been allowed to throw up homes, condominiums, and outlet-centered shopping malls across a formerly bucolic rural landscape. Demand for land was so intense that the asking price for one acre of prime commercial property along Route 1 was as high as $500,000 in 1999.

Critics of the astonishing population growth and commercial expansion along the seacoast have de-

Wilmington's changing skyline in 1998. Courtesy, Delaware Tourism Office

A protester of commercial development along Route 1 displays her feelings about the opening of a K-Mart store in 1994, just north of Rehoboth Beach. Photo by Mark Clery

manded that stricter building and development controls be applied to the area, but they have been frustrated by the perceived inaction of the Sussex County government. Lawrence Lank, Director of Planning and Zoning for the county, admits that mistakes were made in the past, but insists that the county's government has become more active in controlling development since the implementation of a county comprehensive plan in 1997. For the 5.7 mile stretch of Route 1 from Nassau—located a few miles northwest of Lewes—to Dewey Beach, the explosive commercial and residential growth of recent years presents the area's residents with traffic gridlock, significant environmental damage, and the loss of pleasing rural vistas.

While a majority of recent retirees moving to southern Delaware chose to settle along the coast, others found the less developed landscape and small towns of central and western Sussex more agreeable to their aesthetic tastes and more limited budgets. The presence of increasing numbers of tourists and retirees has created new jobs across southern Delaware, which in turn have attracted thousands of younger people to the region. The extraordinary influx of new residents caused Sussex's population to grow an estimated 28 percent (32,000), during the last 10 years of the 20th century. This is approximately twice the growth rate for the entire state during the same period.

For New Castle County, the population increase from 1990 to 2000 is projected at the considerably lower rate of 10 percent. The changes in the landscape, however, have been equally profound, the increase in

traffic congestion was just as serious, and the debates concerning "land use" were every bit as contentious. By 1999, Donald R. Kirtley, a veteran political observer from Westover Hills on the northwest edge of Wilmington, listed heavy automobile traffic, created by rapid commercial and residential expansion, as his major local concern. Other New Castle residents echoed the same complaint because examples of increasingly clogged transportation arteries were everywhere. Just one example was the Kirkwood Highway, connecting Newark and Wilmington, which averaged only 14,000 vehicles per day in 1960; by 1998 the daily number had increased almost three times to 41,000.

Central to the growing debate over "land use" and its implications for highway congestion was the fact that while population was increasing arithmetically, land development and attendant traffic problems were increasing geometrically. From 1984 to 1992, for example, the First State's population rose only 14 percent while land used for commercial/industrial or residential purposes increased by 50 percent.

The construction of new shopping malls, corporate offices and housing developments continued unabated throughout New Castle County from 1985 to 1999. But increasingly, much of this new construction was south of Wilmington and Newark with the Middletown-Odessa region feeling much of the impact. Indeed, during the 1990s, the population of New Castle south of the Chesapeake and Delaware Canal grew at four times the rate for the entire county.

Above
Early stages of a new housing development along the south bank of the Chesapeake and Delaware Canal. Photo by Gary Emeigh

Below
Dover Air Base near Dover which employed approximately 1,000 Delaware civilians in 1998. Photo by Eric Crossan

Since 1985, some of the same commercial and residential expansion, and increasing traffic congestion that has characterized most of Delaware could also be found in Dover and its immediate area. Route 13 by the Dover Mall, for example, averaged 60,000 vehicles per day in 1998. But overall, despite an estimated population increase of 13 percent from 1990 to 2000, Kent County experienced comparatively modest economic growth. In fact, so out-of-step has been most of the county with business expansion elsewhere in Delaware, that columnist Ron Williams was moved to ask in 1999, "What the heck's wrong with Kent County?" The Dover Air Force Base, various state government agencies, Kraft Foods, Playtex Apparel, Playtex Products, International Laytex (ILC), Proctor and Gamble, Bay Health (Kent General Hospital) and numerous retail stores continued to employ many Kent Countians. According to Williams, however, a vigorously expanding private economy that would attract large numbers of job seekers to Kent was still not on the horizon in 1999. Others, however, argued that economic expansion in Kent is heavily dependent on removing the last bottlenecks on Route 1, and that

should take place in the near future. Most of Kent was able to maintain a far higher percentage of its farmland than either New Castle or Sussex counties because it was under less pressure than other areas of the state from commercial developers.

Throughout Delaware, the accelerated pace of land development was made more problematic by its sprawling nature. Urban planner David Ames pointed out that much of the new construction in Delaware

James Sills, who was elected first black mayor of Wilmington in 1992. Courtesy, Office of the Mayor of Wilmington

was dispersed across the landscape, and that fact "is just as important as the amount of new development." When rural fields and mixed pine and hardwood forests gave way to company offices, shopping malls, and housing developments located a considerable distance from town sewer systems, larger lots became necessary to accommodate individual septic systems. The resulting patchwork transformation of Delaware's landscape has literally punched holes in the state's shrinking natural habitat.

By the late 1990s, the drive to make Delaware a more inclusive society could point to both successes and failures. In 1999, African-Americans represented

Return Day Parade moving up West Market Street to the Circle in Georgetown in 1998. This celebration on the Thursday after the Tuesday in November when votes are cast, goes back to the early nineteenth century when voters returned to Sussex County's seat of government to hear the election results read and to participate in parades and parties. It is Delaware's largest folk festival. Courtesy, Delaware Tourism Office

about 19 percent of the state's population compared to 12 percent for the entire nation. Growing numbers of African-Americans were moving into Delaware's middle class, while a much smaller number found themselves in policy-making positions in education, politics, and business. But as a group, Delaware's blacks continued to lag behind their white counterparts in a number of economic indices including household incomes.

Among the African-Americans seated at the table of Delaware's power brokers in the late 1990s were Iris Metts, Delaware's Secretary of Education (1997–1999); James Sills, Mayor of Wilmington (1993–); Stacey Mobley, Senior Vice President and Chief Administrative Officer of the DuPont Company; and Joshua W. Martin, President and Chief Executive Officer of Bell Atlantic, Delaware. Certainly the best example of increased visibility of black decision-makers was found at Wilmington's City Hall. In 1990, African-Americans represented 52 percent of Wilmington's population, and that fact was soon reflected in the racial make-up of the city's political leadership. In 1992 James Sills became Wilmington's first black mayor and would be reelected in 1996. By 1999, in addition to the mayor, seven of 13 City Council members and its President, James Baker, were African-Americans.

Increasing African-American representation also characterized the Delaware General Assembly where four out of 62 members, or 6 percent, were black, in 1999. But this was far below the 19 percent black share of the state's population. Although the exact figures are difficult to come by, it is clear that African-Americans in 1999 were even more under-represented among corporate executives, attorneys, and physicians. In 1994, one estimate maintained that less than 2 percent of Delaware's practicing attorneys were black. In occupations demanding less academic preparation, African-Americans were better represented. Delaware's State Police, for example, was between 8 and 10 percent black during the 1990s, but this was only about one-half of the proportion of blacks in the state's population.

The under-representation of African-Americans in the state's most influential professions and top corporate positions may be partly blamed on the diminished, but still significant presence of racism. But it is also apparent that certain professional and corporate positions that were closed to blacks prior to the civil rights movement of the 1960s and the affirmative action programs that followed, will not be proportionally filled by African-Americans until the academic performances of large numbers of black students can be dramatically improved.

Memorial Hall on the campus of the University of Delaware, Newark. Courtesy, University of Delaware

Delaware's growing Latino population certainly represented more than the official estimate of 3 percent of the state's population in 1999, but considerably less than the national average of 11 percent. Ranging in color from white to dark brown and even black, individual Latinos found that their acceptance in Delaware was based on such variables as skin color, ability to speak English, and educational and income levels. Historically, most of Delaware's Hispanic population lived in the Wilmington area; since 1985, however, large numbers of Latin Americans have left their homelands for southern Delaware to work in the area's broiler processing plants. No downstate community has felt the impact of this recent immigration more than Georgetown. By 1997, an estimated 25 to 50 percent of its population was Latino, primarily Guatemalan. Many long-time Georgetown residents, unused to large numbers of foreign immigrants, reeled from culture shock.

Over the next 20 years, Delaware's Hispanic population is projected to increase at a faster percentage rate

Left
Judge Susan Del Pesco, who was
appointed the first woman on
Delaware's Superior Court in 1988.
Courtesy, Judge Del Pesco's office

Middle
Justice Carolyn Berger, who was
appointed the first woman on
Delaware's Supreme Court in 1994.
Courtesy, Justice Berger's office

Right
Lieutenant Governor Ruth Ann
Minner (1993-2001). Courtesy,
Office of the Lieutenant Governor

than either blacks or whites. That means that the relatively limited political power exercised by Latinos —in 1999, one member of the General Assembly and one member of Wilmington's City Council were Hispanic—will increase significantly in the 21st century.

Delaware's women have continued the process begun in the 1960s and 1970s of making significant, although uneven inroads into the male-dominated professional and corporate world. Overall, this increasing feminization of important power positions in the workplace represents one of the most significant revolutions in Delaware history. The specific nature of these female inroads generally reflected gender enrollment patterns in both undergraduate and graduate education.

Since the 1980s females have outnumbered males in the University of Delaware's undergraduate student body, but in the College of Engineering and in the College of Business and Economics, women made up only 22 percent and 42 percent, respectively, of the undergraduates in 1997. Among the University of Delaware's graduate students, the overall number of women almost matched the number of men. But in the graduate programs of engineering and business, they represented only 20 and 32 percent of the student body. By contrast, at the Delaware campus of The Widener University School of Law (formerly Delaware

Law School), females increased from 33 percent in 1984 to 45 percent of the law students by the spring semester of 1999.

As might be expected by undergraduate and graduate enrollment patterns, the practice of law particularly reflected an increasing female presence. From 1980-84, approximately 30 percent of newly admitted attorneys to the Delaware Bar were women; for the 1994-98 period the figure had risen to 46 percent. The fresh infusion of large numbers of young women increased the female share of Delaware's practicing attorneys from 24 percent in 1991-92 to 29 percent in 1998-99. In medicine, females increased from 17 percent of the state's practicing physicians in 1985 to 24 percent in 1997.

Women became increasingly more visible in significant corporate positions. In DuPont's Delaware-based operations, for example, the female share of managerial and professional positions grew from 23 percent in 1984 to 33 percent in 1999. Women also became more visible in Delaware's political leadership, increasing their seats in the General Assembly from 16 percent of the total in 1985 to 24 percent in 1997. Moreover, Ruth Ann Minner, who has presided over the Delaware Senate since 1993 as Delaware's first female Lieutenant Governor, is a strong candidate to win the Democratic Party's nomination for Governor in 2000. On the Republican side, Delaware Attorney

General Jane Brady is a possible contender for her party's gubernatorial nomination in the same year.

Delaware's gay and lesbian community, its least visible minority, has received greater, but still incomplete legal protection, since 1985. In 1997, for example, attacks on sexual orientation were added to the state's list of hate crimes. But through 1999, no Delaware law protected gays and lesbians against discrimination in housing, employment, credit, and public accommodations. Delaware's Secretary of Labor, Lisa Blunt-Bradley, reported in 1999 that her department "receives 500 complaints a year" from workers who claimed to be discriminated against because of their sexual orientation. Delaware has never recognized same sex marriages performed in the state, and in 1996, the General Assembly passed a law prohibiting the recognition of same sex marriages performed in other states.

For much of Delaware's history, Wilmington has dominated the state's economic and cultural life. The flight of people, corporate offices, and retail stores to the suburbs during the last five decades, however, has caused a significant eroding of Wilmington's once dominant role. A city that contained approximately one-half of all Delawareans in 1920, contained less than one-tenth in 1998. By the latter date, some of Wilmington's most important institutions, such as the *News Journal* and the New Castle County Government, had moved most or all of their offices to the suburbs.

As the end of the 20th century approached, it was increasingly apparent that Wilmington would never again exert the economic and cultural hegemony of earlier years. Since 1985, however, many steps have been taken to restore some of the city's former vitality and self-assurance. Although the alteration of Wilmington's skyline by new bank buildings was the most visible sign of renewed confidence in the city's future, other less visible actions by some of Wilmington's most venerable organizations have done much to assure the city's vitality in the years ahead.

Governor Tom Carper (1993-2001) with school children. Courtesy, Office of the Governor

One example was the 1991 decision by the Historical Society of Delaware to remain on lower Market Street, to anchor the rehabilitation of the area despite the temptation to move to the suburbs where space for physical expansion and additional parking was more readily available. Along King and Fourth Street just east of the Historical Society, the new justice building, a state-of-the-art 12-story structure that will house the Supreme, Chancery, Superior, Common Pleas, and Family courts, was under construction in 1999 at an estimated final cost of $130 million. It, too, will act as a focus for Wilmington's urban renewal because the justice building will soon be surrounded by restaurants and specialty shops catering to the needs of court employees and those using the courts.

Along the north bank of Wilmington's Christina River, where derelict buildings and waste-strewn lots once dominated the landscape, new life was injected by the construction of the Delaware Theater Company's new facility, Frawley Stadium, First U.S.A. Riverfront Arts Center, retail shops and Tubman-Garrett Park. But, as columnist Norman Lockman pointed out, "the toughest challenge in Wilmington's renewal is not Market Street and the Christina riverfront, but the

declining old neighborhoods shot through with blight and ripe for trafficking in crime."

While Wilmington was working hard to reinvigorate its downtown core, Delaware schools turned from the challenge of integration to a growing concern about student academic performances. In 1998, the Delaware State Testing Program was administered to more than 90 percent of the state's third, fifth, eighth, and 10th graders. The results were somewhat troubling because they showed that in mathematics and reading, Delaware's public school students performed at or above the national average until the 10th grade, when their scores dropped to the 45th percentile in mathematics and the 41st percentile in reading.

During the 1990s, the growing call for greater accountability in education led Governor Tom Carper (1993–2001) to demand that teacher evaluations be

Some of the buildings of the Historical Society of Delaware along lower Market Street, which have helped anchor that part of Wilmington against urban blight. Courtesy, Delaware Tourism Office

partially based on their students' test performances. But opposition to the Carper version of teacher evaluations by the Delaware State Education Association—the teachers' union—has blocked state government action on this issue. Ongoing negotiations between the Governor's office and D.S.E.A. during the summer of 1999, however, indicated that the two parties were moving towards a compromise settlement on the issue.

Crime and its growing cost to victims and to taxpayers have also been much on the mind of Delawareans. From 1985 to 1996, reported crimes in the state jumped from 159 per thousand people to 252 per thousand, a 78 percent increase. Reflecting the rising crime rate, the daily number of inmates incarcerated in Delaware's prisons rose from 1,474 in 1980 to 5,703 in early 1999, and by the latter year each inmate was costing the state's taxpayers approximately $21,000 per year. The need to build new prisons and to feed, clothe, and provide programs for dramatically increasing numbers of convicted criminals has pushed the annual budget of the Department of Corrections up from almost $41 million in 1985 to $141 million in 1999.

To pay for the increasing strain placed on the state budget by the rising costs of schools, social agencies, road construction, state police, prisons, and other services, Delaware's government looked for new sources of income. A heavy progressive state tax on high-income earners had worked against economic growth in the 1970s and was scaled back in the 1980s. Although the economic miracle of the 1990s provided dramatically increased amounts of tax money, the state's political leadership searched for other sources of income that would be palatable to taxpayers.

In the meantime, the state's horse-racing industry was suffering from hard times and the solution, suggested by the tracks and certain other interested parties, was for the state to legalize slot machines at each of Delaware's three facilities, Dover Downs, Harrington, and Delaware Park. In 1994, the General Assembly passed the "Horse-Racing Preservation Act," also known as the "Slots Bill," which seemed to offer something for just about everyone. By 1999, the tracks were taking home about 60 percent, the state about 34 percent, and the machine vendors a little over 6 percent of the profits generated by the slot machines. Particularly appealing was the fact that the state income generated by slot machines enabled politicians to consider tax rate reductions.

Delaware's take from slots—for constitutional reasons "video lottery" is the state's preferred euphemism—has been astonishing. By 1997, it was the

Playing the slot machines at Harrington Raceway. Photo by Eric Crossan

state's third largest source of revenue after Delaware's income and corporate taxes. In 1999, the projected state income from this source was $165 million. Best of all, two-thirds of the players were from out-of-state. Governor Carper, who initially opposed the slots bill but allowed it to become law without his signature, concluded in 1999 that the "video lottery" was a good thing for Delaware.

But was this a Faustian bargain with the Devil? Critics argued that only a very hypocritical society preached the virtues of hard work and delayed gratification, while, simultaneously encouraging its citizens to gamble. They pointed out that slots were addictive for players and for a Delaware government that had become increasingly dependent on this painless form of revenue. Moreover, siphoning off profits from gambling to support government programs was a regressive form of taxation that particularly hurts the poor.

Navigating the shoals of this and other issues has been a state government marked, since the early 1980s, by greater harmony between Democrats and Republicans. In the 1960s and 1970s, tendentious divisions over such issues as the Vietnam War and civil rights, combined with a sluggish economy and the fear that the state government would become insolvent, to produce a restless Delaware electorate that routinely turned out incumbent governors and members of the General Assembly. Moreover, the tensions of that era produced a certain mean-spiritedness that marked relations between Democrats and Republicans. Since the early 1980s, however, ideological tensions have declined while the economy rebounded to provide more jobs for Delawareans and increased revenues for their state government. A more satisfied electorate commonly returned incumbents to office, and politicians generally adopted a more civil and cooperative attitude towards each other as Democrats and Republicans set about doing the people's business.

From 1985 to 1999, four Delawareans have largely dominated the state's political arena. Republican Mike Castle served as Governor of Delaware (1985–1993) and then as the state's lone Congressman in Washing-

ton (1993-) where he has emerged as a leader among House Republican moderates. Castle's successor as the state's chief executive, Tom Carper (1993–), has also emerged as a political moderate, albeit the Democrat variety. Since 1985, Delaware's two U.S. Senators, the conservative-leaning Republican Bill Roth (1971–) and the liberal-leaning Democrat Joe Biden (1973–), have exercised considerable political clout in Washington because of their seniority in office. Although at odds on many issues, they usually acted in concert when Delaware's vital interests were at stake. Indeed, all four politicians have exemplified the new civility that has characterized the Delaware political scene in recent years.

CONCLUSION

As the 21st century approaches, most Delawareans are as confident of their state's future as they are proud of its past. The Chesapeake and Delaware Canal continues to geographically divide downstaters and upstaters, but the actual differences between the two

Above
U.S. Senator Bill Roth (1971–) who also was Delaware's Congressman (1967–1971). Courtesy, Senator Roth's office.

Right
Aerial view of Legislative Hall in Dover. Photo by Gary Emeigh

Opposite above
Congressman Mike Castle (1993–) who also was Governor of Delaware (1985–1993). Courtesy, Congressman Castle's office

Opposite bottom
Annual Point to Point Race at Winterthur. Courtesy, Delaware Tourism Office

groups is considerably less than it was 50 years ago, and surely less than politicians and writers, looking for a popular issue or intent on telling a good story, care to admit. One suspects that Delawareans, like the residents of small states and nations throughout the world, have a tendency to exaggerate sectional differences because this somehow makes their state or nation seem a bit larger than it really is.

Delaware's dimensions—only Rhode Island is smaller and only Vermont, Wyoming, North Dakota and Alaska have fewer people—define both its charm and potential. As a number of Delawareans have pointed out, the First State's small size lends itself to innovative ideas that would be difficult to implement in larger states.

But history indicates that Delaware hasn't always been receptive to innovative ideas. Although the first state to ratify the U.S. Constitution, it was among the last to abandon slavery and grant women the right to vote. Indeed, for much of its history Delaware has been reluctant to address significant social, educational, racial, and economic problems. Because the First State so often refused to take the initiative, the federal government or certain members of the du Pont family felt compelled to act. By 1999, however, most of the du Ponts lived outside of Delaware, and the federal government was less disposed than 35 years ago to intervene in the affairs of individual states. Now more than ever before, the future of the First State rests with ordinary Delawareans and their elected representatives.

Among the issues that must be addressed to ensure a better tomorrow for all Delawareans is finding ways to more directly involve a larger percentage of African-Americans in the First State's economic, political, and cultural life. Because legal barriers have disappeared, many blacks have matched white women in dramatic personal advancement. A large segment of Delaware's African-Americans, however, seem mired in apathy and contribute less than they might to the state's economic and social well-being. If some way can be found to stimulate their energies and ambitions, all Delawareans will benefit.

A second issue concerns the need to control the accelerating pace of commercial and residential development that threatens to further erode the quality of life of every Delawarean. For those who live in relatively "undeveloped" sectors of the state, a quick look at the commercial development and traffic congestion that marks most of the greater Newark-Wilmington area and Route 1 in eastern Sussex, or the residential developments that are scarring the once rural land-

Replica of the Kalmar Nyckel (Key of Kalmar) sailing up the Delaware River under the Delaware Memorial Bridge. Photo by Gary Emeigh

scapes of southern New Castle County and punching holes in Delaware's natural habitat everywhere, serves as a cautionary tale.

Without proper controls, the water that we drink and the air that we breathe will suffer further degradation. Moreover, the continued integrity of Delaware's woods, streams, marshes, and bays that protect and sustain our wildlife and spark in each of us that sense of awe and serenity that elevates us as human beings, may not survive the first few decades of the 21st century. Delaware's economic miracle has offered hope and possibilities to increasing segments of the population. But a higher per capita income is not the sole measure of a people's success, particularly when it is purchased at the cost of lowering the quality of life.

If the past serves as a guide, Delaware's future governments may be reluctant to confront these and many other significant issues. Even when previous General Assemblies addressed important problems, they often opted for a cosmetic cure while ignoring the fundamental question at hand. Delaware's continued use of the whipping post long after it had been abolished in every other state is a case in point. In 1935, a Philadelphia newspaper published a photo of a public whipping in Delaware that stirred strong protests inside and outside of the First State. The General Assembly's perverse response to the humanitarian outcry was to outlaw not the whipping post, but the photographing of public whippings. The last public whipping occurred in Delaware in 1952, and the General Assembly finally officially abolished the whipping post 20 years later.

Three and one-half centuries ago, David de Vries first set eyes on southern Delaware. He marveled at Delaware Bay "with whales so numerous," and at the land "so fine for cultivation." Shortly thereafter, Peter Lindestrom waxed euphoric about the Christina River "so rich in fish," and the surrounding countryside so fertile "that the pen is too weak to describe, praise and extol it." History demands of Delaware's past generations an accounting for what they have done with the state's bountiful natural and human resources since the days of De Vries and Lindestrom. A century from now history will demand a similar accounting. The long life of Delaware's whipping post, however, makes clear that when Delawareans and their public officials choose perversity and shortsightedness over empathy and vision, the accounting can be painful.

Marsh at Bombay Hook in eastern Kent County. This and other wildlife habitats are protected by the state. Courtesy, Delaware Tourism Office

"Southern Approaches," a painting by Kevin McLaughlin, depicts a scene familiar to most residents of Northern Delaware. Commuters make their daily trek from their suburban homes to work in Wilmington along well-traveled routes such as Interstate 95. Courtesy, Kevin McLaughlin

CHAPTER IX

CHRONICLES OF LEADERSHIP

Delaware's fortunes have always been strongly tied to its hundreds of miles of shoreline along the Delaware River Bay and Atlantic Ocean. The fertile coastal plain, combined with waters teeming with marine life, attracted European settlers as early as 1631.

The first settlers, a small band of Dutch fishermen, lived briefly near Lewes before being massacred by Indians. They were followed in 1638 by Swedish and Finnish settlers, who sailed farther into the bay to establish New Sweden at the mouth of a deep-flowing river they named the Christina.

Later the Scotch, Irish, Welsh, and English arrived, as well as other settlers from Western Europe. By the early 1700s another community, Willingtown, was established nearby. When chartered in 1739 the two settlements were renamed Wilmington.

During and after the American Revolution, the city prospered. Lumber, grains, paper, and textiles were milled along the plentiful streams that were the sources of power for the mills as well as conduits to outlying areas.

In 1801 a French immigrant named Éleuthère Irénée du Pont began operating gunpowder mills on Brandywine Creek. His choice of location was to have a profound effect on the state. The powder mills were the forerunner of the modern-day enterprise that bears his name, the E.I. du Pont de Nemours Company, Inc., the state's largest employer.

In the lower counties, forests of cypress, cedar, and white oak provided a thriving lumber trade. Fishing, crabbing, and oystering provided food as well as goods for trade.

By the beginning of the nineteenth century shipbuilding had become important to the state's commerce. Shipyards in many coastal and river towns produced wooden sloops, schooners, and fishing boats.

The railroad brought profound changes to lower Delaware. In 1856 the first train from Wilmington reached Seaford on a new line built by the Philadelphia, Wilmington & Baltimore (PW&B) Railroad. The downstate line opened all of Delaware to trade.

Farmers in Sussex and Kent counties planted large fruit orchards and strawberry fields and sent the crops to city markets. Lower Delaware was a major producer of peaches, pears, and strawberries well into the twentieth century. The development of a year-round broiler industry in the late 1920s was also furthered by the new overland access.

Today Delaware is known worldwide as headquarters for three major chemical firms. Nearly half of the nation's *Fortune* 500 companies claim Delaware as their corporate home. During the early 1980s an increasing number of banks and insurance companies have built large offices and computer operations here. Tourism is also a growing industry, and the Port of Wilmington draws ships from around the world.

In Kent and Sussex counties the broiler industry is still king, and the fertile land continues to yield vegetables and grains. The coastline provides towns like Rehoboth, Lewes, and Bethany with a thriving tourism business.

Today First Staters enjoy the same riches that attracted the earliest settlers. The rich land provides plentiful grains and food, and the Delaware Bay still yields a rich marine harvest for table and trade.

The organizations whose stories are detailed on the following pages have chosen to support this important literary and civic project. They illustrate the variety of ways in which individuals and their businesses have contributed to the state's growth and development. The civic involvement of Delaware's businesses, institutions of learning, and local government, in cooperation with its citizens, has made the First State an excellent place to live and work.

AMERICAN LIFE INSURANCE COMPANY

An overseas company with a local address—this is the American Life Insurance Company (ALICO). Although ALICO's headquarters are in Delaware, the company remains unknown to many Delawareans. ALICO operates in over 50 countries and territories worldwide, excluding the United States. More than 5,000 employees and 20,000 agents encompass and define ALICO's rich history that spans over 75 years.

It all started in 1921, when Cornelius Vander Starr, a 27-year-old Californian, opened an agency called American Asiatic Underwriters in Shanghai. His business began in a two-room office selling 20-year endowment policies. Two years later, Starr's entrepreneurial spirit led him to create the Asia Life Insurance Company. Within 20 years of Starr opening his agency, Shanghai became the insurance mecca of the Far East. Starr was one of the city's most successful entrepreneurs.

In 1926, he opened ALICO's first U.S. office, in New York. The global expansion continued with representation in Central and South America.

During World War II, insurance operations ceased temporarily in China, Hong Kong, and Southeast Asia. Starr's amazing business insight and leadership led the firm to phenomenal growth in wartime. ALICO's growth continued after WW II.

In 1951, Asia Life was renamed American Life Insurance Company and opened operations in the Caribbean, Middle East, and African nations. In 1968, Starr died, leaving a legacy of growth and insight for a thriving company that would persevere and expand in the Starr spirit.

In 1969, ALICO decided to relocate its headquarters from Bermuda to the acclaimed American International Building in Wilmington, Delaware. ALICO's success overseas persisted when ALICO became the first foreign life insurer fully admitted to the Japanese market, in 1972.

In 1985, ALICO's headquarters moved to One ALICO Plaza in Wilmington, Delaware, where it is located today. The building has nine floors of offices and a 10-floor penthouse-training center.

ALICO's expansion throughout the '90s is representative of ALICO's commitment to global expansion, aggressive growth in revenue, earnings, and market share. In the first half of the 1990s, ALICO expanded to The Czech and Slovak republics, Hungary, Poland, Argentina, Peru, Columbia, Venezuela, Pakistan, and Turkey. The most recent expansions were to Egypt, Uruguay, and Brazil. ALICO is now one of the largest international life insurance companies in the world, with $173 billion of life insurance in force.

In the final analysis, an insurance company is only as good as its ability to honor the commitments and promises it makes to its policyholders. Standard and Poors rates ALICO "AAA" (Superior) for claims paying ability. This is the single highest rating awarded to an insurance company.

Entrepreneurial, highly motivated people; a strategy of pioneering the establishment of insurance operations with local talent in emerging markets; and the financial strength to honor company commitments to policyholders and employees alike—all of these contribute to ALICO's long history of success and industry leadership. ALICO remains fully committed to this path, confident that the company's future will be even brighter than its past.

ARTISANS' BANK

The year was 1861. Abraham Lincoln was to become President. The Civil War had begun. The country was in turmoil and commerce was chaotic. It was a time that called for people of vision. Ten Wilmington, Delaware businessmen rose to the occasion. Despite the uncertainties and pressures on the economy brought on by the war, these 10 men boldly suggested the creation of a bank for working people: the "Artisans." They envisioned a unique financial institution—one that returned money to its depositors in the form of mortgages, loans and interest on savings. A bank owned mutually among the depositors.

The 10 founders each put up four dollars. Faith and $40 were all they had. Of that amount, $12 paid for a charter and certified copy, 50¢ for a minute book, and other disbursements for stationery. The charter was granted by the state legislature on February 28, 1861. Artisans' Savings Bank opened for business on April 1, 1861 at 117 Market St. in

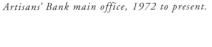

Artisans' Bank main office, 1972 to present.

Wilmington, with William S. Hillis as the Bank's first president.

After three years, the fledgling Artisans' proudly repaid each original investor four dollars, plus 72¢ interest. The Bank's secretary, Mr. John P. McLear, in his letter to the original investors dated April 15, 1864 concluded, "...that the influence of the institution throughout its history will be so marked for good as to cause you to remember with satisfaction that you had a part in its small beginnings."

The Bank steadily grew and in 1865 moved to larger quarters at 602 Market St. Artisans' Savings Bank moved again in 1871, when it purchased the historic Indian Queen Hotel on the corner of Fifth and Market Streets, and in partnership with other institutions, built the Clayton House on this site. For many years, the Clayton House enjoyed the reputation of being one of the finest hotels in the east, with the Bank occupying offices on its first floor. In 1908, the Bank moved to 505 Market Street. It stayed at that location for 64 years, until moving in 1972 to its current location at Ninth and Tatnall Streets.

In 1959, Artisans' Savings Bank began to open branch offices. Today,

Clayton House, Artisans' Bank main office, 1871 to 1908.

eight branch locations serve the community. To meet the challenges of the future, the Bank's charter was modernized in 1996. The word "Savings" was dropped from its name, and Artisans' Bank's products and services grew and expanded to provide a full-range of financial coverage, including internet banking, for its community.

The vision of the original founders continues. As a mutual community bank, Artisans' Bank continues meeting the financial needs of working men and women, retirees, students, small businesses, developers and craftspeople: the "Artisans." At year end 1998, the Bank had over $365 million in assets and just under $35 million in capital. A strong financial institution, serving its community. All the result of faith and $40.

ASHBY & GEDDES

The founding partners were ahead of their time. Attorneys at one of the major Delaware firms involved in corporate litigation, Rod McKelvie and Jim Geddes decided there was room for a small, responsive firm to handle the specific litigation needs of major clients cost-effectively while encouraging all its people to become the most they could be.

In 1979, when McKelvie and Geddes established their offices, there were "three or four" large firms doing corporate work and many smaller firms handling real estate and small local matters, recalled Larry Ashby. Ashby, in 1982, left a partnership in another of those large firms to share McKelvie and Geddes in their conviction.

Twenty years later, with their company numbering a dozen attorneys, Ashby and Geddes have carved out an identity for their partnership as a premier small litigation firm and an excellent place to work. (McKelvie left in 1992 for a judgeship on the United States District Court for the District of Delaware.)

At the beginning of the 1980s, accepted wisdom was that large corporations needed large firms of attorneys to do their work. The idea of closely monitored time and cost-effective legal billing would not become part of the corporate mindset until the decade's mergers and acquisitions boom had washed over the stock markets and begun to drain away from the mountains of debt it created. "We provided itemized bills before it became corporate practice," said Ashby.

Promoting its attorney's litigation skills, the new firm developed a team philosophy, allowing greater flexibility in bringing its staff's skills to bear on client needs while permitting its attorneys to put aside the profession's workaholic stereotype. Teamwork allowed them to back each other up. For the clients, this meant a cadre of attorneys familiar with their case. For the attorneys, it meant they could plan a vacation with little fear of the case being overtaken by unexpected

motions that only they could handle. Each attorney willingly worked long hours when necessary, enabling them to maintain family, community commitments, and the other attributes of a productive personal life.

More than that, the partners recognized that everyone, from receptionist and runners up to the managing partner, was worthy of respect and the opportunity to grow. Everyone on the team was needed to get the final product out. One employee, who started as the receptionist and later worked her way up to bookkeeper, to paralegal, and eventually to office manager, recalled, "My favorite saying was, 'We want to treat people fairly, not necessarily equally,' and being small meant we could do just that. If people had a personal problem and needed additional time off, they could take it."

The partners' concern for quality of life created a high degree of internal loyalty, with people who joined the staff staying. And, as an efficient litigation boutique, Ashby & Geddes offered a broad range of opportunities to its attorneys, allowing them experience that developed their careers more rapidly than would be likely in a traditional large firm. This burgeoning skill and long-term commitment built for the firm a reputation for responsiveness and excellence across its practice areas.

In its early days, Ashby, McKelvie and Geddes established themselves as specialists within the broad spectrum of corporate practice, handling Delaware matters in chancery and federal courts for national corporations. Their areas of practice expanded over the years to include commercial matters, bankruptcy, corporate transactions, administrative law, asbestos defense, environmental litigation and personal injury and medical malpractice cases. Clients ranged from Fortune 500 companies to individuals with small personal matters, and the firm counseled clients from across the United States and from a number of foreign countries, in connection with Delaware law.

Perhaps the most visible contract dispute the firm handled involved the 1994 battle over the firing by Dart Group Corporation's Herbert Haft of his son, Robert, as president of Dart and Crown Books. Ashby & Geddes was Delaware counsel to Robert in the dispute within the family-run operation. The case resulted in Robert recovering $40 million on his employment and option contracts.

Activity under the bankruptcy laws, which cover reorganization of viable companies (Chapter 11) as well as dissolution of those that fail (Chapter 7), is substantial in Delaware since it is legal home to many companies. Ashby & Geddes' first client in this arena was a consortium of French banks in the mid-1980s reorganization of Phoenix Steel. In the years that followed, the firm has represented nationally-based clients in most of the larger Chapter 11 reorganizations that took place in Delaware, including major secured and unsecured creditors in the Continental Airlines, United Merchants, TWA, Montgomery Ward, HomePlace, Crown Books, Days Inns, Discovery Zone, Harvest Foods, and Peter J. Schmitt reorganizations, among others.

Ashby & Geddes' corporate transactional practice involved representing corporate clients, directors, and officers in stockholder derivative and class actions, proxy contests, takeovers, going-private transactions, and other such matters. Its attorneys served as counsel to boards of directors or board committees in connection with proposed mergers or dissolutions of companies, and provided advice and opinions on Delaware law in these matters. They handled incorporation and setting up partnerships in the state.

In the corporate arena, the firm participated on behalf of the Investment Company Institute in the 1985 case that challenged the stock structure, developed by Household International, which became known as the "poison pill." It was the first such case in the state and the Dela-

The current partners at Ashby & Geddes: standing, Rich Heins, Lee Trainer, Bill Bowden, Gina Iorii; seated, Jim Geddes, Larry Ashby, Randall Robbins; absent are, Steve Jenkins and Steve Balick.

ware Supreme Court eventually affirmed the plan, paving the way for widespread use of the "poison pill" as a takeover defense.

The firm also represented Texaco against shareholder suits filed after the oil giant's takeover battle with Pennzoil over Getty Oil in the mid-1980s. The derivative suits sought to regain control over the Company's claims for its Board of Directors. Ashby & Geddes won.

As part of its administrative law practice, Ashby & Geddes is special counsel to the Governor and the Attorney General in connection with the Delaware Public Service Commission, the agency with jurisdiction over investor-owned gas and electric utilities. This included acting as staff counsel on behalf of all ratepayers in adminis-

trative proceedings, and representing the Commission in appellate work.

Even as their convictions became mainstream, Ashby & Geddes concentrated on the needs of its clients and employees. In the words of one employee, "the firm knew what it was good at, put out the best product going, found good people to work there and treated them with common sense, kindness and a respect for their strengths and allowance for their weaknesses." The firm has maintained its belief that its clients had the right to expect the very best service and finest quality work for a reasonable, fair and readily understandable fee, and that satisfying those expectations on a consistent basis was the best way to assure their own continuing growth and success.

ASTROPOWER, INC.

AstroPower is the successor to a business founded by Dr. Allen M. Barnett in 1983, to make a better solar cell for the direct conversion of sunlight to electricity. The business was an outgrowth of solar cell research at the University of Delaware in Newark. AstroPower develops and manufactures better solar electric power products to meet the large, unmet need for clean, renewable energy. AstroPower became an independent company in 1989, and a public company in 1998. It is the largest U.S.-owned manufacturer of solar cells, and the fifth largest in the world.

The electric power industry comprises one of the world's largest economic sectors, with annual revenues over $1 trillion. The current market for electric power equipment is over $200 billion with roughly 10 percent of this market dedicated to distributed generation equipment such as diesel generators and solar electric power systems. The solar electric power systems account for about 10 percent of the distributed generation equipment market, or $2 billion. The solar electric power industry shipments have increased every year since 1980, at an average rate of 23 percent. Market growth accelerated to over 40 percent in 1997, and forecasts for the future are bright. Three major areas affected by this rapid growth are: telecommunications and transportation infrastructure; electrification of rural homes for lighting and wireless power; and on-grid application where solar power systems are used to provide clean, silent, reliable electricity to consumers already connected to the utility grid.

Much of the market is very price sensitive; AstroPower responded to this by creating a proprietary product known as Silicon-Film™, a revolutionary high-speed process to produce silicon wafers. These wafers are then finished into APex™ solar cells, which in turn

can be assembled into modules for a variety of applications. This new patented process is conceptually similar to modern low-cost manufacturing techniques for sheet steel or plate glass, and offers a cost advantage of over 50 percent compared to batch-style wafer production. A decade's worth of research went into creating this product. AstroPower also produces single-crystal solar cells by reclaiming silicon wafers from the semiconductor industry. The company is developing a next-generation solar cell product that offers even higher levels of features and performance

AstroPower's first Silicon-Film™ module shown with the developers, in 1991. This first, new technology photovoltaic product was enabled with a 36% cost-sharing from the U.S. Department of Energy.

than APex™. Although such a product is still several years away from high volume production, the potential of this effort was recently substantiated when the U.S. Department of Energy awarded AstroPower a three-year, $3.5 million development contract.

The company moved its manufacturing facility from the center of the University of Delaware campus to a larger space on the edge of campus, in 1991. With its primary mission accomplished to build a better solar cell, AstroPower set out to create a better company. In 1992, the firm began recruiting a commercial team with substantial business experience to lead Silicon-Film™ commercialization and production scale-up. As a key stage in this transition, AstroPower made a significant investment in 1996 to finalize the technical development of its Silicon-Film™ technology, contributing to a loss for that year. Since that investment, the company has been profitable for nine successive quarters. In February 1998, AstroPower completed an Initial Public Offering that raised approximately $17.1 million. The IPO proceeds have significantly strengthened the organization, and were used to open a second manufacturing facility in Newark.

Today, AstroPower is one of the leading manufacturers of solar cells and solar electric power modules. Product revenue has grown at an average of 65 percent each year since 1992, making AstroPower one of the fastest growing solar electric power companies in the industry. The company has not strayed from its primary product focus, solar cells, and AstroPower's proprietary technology for low cost manufacturing has made the firm one of the most profitable solar electric power enterprises. The Silicon-Film™ product is considered revolutionary; the company has been steadily adding to its technology, which will lead to the next generation of thin-film and advanced products. AstroPower employs over 300 people, and plans to double its manufacturing capacity by the end of 1999. AstroPower's technology, talent and opportunity make the future bright. With continued progress in innovation and operational development, AstroPower is poised to continue its rapid growth.

Above
APex™ continuous-sheet technology, is currently being scaled up in the new Pencader plant. This technology will carry the company to significantly higher levels of production capacity while further improving their cost position. APex™ solar cells are made by using a revolutionary new continuous high-speed process called Silicon-Film™ that produces silicon wafers in a matter of minutes, similar in many ways to modern, low-cost methods for manufacturing plate glass or sheet steel.

Below
One of the first Silicon-Film™ panels. It was installed in a 17 kilowatt, grid-connected system. This system has demonstrated no measurable change in performance over 4½ years. It is operating at the PVUSA site in Davis, California.

BAYHEALTH MEDICAL CENTER
MILFORD MEMORIAL HOSPITAL

The present-day Milford Memorial Hospital, established in 1938, can actually trace its beginnings to the first hospital in downstate Delaware, the Milford Emergency Hospital, founded in 1913. Mary Louise Donnell Marshall is credited as being the founder of Milford Memorial Hospital. As early as 1907, she enlisted the help of her friends to establish a local hospital. After several failed attempts, she was successful in her efforts, when during the 1912-1913 session of the General Assembly of Delaware, House Bill 194 authorized the establishment of the Milford Emergency Hospital. On July 1, 1921, Milford Memorial Hospital was relocated to 123 N.W. Front Street.

In 1915, Milford Emergency Hospital established a school of nursing, located on the upper floor of the hospital. Over the years it moved a number of times, but finally came to occupy the G. Layton Grier Building on the present hospital grounds. The school of nursing was closed in 1976.

In the mid-1930s, it became apparent that a larger community hospital was needed. A fund-drive was started and the new 100-bed hospital, renamed Milford Memorial Hospital, was opened on April 9, 1938. In 1954, a four-story clinical addition was added to the existing hospital and a separate three-story building (the Grier Building) was constructed to house the school of nursing, and housing for the nursing students.

Existing facilities continued to be renovated and equipment upgraded throughout the 1950s and '60s. In 1969, another four-story wing was dedicated. This new addition housed an emergency department, cardiopulmonary, radiology, physical therapy, central supply and pharmacy services. In 1974, Milford Memorial Hospital constructed the 12-suite Medical Arts Building for use by medical staff members. In 1985, the most recent addition to Milford Memorial Hospital was dedicated—the Burton-Fischer

Milford Memorial Hospital today.

Wing. This addition provided expanded quarters for the emergency, laboratory, radiology, and physical therapy departments.

The present-day Milford Memorial Hospital campus is made up of the main hospital building, the Grier building, a 12-suite Medical Arts Building and the Regional Rehabilitation Center.

In addition to the Milford campus, the hospital owns outreach offices in Frederica, Harrington, Georgetown and Milton.

From its humble beginnings as a 12-bed hospital to its current compliment of 163 beds, Milford Memorial Hospital has always enjoyed tremendous community support. For, just as community health needs have always determined the types of services

Milford Memorial Hospital offers, community philanthropy has always helped to finance the new initiatives. Donations of bedroom slippers and furniture helped to equip the first hospital. The 1985 capital campaign generated $1.7 million dollars (113% of goal) to build a new wing, and the 800+ current auxiliary members contribute more than $100,000 annually for the purchase of needed capital equipment. From these examples, it is clear that the community has always been actively involved in the growth and development of its hospital.

Milford Memorial Hospital in the 1970s.

BAYHEALTH MEDICAL CENTER
KENT GENERAL HOSPITAL

Kent General Hospital main campus.

More than 70 years ago, the Dover Rotary Club recognized central Delaware's need for a health-care facility, and sponsored a project to develop a hospital in Dover. The $190,000 required was raised through a community fund drive, a special bequest, and a bond issue. The result was a 40-bed hospital, opened in 1927, known as Kent General Hospital.

During the Hospital's first year of operation, 583 patients were admitted, and 169 were treated in the dispensary. The operating expense for the first year was $32,700.

The population of central Delaware was rapidly growing, and additional bed space became a necessity. In the mid-1940s, just 20 years after the Hospital was founded, the second major building campaign was organized. A community fund drive and Federal grants helped speed the building program, and a new wing opened in 1951, making Kent General a 93-bed hospital.

In the 1950s and 1960s, demand for hospital services increased tremendously. Kent General expanded its laboratory, special care units, and labor and delivery facilities in 1950s. The laboratory and radiology departments expanded, beds for medical/surgical and post-partum patients were added, and a new nursery was built in the 1960s. During this time, physical therapy was introduced, and a special care unit opened that offered advance-monitoring equipment for cardiac patients.

As Kent General celebrated its 45th anniversary in the 1970s, the Hospital completed another major building program to upgrade outpatient services and expand emergency services.

In the early 1980s, central Delaware's first inpatient psychiatric unit—ADAPTS (Adult and Adolescent Psychiatric Treatment Services) was opened at Kent General, as was a new state-of-the-art radiology and imaging department. Also during this time, Kent General's operating room was enlarged to six suites, the pediatrics department was expanded and relocated, and a birthing room was added to the maternity ward.

In the mid-1980s, Kent General embarked on another major building project that resulted in a four-level addition and improvements to older parts of the hospital. The number of beds increased to 157. The Central Delaware Oncology Center opened in 1987—bringing radiation oncology services to the region.

Construction continued in the 1990s, as Kent General sought to keep up with the needs of the growing population. A new emergency department was dedicated and named the J. Allen and Esther Frear Emergency Medical Pavilion, in October 1994. In 1995, Kent General dedicated a new Outpatient Rehabilitation Center and a Women's Care Center.

In 1996, psychiatric services moved off-campus to a new location at the St. Jones Center for Behavioral Health, a 48,000 square-foot psychiatric facility located on 31 acres east of Dover. A new Outpatient Services Center also opened in 1996.

In January 1997, Kent General Hospital and Milford Memorial Hospital merged to form Bayhealth Medical Center. Several major building projects are planned for the future to keep pace with the healthcare needs of friends and neighbors in southern Delaware.

St. Jones Center for Behavioral Health is located east of Dover on 31 acres of land.

BELFINT, LYONS & SHUMAN, P.A

In 1923, Charles I. Belfint started a small accounting practice in Wilmington. Over the years, this practice, now known as Belfint, Lyons & Shuman, P.A., evolved into one of the largest certified public accounting and business consulting firms in the state of Delaware. The firm is now celebrating its 75th anniversary.

Belfint, the original founder of the firm, was born in London, England, in 1902. When he was two years old, he emigrated to the United States with his family, who eventually settled in Delaware. Belfint graduated from Wilmington High School in 1920, and attended The Wharton School of the University of Pennsylvania, where he graduated with a B.S. degree in accounting in 1925. While pursuing his degree in the evenings, he worked in the general accounting offices of the Pennsylvania Railroad Company. It was during this time, that he first practiced as a public accountant. Belfint earned his Delaware CPA Certificate #16 in 1927 and, over the years, was instrumental in helping to shape the public accounting practice in Delaware. He served on the Delaware State Board of Accountancy for 35 years and with the Delaware Society of CPAs, in addition to other professional and charitable organizations. Belfint made many contributions to his chosen profession and to the local community of Wilmington during his many years in public accounting. He was married, with no children. Belfint died in 1987.

In 1958, Norman J. Shuman, CPA, PFS, and current president of the board of directors of Belfint, Lyons & Shuman, joined the firm as senior accountant. At the time, the firm totaled six employees. Born in 1932, in Baltimore, Shuman attended high school there and went on to The Wharton School of the University of Pennsylvania, where he earned a B.S. degree in economics in 1954. Later, he attended the University of Baltimore Law School and New York University Extension Institutes. He received his CPA certification from the state of Maryland in 1957, and

Charles I. Belfint, founder.

from Delaware in 1960. Shuman became a partner of the firm in 1968 and managing director in 1972. He remained managing partner of the firm until 1978, when he was named president. He has been actively involved in leadership positions with the Delaware Society of Certified Public Accountants, the American Institute of Certified Public Accountants, and served as a board member of the International Group of Accounting Firms. He is married, with five children and three grandchildren.

In the 1960s, Desmond A. Lyons joined the accounting firm. Lyons' tenure, however, was short lived. He died in the '70s.

Today, the firm of Belfint, Lyons & Shuman is comprised of some 56 people, led by eight directors. Its

accounting professionals total 39. Located in Wilmington, the firm offers a wide range of accounting and business consulting services that include: tax planning and preparation; accounting and auditing; personal financial and estate planning; litigation support; business succession; management information support; and Delaware investment-holding company services. Overall, the firm serves a wide range of clients that include individuals; small, privately held businesses; nonprofit organizations; contractors and construction firms; real estate development and financial service companies; manufacturers; wholesalers; retailers; and various professional service organizations, such as medical, dental, legal, and employee benefits.

Belfint, Lyons & Shuman's objective is to offer the highest quality cost-effective financial services, through one-on-one interaction with its clients. The firm is committed to excellence in caring for its clients' present and future needs. Each accounting engagement is approached as a new challenge, with the individual needs of the client being foremost in importance. In keeping with a tradition that started more than 75 years ago, clients have come to rely on those services. Belfint, Lyons & Shuman is proud of the role it has played in helping to shape the accounting industry in Delaware and looks forward, with confidence, to playing a major role in its future.

Belfint, Lyons & Shuman employees at 75th anniversary event. Photo by Lynn Mascalco

BLUE CROSS BLUE SHIELD OF DELAWARE

The First State's first health insurance company was Blue Cross Blue Shield of Delaware.

As millions of Americans faced financial struggles during the Great Depression, the first Blue Cross plans were founded to help make hospitalization affordable. In 1935, Harold V. Maybee, who helped set up a Blue Cross plan in Washington, D.C., came to Delaware to start a similar plan.

With Mr. Maybee's guidance, Wilmington's hospitals, business leaders and physicians created a corporation called Group Hospital Service, Inc. It was the nation's thirteenth Blue Cross plan and the forerunner of today's Blue Cross Blue Shield of Delaware. And, it was an idea whose time had come.

The company grew rapidly as businesses and individuals embraced the new coverage for hospital expenses. In 1943, Group Hospital Service introduced Blue Shield plans for surgical and medical insurance. Three years later, Group Hospital Service was a pioneer in expanding coverage to include psychiatric care. Before long, the company introduced Delaware's first major medical and extended benefits. As the demand for health benefits continued to soar, the company developed a broader range

The headquarters of Blue Cross Blue Shield of Delaware is at One Brandywine Gateway in Wilmington.

A 1952 street banner in Milford announcing Blue Cross Blue Shield of Delaware.

of health plans. In 1965, Group Hospital Service changed its name to Blue Cross Blue Shield of Delaware.

Throughout its history, Blue Cross Blue Shield of Delaware (BCBSD) has been recognized for its innovation and dedication to providing the highest quality health benefit programs. Innovations included: opening the first HMO in Delaware; creating managed care programs for health, mental health, and substance abuse; and bringing the first point-of-service plans to Delaware. Offering a full portfolio of traditional and managed care plans, BCBSD covers more Delawareans than any other health insurer. The

comp-any prides itself in providing superior customer service to its members. It also applies the latest technology to efficiently process claims.

Blue Cross Blue Shield of Delaware is now at the forefront of bringing Blue's benefits to citizens of other countries. In 1994, BCBSD established Blue Cross Blue Shield of Uruguay, that country's first private health plan. Four years later, BCBSD launched Blue Cross Blue Shield of Argentina. In 1999, BCBSD became the first company licensed to sell health insurance in Taiwan. The company is continuing to form partnerships worldwide.

Despite its broad horizons, BCBSD is deeply rooted in Delaware. Over the years, the company has built close, productive relationships with the business and medical communities and its customers, all of which enable it to provide the best in health benefits and service. And BCBSD's employees touch people's lives as volunteers in more than 50 different organizations statewide.

As Delaware's leading health benefits organization, BCBSD is dedicated to keeping the promise of quality service, exceptional access and unparalleled value for the people it serves at home and around the world.

CARAVEL ACADEMY

Caravel Academy, from concept to accomplishment, was guided by its founder, Robert C. Peoples—builder, teacher, father, and philanthropist. His vision, dedication, financial support and commitment provided the cornerstone on which the school is built. So well has the school served the needs of the growing community, that Caravel Academy has become one of the finest full-program college preparatory academies in the East.

Located on 75 acres in the heart of residential developments in the Bear/Glasgow area, the campus includes educational facilities that range from preschool to 12th grade. At the Academy's inception in 1979, six classrooms were built for 172 students, quickly followed by six more classrooms in 1980 and another six in 1981. In 1981, the Board decided to add high school classes, and a large expansion took place in the next few years with construction of a cafeteria, library and nine classrooms. In 1982, a modern gymnasium capable of seating 1,200 was added to the complex of classrooms linking the lower, middle and upper schools.

In 1984, to suit the needs of the growing community, a preschool building was erected adjacent to, but separate from, the main buildings. This structure is situated with ample room for a large playground area

President of Board Mrs. Dorothy M. Peoples.

with attractive recreational equipment and a natural area for walks and observation of flora and fauna. From the age of three through kindergarten, students learn to work cooperatively with each other and to appreciate themselves as individuals. Children and parents delight in walking into the foyer, which is enhanced by cheerful wall murals. Both inside and out, the preschool building provides a nurturing environment for young children.

Because the board wished to increase opportunities available to all Caravel students, a second gym and eight classrooms followed in 1989. In addition, a lighted stadium provided fields for football, soccer, hockey and lacrosse. The newest facility, added to the complex in 1996, is a lower school library and a band room, both of which include enhancements proving that Caravel Academy is a shining example of a supportive, educational environment.

Building expansion has been matched with equipment purchased and updated. Two classrooms serve as computer labs with 30 stations of computers. Each classroom in the school has at least two computers, in addition to the teacher's. Both the upper school and lower school libraries have a bank of computers, and each classroom is wired to library card catalogs. The grade reporting

Artist's rendition of Caravel Academy. Painting by Shawn Faust

system is electronic, giving teachers the capacity to keep grades up-to-date and to transport report card grades to the central office.

Not only the philanthropy, but also the philosophy of the founder Robert C. Peoples, has inspired the amazing growth of Caravel Academy. His belief in the value of hard work and honest effort underlies the school's emphasis on traditional American values. Students are expected to be respectful of others, honest in interpersonal relations as well as academic pursuits, and to be sincere in efforts to achieve improvement for themselves and others. Students are required to dress and to conduct themselves in manners which uphold the high standards of the school's code of conduct.

The curriculum of the Academy is directed to the student seeking a college preparatory program. As students move through lower school, they find they are challenged to think creatively, as well as to achieve academically. In the middle school, students begin to assume more responsibility, as their instruction changes from a centralized classroom to a departmentalized team approach. A wide variety of activities is offered to all middle schoolers, and by the sixth grade, all students are required to participate in two extracurricular activities per year.

Academics are the first priority: English, math, history, languages, science and computer studies form the core of the program. Students in the upper school have the opportunity to choose advanced placement classes in many of the academic areas. Ideally, upon graduation, each student will not only have prepared him or herself for higher education, but will also have developed a love of learning that fosters a pattern of lifelong learning. Because of the quality of the program, Caravel students have had no trouble being accepted by many of the country's finest colleges and universities.

Academic achievement is not the only goal of the Caravel program.

Building and athletic fields of Caravel Academy. Photo by Eric R. Crossan

An educated person is a responsible, contributing, humane and sharing individual who possesses mature values as well as a mature mind. Music, art, drama and sports opportunities are offered to all students, and service to the school and community is a requirement for graduation. Through these experiences it is hoped that students develop integrity, character, courage, leadership and loyalty.

As Caravel Academy enters its third decade of existence, plans are underway to add to the campus a field house, which will be the finest high school facility in the state. In addition, classroom space will be enhanced and more classes of advanced placement status will be offered. Both physically and intellectually, Caravel Academy is advancing. Like the caravels Columbus used to discover a New World, Caravel Academy is a setting a course for students to discover their potential.

Members of the Board of Education of Caravel Academy: Carol Manubay, Paul Manubay, Dorothy Peoples, Robert Peoples, Jr., Thomas Peoples and Harrison Peoples.

CORRADO AMERICAN, INC.

The beginning was not auspicious. It was August 1945. Joe Corrado decided to start a new business. He and his brother planned to do landscaping for Wilmington's upscale Westover Hills neighborhood. They operated from the kitchen table in Joe's home, and their startup equipment consisted of a pickup truck, some picks, and a few shovels. As the business expanded and they ventured into new endeavors, Joe hired employees to assist him. The payroll totaled less than $500 each week for a staff of ten, and Joe usually just brought the entire week's payroll to the office in the pocket of his work pants. Laborers earned about 40¢ per hour, and equipment operators were paid about $1.40 hourly.

In those early days, following closely on the heels of World War II, countless other entrepreneurs set out along a similar path. Men and women returned from "over there" and invested their time, energy, and resources to establish companies throughout the Delaware-area as peacetime prosperity was restored. There were many men like Joe Corrado, who climbed onto a piece of heavy equipment, determined to forge a new path. But Joe's turned out to be a different kind of story.

Original office at 2400 West Fourth Street, Wilmington.

Joe Corrado was never content to ride along. Instead, he drove his bulldozer to the top of the mountain. Today, he sits as chairman of the board of Corrado American, Inc., one of the largest site-development contracting companies in the tri-state area comprising Delaware, Pennsylvania, and Maryland. Even at age 80+, he continues to turn up in the office each day—not just to sit and reminisce, but to run the business in much the way he always has: with 150% commitment to excellence in everything the company undertakes, and with loving attention to his 500+ employees. The lone pickup truck Joe started with in 1945 has given way to more than 200 pieces of heavy equipment. The kitchen table that was their original workspace has metamorphosed into a two-story, 16,000 square-foot office building in burgeoning New Castle. Corrado American has played an integral role in the development of Delaware, and in many ways its story echoes the growth of the region.

When the kitchen table threatened to collapse beneath the weight of new business plans, the Corrados moved their operations to a small office behind their machine repair shop at 2400 West Fourth Street on Wilmington's west side. Those close quarters remained the business

Joe Corrado's D2 bulldozer, circa 1940.

headquarters for almost 35 years. In 1980, Corrado American moved to its present location at 200 Marsh Lane in New Castle, where the office building is augmented by a machine shop, a warehouse, and a storage yard for heavy equipment. Joe Corrado's first piece of heavy equipment was a Caterpillar D2 bulldozer. He ordered the equipment without any idea how to operate it. The salesman who delivered the bulldozer quickly showed Joe how to pull the rope to turn the engine over, and then departed, never to be seen again. Joe spent the next three days nursing an extremely sore shoulder, worn out from his ripping the cord repeatedly to revive the bulldozer's stalled engine. That first bulldozer was just an inkling of the dump trucks, rollers and backhoes that would become part of the Corrado fleet. The company now owns virtually every piece of dirt-moving equipment manufactured today, including some of Caterpillar's largest machines.

Joe Corrado is the first to acknowledge that the success of Corrado American reflects the hard work of countless people, past and present. Among the most important contributors are his two sons, Joseph J. Corrado ("Butch") and Frank Corrado ("Gogo"). Frank has assumed primary responsibility for field operations, supervising employees who work on site-development projects including excavating, installing underground utilities, paving, and curbing. Joseph J. has concentrated on administrative responsibilities, marketing the company's services and developing related businesses. The concerted efforts of father and sons has expanded the Corrados' business group, which now includes asphalt-batching plants, stone depots, cement plants, and two manufactured housing communities. The Corrados have formed partnerships with numerous other enterprises throughout Delaware to operate these businesses, always with a firm commitment to producing their own materials and strengthening the site-development business that remains the cornerstone of their operations. In 1999, Joe Corrado's grandson, Joseph J. Corrado Jr., will complete his college degree in construction management. He plans to follow in the footsteps of his grandfather, his father, and his uncle—and he hopes to have a hand in guiding Corrado American into the new millennium.

Corrado American, Inc., has left an indelible mark throughout Delaware. On major construction projects from Claymont to Selbyville, it's likely that Corrado employees are among the first and

Left to right: Frank Corrado, Joseph J. Corrado and Joseph S. Corrado

Company headquarters, 200 Marsh Lane, New Castle.

last on the scene—excavating the foundation for a new building, shaping the site, and putting the finishing touches on the sidewalks, curbs, and parking lots surrounding it. The company's painstaking work shines brilliantly in the area, including the Brandywine Town Center, the Christiana Mall, the General Motors Boxwood Road Plant, the Texaco Refinery, the Port of Wilmington, and the Medical Center of Delaware. The history of Corrado American, Inc. is,

ultimately, a micro-history of the state of Delaware. Just as Joe Corrado's small landscaping jobs led to major construction projects, quiet, rural Delaware has become a thriving state with busy metropolitan centers. Neither Corrado American nor Delaware has ever lost sight of the roots that keep it grounded, even as it grows.

Although Corrado American, Inc., long ago set its sights beyond small landscaping projects in Westover Hills, the company and the family that leads it have never wavered from the dedication that paved the way for its success. For nearly 55 years, the guiding philosophy has always remained clear: completing the job on time (no matter how tight the schedule), delivering a superior product, operating safely every day, and remaining mindful of the well-being of all employees. All of the individuals who are part of Corrado American, Inc.—and thereby part of Joe Corrado's family—look forward to climbing on a bulldozer and moving the company forward, mission intact, into the 21st century.

DAIMLERCHRYSLER CORPORATION

The history of the DaimlerChrysler Corporation assembly plant in Newark, Delaware began on December 22, 1950. On that day, Army Ordnance officials announced that they had selected Chrysler Corporation to build and operate a new facility called the Chrysler Delaware Tank Plant. Chrysler would produce a new medium tank, the Patton M-48, as well as a new heavy tank, designated the T-43. Tank production continued at the plant until 1956, when conversion to car production began in the main assembly building. Tank production at the Chrysler Delaware Tank Plant totaled over 2,500 units.

On April 30, 1957, the Newark Assembly Plant built its first passenger car, a Plymouth Plaza. It was reported by the Wilmington *Morning News* to be a "snappy, two-tone, four-door sedan, meadow green with sand dune white trim." By the end of 1957, the number of employees at the Newark plant had grown from 850 to over 1,300. The plant had a total payroll of $6.2 million and produced 34,023 cars in its first year.

Over the next 42 years, the Newark Assembly Plant has produced Plymouths, Dodges, and Chryslers. It has built sedans, hardtops, coupes, convertibles, station wagons, and beginning in 1997, sport utilities. On October 23, 1998, Newark Assembly celebrated the production of its 7,000,000th vehicle.

Newark Assembly, during its first 42 years of car and truck production, was part of the Chrysler Corporation. Chrysler, headquartered in Auburn Hills, Michigan, was established on June 6, 1925, when Walter P. Chrysler decided to buy the Maxwell Motor Corporation where he was chairman. He had revitalized Maxwell with the development of the Chrysler Six, America's first medium-priced, high-styled automobile. By January 1924, Maxwell had set an industry record when sales of the Chrysler Six reached 32,000 units.

Walter P. Chrysler's leadership and innovation resulted in early success for the company that bore his name, and by 1928, the Chrysler Corporation was producing Chrysler, DeSoto, Plymouth, and Dodge automobiles.

Chrysler's commitment to engineering excellence was apparent during the 1930s. It resulted in innovations such as the patented "Floating Power" engine mounting system that provided a much smoother ride than previous vehicles. The Chrysler and DeSoto Airflow vehicles, introduced in 1934, were radical departures from conventional designs, and proved to be devastating financial failures. Despite the public's lack of interest, the car's streamlined shape, superior ride quality, and improved body construction would influence car building for years to come.

In the 1940s, America shifted industrial production from consumer goods to defense equipment. Chrysler Corporation contributed to this effort by producing tanks, aircraft engines,

tactical trucks, boats, ammunition, compasses, and other material.

Postwar prosperity resulted in strong consumer demand for cars and trucks, and Chrysler responded by buying or building 11 plants between 1947 and 1950.

Chrysler's history during the 1950s and '60s reflects engineering innovation and dramatic styling change. Industry firsts such as power steering, hemispherical combustion chamber V-8 engines (Hemis), all-transistor car radios, rear facing 3rd seats in station wagons, airfoil windshield wipers, and unibody construction continued Chrysler's leadership role in engineering.

Financial problems plagued the company, however. Gasoline shortages, political uncertainty, high interest rates, severe inflation, and weakening consumer confidence drove Chrysler into financial crisis in the late 1970s, and the company's survival became an issue of national debate.

In December 1979, Congress passed the Chrysler Corporation Loan Guarantee Act, which provided Chrysler $1.5 billion in federal loan guarantees. Delaware Governor Tom Carper, then a newly elected State Treasurer, played a pivotal role in securing the support of Delaware in that effort.

Chrysler's revival began with the introduction of the K-cars. The simple, front-wheel-drive platform was used to create various models for all of the company's car divisions. They succeeded, and slowly "The New Chrysler Corporation" began to emerge from its financial problems.

The employees of Newark Assembly Plant were an important part of that rejuvenation and began production of the Dodge Aries and Plymouth Reliant on September 3, 1980. Chairman and CEO Lee A. Iacocca led the ceremonies, driving the first K-car off the line.

The K-cars, soon to include a Chrysler version, became a success after some initial public wariness, and Chrysler sold 15,086,050 K-based

1,000th Patton M-48 Tank built at the Chrysler Delaware Tank Plant.

cars from 1980 through 1995. On July 13, 1995, Newark Assembly produced the last K-based vehicle, a Chrysler LeBaron convertible, and an important era in Chrysler's history ended.

In 1983, two events signified the progress made by the corporation. First, Chrysler paid off the federal loan guarantees seven years early, at a profit to the U.S. Government of $350 million. Second, Chrysler began production of its new minivans. The Dodge Caravan and Plymouth Voyager created a new market segment, and changed the way Americans viewed family transportation.

The late 1980s and early 1990s were exciting and dynamic times for both Chrysler and Newark Assembly. Chrysler made its biggest acquisition in 1987, when it purchased American Motors Corporation, including the world famous Jeep®.

Newark Assembly launched the corporation's replacement for the original K-cars, the Dodge Spirit and Plymouth Acclaim, on October 10, 1988. The cars were produced for seven years at Newark Assembly and proved to be one of the highest quality and most reliable vehicles in Chrysler's history.

During that launch, management and the leadership of the U.A.W., along with the people of Newark Assembly,

developed and began implementing a Modern Operating Agreement based on respect, trust, shared responsibilities and joint decision-making. One of the agreement's key objectives is to "make full use of the knowledge, skills and abilities of all our employees." Newark continues today to emphasize full participation by all employees as a foundation of its success.

Chrysler continued its financial recovery and began a restructuring that would revolutionize the way cars and trucks are designed and built. Platform teams were organized, teaming representatives from such diverse departments as design, engineering, purchasing, manufacturing, and marketing to work together on a single vehicle line through its entire life cycle.

This new approach resulted in some of the most exciting new vehicles in the world. Dodge Viper, a V-10 roadster, came to the public almost unchanged from its rave reviews as a concept car. The totally new Jeep Grand Cherokee in 1992 redefined the sport utility market. Then, in 1993, a new line of family sedans with innovative cab-forward design excited the imagination of the American public. The Eagle Vision, Dodge Intrepid, and Chrysler Concorde were critical and popular successes as soon as they reached the showroom.

Again, Newark Assembly played an important part in this critical phase of Chrysler history. Newark began production of the Dodge Intrepid on August 2, 1993, making it one of the most complex car assembly plants in the world. During 1993 and 1994, Newark Assembly built, on one assembly line, 35 different versions of three completely different vehicle platforms, using almost 7,000 parts, for shipment to North America, South America, Europe, and Asia.

Recognizing the important contribution that the plant makes to Newark and the entire state of Delaware, the celebration of the Intrepid launch was attended by Governor Thomas R. Carper, Senators William V. Roth, Jr. and Joseph R. Biden, Jr., and Congressman Michael N. Castle.

In the midst of launching three different car lines, Newark received the "State of Delaware Quality Award" in 1993. Robert J. Eaton, Chairman of the Board and CEO of the Chrysler Corporation, accepted this prestigious award for Newark Assembly on November 8 at the Hotel DuPont.

During 1994 and 1995, however, the future for Newark Assembly was a matter of major concern for the employees, the State of Delaware, and Chrysler Corporation.

The marketplace had made a dramatic shift toward trucks and sport utility vehicles, and away from cars. July 1995 marked the end of LeBaron convertible production. In December 1995, Dodge Spirit, Plymouth Acclaim, and Chrysler LeBaron sedan production ended.

Newark's future was dim, and many expected that the plant would close. Demand for the product produced at Newark was down. The plant operated on one shift and at a substantially lower production rate.

Even during this time, however, the spirit of trust and cooperation in the Modern Operating Agreement surfaced. An innovative and remarkable agreement between Union and Management provided for two-week rotations of two production crews. This enabled the plant to retain a two-shift work force, even on the single-shift production schedule.

In November 1996, the future of the Newark Assembly Plant and its employees brightened considerably. Chrysler announced that Newark would build its newest entry into the red-hot sport utility market: the all new Dodge Durango.

Aggressive looks, terrific handling and great performance make Dodge Durango a favorite in the sport utility market.

Through the cooperative efforts of Chrysler, the U.A.W., and the State of Delaware, Newark Assembly would be the only plant in the world building the Dodge entry in the growing sport utility segment. Dodge Durango went from concept approval to production in just 23 months, a record time.

The corporation spent $623 million to bring the Durango to Newark, including an all-new state-of-the-art paint shop that not only provides a beautiful paint finish, but makes significant improvements in environmental controls.

The 3,200 employees of Newark responded to this new opportunity with the dedication and energy it required. A small team of Newark employees spent over a year in Michigan, working with engineers, suppliers, and designers to ensure that the Durango was ready before it came to Newark.

Production processes were tried, modified, and perfected in a new facility at Newark called the Process Simulation Building. Workstations were simulated on moving assembly lines, even while the main plant was undergoing a total renovation.

Inside the plant, the ceiling and walls were painted for the first time since 1951 (84,000 gallons of paint). The entire plant was relamped (5,100 new fixtures). The cafeterias were refurbished, the parking lots resurfaced, and the plant ventilation and water systems were improved. A new, permanent training facility with 14 classrooms was constructed, and in a joint program with the U.A.W., a new exercise facility was built. The administration building was gutted and completely renovated for the first time since the 1950s.

On September 5, 1997, Newark Assembly was again the site of a new vehicle launch celebration. Chairman of the Board Robert J. Eaton said that, in order for the Durango to be a success, it would take "...teamwork. In other words, an everyday renewal of the training, hard work, attention to detail, and customer focus that got the Dodge Durango here in record time, and gave Newark Assembly Plant the opportunity to show the world just how good you are."

As Newark Assembly enters the 21st century, it is part of the DaimlerChrysler Corporation, a multi-national organization combining the strength and creativity of Chrysler and Daimler-Benz to form a transportation and services company second to none. There is every reason to believe that Newark Assembly will play an important role in the success of DaimlerChrysler for years to come.

COHEN'S FURNITURE

The Cohen family has been a force on the Wilmington scene since the early 1920s. Initially in the food business, the Cohen sons learned about hard work and community service as they fed Wilmington families during the Depression. When World War II came to the U.S., the sons went to war, serving in both the European theater and the South Pacific.

The Cohen's first venture into home furnishings was rebuilding home refrigerators. Joseph Cohen, a welder at the Dravo shipyards during World War II, also dabbled in used furniture and antiques before founding Cohen Furniture in 1942. Their first showroom was a converted 900 square-foot space at 825 Walnut Street. Herman Cohen joined the firm in February 1946, following his discharge from the army. He was a non-commissioned officer in the Americal Infantry Division Signal Company.

In the early days, the staff at Cohen Furniture consisted of Joseph, Herman and a helper. Herman received a paycheck of $20.00 per week. Many of their customers were local people who knew the Cohen brothers from the family food business.

Gambrinus, mythical king of beer. Old brewery converted to Cohen's warehouse facility and wholesale distribution center.

Remodeled and expanded store for the millenium at 4014 N. DuPont Highway, New Castle, DE.

As business grew, the need to expand drove the brothers to search for larger quarters. In 1947, they purchased 504 Madison Street, giving them 2,000 square-feet of display space. In 1951-52, the brothers built a new facility at 509-11-13 Madison Street—an 8,000 square-foot, three-story colonial structure with an interior modeled after the Independence Hall Building.

Expansion continued in the 1950s and 1960s. In 1957, Joseph and Herman purchased the six-story Stoeckel Brewery at 5th and Adams Streets. The State Highway Department bought the Brewery for the construction of I-95. In 1962, Joseph and Herman found warehouse and retail space at the old Lippincott building at 308-314 Market Street.

When one of their buildings was burned during the Wilmington riots in 1968, the Cohen brothers decided to relocate out of downtown Wilmington. With the help of a small business loan, they purchased four acres on North DuPont Highway in 1970, and built the initial structure of the present complex. Joseph retired in 1984; Herman added the warehouse at the rear of the store that same year. In 1995, he expanded the warehouse another 250,000 cubic feet, giving the present location 21,000 square feet of display space and 700,000 cubic feet of warehouse storage.

Cohen Furniture's reputation for selection, good service and value at reasonable prices has spread beyond Wilmington and New Castle Counties.

Customers now span a four-state area, including Delaware, Maryland, New Jersey, and Pennsylvania. In 1996, Cohen Furniture was recognized as the Tri-State Furniture Association "Retailer of the Year," one of the few Delaware stores to receive the award in the past 50 years.

In 1997, Cohen Furniture began to prepare for the new millennium with a major remodeling effort. The new facade updated the look of the store; the new interior was designed to make the shopping experience delightful for customers, as they flowed through various departments.

In 1984, when Joseph retired, Herman's wife Mildred, joined the business. Herman describes his proudest moment as when his wife decided to be his business partner as well as his life partner. Today, son Arnold is co-owner, and Arnold's wife, Pam, and her son Brian, work part-time at the store. Mr. Herman Cohen's other son Phillip, has chosen a career in the food industry. His daughter Sharon is the founder and executive director of *Figure Skating in Harlem* which is a non profit foundation in New York City.

After nearly six decades of growth and expansion, Cohen Furniture remains a "family" business in every sense of the word.

The "Our Family to Your Family" tradition has extended and includes over 40 co-workers who enthusiastically endorse the total service philosophy of Cohen Brothers Furniture.

DELAWARE STATE MUSEUMS

Delaware State Museums, founded in 1949, is an administrative unit of the Division of Historical and Cultural Affairs, Department of State. Exhibits, tours, and programs offered at the Museums' eight historic sites, enable guests to learn multifaceted aspects about Delaware's rich historical and cultural past. Presentations highlight a myriad of topics, including: abolition, agriculture, archaeology, architecture, decorative arts, economics, geography, government, history, law, manumission, multiculturalism, politics, prehistory, and slavery. Staffs provide meaningful encounters by depicting people, places, and events through unique learning experiences based on research, archaeological discoveries, and a study of historic building materials.

Approximately 96,000 guests visit Museums' eight historic sites annually. International visitors representing a number of foreign countries, including India, Senegal, Uzbekistan, Greenland, Israel, Kuwait, and Australia, are among the individuals who learn about Delaware history through site activities. Many professional organizations, including: museums, art leagues, private industries, church groups, service organizations, family reunions, rehabilitation and treatment centers, schools,

Separation Day at New Castle Court House.

Mural of Delaware State Museums painted by exhibits arts specialist, Adrian Guajardo.

colleges and universities participate in Delaware State Museums' programs.

Museums is also responsible for maintaining two state conference centers in historic buildings listed on the National Register of Historic Places–Buena Vista and Belmont Hall. Elected and appointed officials, national and foreign dignitaries, state employees, and special committee members are among the 14,000 guests received at these centers, annually.

Educational outreach is an important dimension of Museums' operations. Staff members loan miscellaneous educational portfolios and resource materials to educators. These materials complement classroom studies dealing with the American Revolution, the Federal Constitution, World War I and the Holocaust, and highlights a premiere Delaware artist

before 1950. Journals, letters, primary resource documents and an autobiography, provide literary genres through which students explore issues regarding slavery, manumission, and abolition. Interpretive goals and objectives developed

Learning activity at Zwaanendael Museum.

for programming activities reflect the state of Delaware's established content standards for social studies as well as visual and performing arts.

Delaware State Museums invite guests to visit their sites and learn about Delaware. The Visitor Center provides general information, a museum store, and a changing exhibit gallery. Delaware Museum of Small Town Life provides a "Main Street" theme that enables guests to explore businesses and economics characteristic of Delaware communities around 1900. The Delaware

Archaeology Museum highlights information about the science of archaeology and showcases artifacts associated with Delaware's Native American cultures. The Johnson Victrola Museum is a tribute to Eldredge Reeves Johnson, founder of the Victor Talking Machine Company and the technological development of the recorded sound industry. The State House is a restored structure representing the state's Capitol in 1792. Discussions reveal how Delaware's legislative and judicial systems impacted the lives of men, women, and children more than 200 years ago. The John Dickinson Plantation features a 1740 residence

Above
Delaware memorabilia relating to thematic tours are sold at museum stores administered by Delaware State Museums.

Below
Mattress stuffing activity at John Dickinson Plantation.

Above
John Dickinson Plantation, a National Historic Landmark.

surrounded by a reconstructed farm complex. This National Historic Landmark showcases the life of John Dickinson, a Delaware signer of the Constitution and noted "Penman of the American Revolution," father, farmer, landlord, and slave-owner. Zwaanendael Museum features exhibits and interpretation devoted to the 1631 Dutch settlement of Lewes, Delaware's changing coastline, the Cape Henlopen Lighthouse, and recovered artifacts from the British brig *DeBraak,* which sank off the coast of Lewes in 1798. The New Castle Court House, a National Historic Landmark, showcases information about Colonial Delaware, the First State Assembly, William Penn, Delaware's boundaries, government, slavery, and the abolitionist trials of Thomas Garrett and John Hunn.

DIVISION OF STATE SERVICE CENTERS—DELAWARE

When it comes to human services, Delaware could be called the little state with the big heart. Although the Division of State Service Centers (DSSC) employs only 150 people at 17 sites, the DSSC impacts the lives of thousands of Delaware residents each year. Throughout its 27 years of service, the DSSC has expanded and adapted to meet the changing human services needs of Delaware residents.

Established by an Executive Order signed by Governor Russell W. Peterson on September 18, 1972, the DSSC provides more than 160 services and programs, ranging from prenatal care to services for the aged. Under the current leadership of Director Anne M. Farley, the DSSC has developed the concept of a "health and human services campus," to provide access to various public and private agencies and training programs in one location.

The mission of the DSSC is "to alleviate crises, improve the standard of living, develop self-sufficiency, provide volunteer and community service opportunities, address the causes and conditions of poverty and provide universal access to information and referral for appropriate services for all Delawareans."

To accomplish its mission, the DSSC administers a statewide network of safe, secure, well-maintained and efficiently-operated service centers. The 14 main centers serve as multi-service facilities, with various public and private agencies under the same roof. Through the DSSC, agencies share the common goal of promoting access to Delaware's health and human services system. Division staff specialize in community resources and client support services to promote increased accessibility, enhanced service integration and efficient service monitoring of programs and services.

Delaware residents make good use of the efficient statewide service centers, with more than 600,000 visits made to state service centers throughout Delaware each year. Based on demographic analyses and com-

Charles Hyghe Debnam (1930-1996) was the visionary behind the integrated, statewide network of community-based neighborhood service centers as we know them today and which, subsequently, became a national model for administering quality human services to the public. Mr. Debnam served as the Director of the Division of State Service Centers from 1972 to 1983 and served Delaware Health and Social Services for more than 30 years.

munity outreach, each service center provides a mix of services appropriate to the communities that it serves.

The multi-purpose service center concept originated in the late 1960s. The Foster Grandparent Program was started by Delaware's Office of Economic Opportunity during that

period. In 1970, the First State Health and Social Services Center was officially inaugurated. Located in northeast Wilmington, it housed the State Divisions of Public Health, Mental Health, Social Services, Juvenile Corrections, Vocational Rehabilitations and Community Legal Aid, along with a private medical group practice.

With the success of the center that became known as the Northeast Center, state officials began planning for the network of service centers throughout Delaware. The proposal included plans for four regional centers—one in each county and one in Wilmington—and 10 satellite centers in areas of high need. The first satellite center opened in Belvedere in southwest Wilmington, in 1971.

In keeping with the trend toward the consolidation of scattered services, the Model Cities Neighborhood of downtown Wilmington moved its facilities into the Winder Laird Porter Center, which opened in June 1972. Neighborhood workers provided crisis alleviation services and

The Charles H. Debnam Building was officially dedicated on July 15, 1998, to the late Charles Hyghe Debnam. The Debnam building houses the DHSS Division of State Service Centers' Administrative Offices and DHSS Applicant Services.

Northeast State Service Center: The present site of the Northeast State Service Center at 1624 Jessup Street in Wilmington, Delaware. Northeast State Service Center was the First State Health and Social Services Center, which officially opened in 1970.

the Volunteer Services' "Adopt-A-Family" program was created in the same year.

After the official establishment of the Division of State Service Centers by Executive Order in 1972, county and satellite centers soon followed. The Laurel Center, Susssex County's first State Service Center, opened in March 1973, followed by the Bridgeville Center in July. In the same year, Retired Senior Volunteer programs were initiated in Sussex and New Castle counties.

Services were expanded to the large rural population of southwestern Sussex County in 1974, with the opening of the seventh center near Frankford. The building's construction was financed with estate funds from the late Edward W. Pyle, a prominent Sussex County resident and philanthropist. In northern Delaware in 1974, the DeLaWarr Center opened south of Wilmington, as a result of the partnership among residents, New Castle County and state and federal governments.

The Floyd I. Hudson Center in Newark was the second major center

to open in 1975, the same year that DSSC began the Statewide Information and Referral program, the precursor of Delaware Helpline, the telephone service that operates today. Another ongoing and valuable service began in 1975 with the first Directory of Human Services. For 24 years, Delaware residents have consulted the directory for information on public and private human service agencies.

The next year saw the opening of Delaware's third major service center, the James W. Williams Center in Dover. Kent County established its

first satellite center in 1977, in Milford. The original vision for the DSSC was partially completed by 1977, with the opening of the fourth major state center in Georgetown.

Expansion of the DSSC continued in the 1980s, as additional agencies came under the DSSC umbrella. The CHEER Senior program was added at the Georgetown State Service Center in 1982, the same year that the Division of Volunteer Services was formed within the State Department of Community Affairs. The activities of the Office of Economic Opportunity were also added to the Department of Community Affairs.

In 1986, the Emergency Assistance Program was transferred to the Division of State Service Centers, along with the Needy Family fund, providing a safety net for at-risk Delawareans. The Volunteer Clearinghouse also became the Volunteer Link in 1986, and volunteer opportunities came under the administration of the Division. Another satellite center, the Anna C. Shipley Center, opened in Seaford in 1987.

For more than 25 years, Delaware Health and Social Services' Division of State Service Centers has served as a safety net for hundreds of thousands of Delawareans annually, working hand in hand with communities to provide emergency one-time or long-term assistance to families in need.

An increased need for services in the Milford-area resulted in the opening of the Milford Annex Center on Front Street in Milford, in 1988. In that year, the DSSC also tackled the growing problem of homelessness, with the creation of the Emergency Shelter program.

The 1990s continued the trend toward partnership and consolidation of human services. The United Way of Delaware merged its hotline, Delaware's First Call for Help, with the DSSC Information and Referral Services to create Delaware Helpline in 1990. In 1991, the DSSC received two new agencies when the State Department of Community Affairs was disbanded. Volunteer Services and Community Services were transferred to the Division of State Service Centers, and subsequently renamed the State Office of Volunteerism and the Office of Community Services.

The State Office of Volunteerism facilitates connections among volunteers, public and private agencies and people in need. It administers the Foster Grandparent Program, the Retired and Senior Volunteer Program, Volunteer Link, AmeriCorps and Learn and Serve Programs. The Office of Community Services works to fill in the gaps in the public and private network of community services with federal funds and block grant programs.

Programs that the Office of Community Services administers include the Low Income Energy Assistance Program, the Weatherization Assistance Program, Community Services Block Grant, Emergency Housing fund, Community Food and Nutrition Program and Emergency Community Services Homeless Grant Program.

Other community developments in 1993 included the founding of six Family Service partnerships throughout Delaware. This collaboration among communities, schools, public and private agencies was developed to strengthen families and communities. Governor Thomas R. Carper's

mentoring program was also initiated in 1993 through the State Office of Volunteerism.

In 1994, community service received another boost with the inauguration of the AmeriCorps program. Nineteen ninety-four was also a significant year in the forward direction of the DSSC, with the development of the concept of a health and human services campus taking shape in Milford.

A program to recognize the many young volunteers from around the state was initiated in 1995, with the first statewide Youth Volunteer Awards. Family Visitation Centers were also opened at the Hudson and Milford State Service centers in 1995, providing facilities for custodial exchange of children for families.

The innovative concept of the health and human service campus was further developed at the "Milford Campus" in 1996. The Child Development WATCH program and the Division of Services for Aging and Adults with Physical Disabilities moved into the Milford State Service Center's Walnut Street Building. The Division of Family Services of the Department of Services to Children, Youth and their Families

was also established in 1996 in the Draper Building on the Milford campus.

A three-year renovation and expansion project was completed at the Georgetown State Service Center in 1996, making the center the largest State Service center, with 55,000 square-feet. Two new State Service centers were opened the following year—Claymont Center in New Castle County and Appoquinimink Center in southern New Castle County. With the opening of the two centers in New Castle County, the original vision of 14 state service centers to create an integrated statewide network of community-based human services delivery, was finally complete.

In 1997, the DSSC launched a ser-vice integration pilot program, called No Wrong Door, setting the stage for the future of social service delivery in Delaware. The guiding principles of the DSSC provide a simple and ongoing framework for the Division and its vital work in the community: "We offer courteous service, timely response and effective solutions to the unmet needs of the individuals and communities that we serve."

The 14 State Service Centers are located throughout Delaware:

New Castle County Service Centers
Appoquinimink State Service Center, 120 Silver Lake Road, Middletown
Belvedere State Service Center, 310 Kiamensi Road, Wilmington
Claymont State Service Center, 3301 Green Street, Claymont
Delaware State Service Center, 500 Rogers Road, New Castle
Floyd I. Hudson State Service Center, 501 Ogletown Road, Newark
Northeast State Service Center, 1624 Jessup Street, Wilmington
Winder Laird Porter State Service Center, 509 W. 8th Street, Wilmington

Kent County Service Centers
James W. Williams State Service Center, 805 River Road, Dover
Milford Campus—Milford State Service Center, 11-13 Church Avenue, Milford
Milford Annex, 13 S.W. Front Street, Milford

Milford Draper Building, 10-12 N. Church Street, Milford
Milford Walnut Street Building, 18 N. W. Walnut Street, Milford

Sussex County Service Centers
Bridgeville State Service Center, Cannon Street, Bridgeville
Edward W. Pyle State Service Center, Omar-Roxana Road, Frankford
Laurel State Service Center, Mechanics Street, Laurel
Georgetown State Service Center, 546 S. Bedford Street, Georgetown
Anna C. Shipley State Service Center, 350 Virginia Avenue, Seaford

Other Locations
C. H. Debnam Building, 1901 N. Dupont Highway, New Castle
First Federal Plaza, 704 N. King Street, Suite 605, Wilmington
Carvel Building, 820 N. French Street, Wilmington

DELAWARE HOSPICE

No one is truly prepared to deal with a limited life expectancy. However, when recovery is no longer possible, Delaware Hospice can help. Focusing on care not cure, Delaware Hospice ensures that patients and their families receive the care, comfort and support at a time when it is needed the most. Pain and symptom management and emotional support are provided in the familiar surroundings of home regardless of the ability to pay.

Delaware Hospice has provided this unique service since 1982 and is the only JCAHO (Joint Commission on Accreditation of Health Care Organizations) accredited non-profit hospice in Delaware. Comprised of a special team of professionals and trained volunteers, Delaware Hospice is dedicated to enhancing the quality of life so patients and their families may find joy in each remaining day.

Delaware Hospice works as a team of professionals and specially trained volunteers to provide care and support, in collaboration with the primary care physician, to address the distinctive needs of each patient and family.

The team includes a registered nurse who is responsible for all physical care. The RN performs skilled nursing procedures and provides aggressive pain and symptom management. Delaware Hospice nurses are available 24 hours a day if an emergency arises.

A personal care assistant is assigned to aid with all personal care, such as bathing, changing beds, and hair and skin care.

A social worker meets with the patient and family to set up regularly scheduled visits. These visits establish a special relationship that helps monitor the coping skills and address the emotional needs of both the patient and family.

Upon request, the spiritual care coordinator arranges visits to the patient from their own clergy or Delaware Hospice chaplains.

Specializing in grief and loss, bereavement counselors help survivors identify and express their feelings concerning the loss of a loved one. Individual counseling and support groups are available for up to one year.

Each volunteer completes an intensive training program where they gain understanding of the needs and experiences of those living with a limited life expectancy. Volunteers provide emotional support for the patient and respite care for the family. They run errands, provide transportation, deliver medications, or pick up prescriptions.

The New Hope Program, unique to Delaware Hospice, was founded especially for children and teens, to help young people cope with the emotions associated with the illness and death of a loved one. The yearlong program provides information, counseling, workshops, a 4-day summer camp, and support groups.

Most insurance plans, including Medicare and Medicaid, cover Delaware Hospice care. Costs are reimbursed by health care insurance plans, and by the generous donations of individuals, families, churches, corporations, and foundations.

Camp New Hope participants and volunteers.

DUPONT

DuPont is one of the oldest, continuously-operating industrial enterprises in the world.

The company was established in 1802 near Wilmington, Delaware, by a French immigrant, Eleuthére Irénée du Pont de Nemours, to produce black powder. E. I. du Pont brought to America some new ideas about the manufacture of consistently reliable gun and blasting powder. His product ignited when it was supposed to, in a manner consistent with expectations. This was greatly appreciated by the citizens of the fledgling republic, including Thomas Jefferson, who wrote thanking du Pont for the quality of his powder, which was being used to clear the land at Monticello. Many other heroes of early America owed their success, and their lives, to the dependable quality of DuPont's first product.

DuPont has transformed itself many times since then. The first transformation began at the start of the 20th century when the company lost its competitive advantage in gunpowder to burgeoning competi-

E. I. du Pont.

DuPont Company's Experimental Station in Wilmington, Delaware.

tion. Shareholders voted to sell the assets to the highest bidder, but three great-grandsons of the founder—Thomas Coleman du Pont, Alfred I. du Pont, and Pierre Samuel du Pont—offered to buy and operate the firm, issuing notes and stock in a new corporation. The offer was accepted and in 1902 the company was restructured to look for new business and create new products through

research. DuPont's research organization dates to this time, with the foundation of the Eastern Laboratory in New Jersey. Construction of the Experimental Station, just outside Wilmington, quickly followed. The "Ex Station," as it became known, originally had responsibility for process research, but by 1909, had expanded into new fields such as the investigation of synthetic fibers. This period marked the beginning of DuPont's transition from an explosives manufacturer to a diversified chemical company.

Another major restructuring took place during the severe economic recession of 1920-21, when the company reorganized into autonomous operating departments. This also marked the beginning of globalization as, soon after the reorganization, the company expanded through acquisitions and joint ventures in the United States, Latin America, Europe and Japan.

Toward the end of the 1920s, the next important breakthrough for the company came as a result of fundamental, rather than applied, research. The head of research noted at the time: "We are including in the budget for 1927 an item of $20,000 to cover what may be called, for want of a better name, pure science or fundamental research work...the sort of work we refer to...has the object of establishing or discovering new scientific facts." In a short time, the group that had been put together under this budget had developed an understanding of radical polymerization and established the basic principles for condensation polymerization and the structure of condensation polymers. This led to the invention and commercialization of nylon in 1938—the beginning of the modern materials revolution. (Prior to this, the group yielded neoprene synthetic rubber in 1933.)

Many synthetic materials cascaded from DuPont research in the next two decades, forming the basis for many global businesses and products, including household names such as

Teflon® fluoropolymer resins and SilverStone® certified non-stick finishes; Stainmaster® flooring systems; Kevlar® brand fiber; Nomex® brand fiber and paper; Lycra® elastane; Sontara® spun-laced fabric; Mylar® polyester film; Tyvek® spunbonded olefin; Cordura® nylon fiber and Corian® solid surface material.

Through the 1980s and into the 1990s, DuPont research continued to be aimed at developing materials and systems to help its customer companies achieve competitive advantage. DuPont products touch the lives of millions of people around the world everyday. DuPont materials may be as everyday as hosiery, packaging and kitchen countertops, or they may be as exotic as the parachute that lowered the Galileo probe into the atmosphere of Jupiter.

Also during this time, the company realized that developments in biology were poised to change the industrial world of the 21st century as dramatically as developments in chemistry and physics changed industry in the 20th century. Well before biotechnology was a household word, DuPont had begun to develop a research capability in this powerful new tool for science and industry. DuPont is keenly aware of its heritage and history as one of the world's premier science companies and is determined to sustain its tradition of science in the service of human needs. DuPont is now a leader in biotechnology, based on in-house science and an aggressive program of acquisitions and alliances to drive growth in the bio-industrial, pharmaceutical, agricultural, and feed and food industries. At the same time, the company is committed to building on its position as a leading supplier of materials, based on the premise that chemistry and biology will become increasingly integrated at the industrial level, as in the production of chemical intermediates or synthetic fibers through microbial activity. In keeping with this focus, the company adopted a new slogan *The miracles of*

Historical photo of the DuPont Powder Mills along the Brandywine River in Wilmington, Delaware.

science™ to replace "Better Things for Better Living," in 1999.

No overview of DuPont would be complete without mention of the company's historic contributions to industrial safety. DuPont is one of the safest companies in the world. In the U.S., its safety performance is typically 30 times better than the average for all of industry. In 1998, the company created a new business called DuPont Safety Resources, with the objective of converting its 200 years of safety knowledge and performance into a high-growth business that can help other industries and sectors of society reduce hazards and operate more safely. In the related area of environmental performance, the company also has been a leader. DuPont was the first global industrial company to commit to a target of zero

DuPont's Agricultural Products Greenhouse.

for waste and emissions, and has been a strong advocate of sustainable growth.

Today, DuPont is a science company delivering science-based solutions that make a difference in people's lives in food and nutrition; health care; apparel; home and construction; electronics; and transportation. The company operates in 65 countries and has 92,000 employees. The DuPont brand is one of the world's most trusted and respected.

The DuPont that has emerged from the company's transformation of the 1990s has often been described by people inside and outside the company as "the new DuPont." This characterization is only partly appropriate, because while DuPont has changed, there are many things that remain the same. The core competency in science and technology, the commitment to safety, the concern for people, the feeling of community, the emphasis on personal and corporate integrity, the future focus, and indeed the willingness to change—these are not "new" characteristics—they are constant forces in DuPont's culture, as the company anticipates its bicentennial celebration in July 2002.

FIRST USA

Delaware has a rich tradition as the "First State"—the state that led the new nation into constitutional independence. Today, First USA has followed Delaware's lead, ranking as the largest VISA credit card issuer in the world, and first in helping its customers achieve financial independence.

Like Delaware, First USA knows the value of being first and remaining on the cutting edge. First USA, a subsidiary of Bank One Corporation, is actively entering new areas of service, including mortgage loans, insurance, installment loans and online banking services. These new First USA products are designed to strengthen the relationship between the company and its customers, in much the same way that First USA has been building a stronger relationship with the citizens of Delaware since moving to Wilmington, in 1985. First USA also leads its competitors in product innovation, uses of technology, and superior customer service.

When First USA initially moved its credit card operations into Wilmington's Delaware Trust Building in 1985, it had approximately 200 employees and two domestic locations. First USA's ranking in the United States credit card services industry was 27th and its outstanding loans totaled $400 million. Today, First USA employs 3,500 people in Delaware and more than 22,000 employees internationally. It has 14 locations in the United States, in addition to three international locations in Ottawa, Canada; Cardiff, Wales; and London, England. Its outstanding loans exceed $100 billion, and its line of products includes not only credit cards, but also other consumer lending products including home equity loans and installment loans. First USA is the largest VISA credit card issuer in the world, with more than 58 million cardmembers worldwide.

Growing Hand-in-Hand With Delaware. First USA's remarkable growth has been fueled by a partnership with Delaware, and has paralleled

First USA's headquarters located in downtown Wilmington.

the state's prosperity. Since 1985, when First USA first relocated to Wilmington, 106,100 new jobs have been created in Delaware—a 36.2 percent net increase. Delaware's population over the same period grew by 6.4 percent , compared to a national growth rate of 4.2 percent.

Today, more than half of the Fortune 500 firms are incorporated in Delaware.

"Delaware has been a perfect fit for us, offering a progressive business environment and outstanding community resources, all of which have helped us in our efforts to make First USA a leader in credit card lending," says Dick Vague, chairman and chief executive officer of First USA.

First USA has been eager to encourage the development of

Wilmington's business, residential and cultural climate, making the relationship between the community and the company truly symbiotic. First USA has made significant contributions to the redevelopment of the Christina Riverfront, with its sponsorship of the First USA Riverfront Art Center. First USA is also a leader in other economic development initiatives, including Wilmington Housing Partnership, the Wilmington Renaissance Corporation and the Delaware Community Investment Corporation. In addition, First USA has deep relationships with and provides support to many community and social service organizations. All of First USA's community involvement is with the goal of helping to make Delaware a better place to live and work.

Other Roots of First USA's Success: Customer Service and Industry Changes. First USA's success comes from a solid growth strategy and from recent developments in the banking and credit card services industry. The U.S. banking industry has undergone tremendous deregulation in recent years, permitting greater competition in the open market. As a result, only companies that are innovative and customer-oriented have continued to be successful and grow. First USA has long been highly customer-oriented, offering services specifically tailored to the needs of individuals, which has enabled the company to take advantage of competitive opportunities and aggressively grow its business. In addition, First USA has capitalized on other opportunities, participating in the industry's rapid consolidation, by purchasing credit card portfolios including portfolios from Chevy Chase Bank, GE Capital and First Commerce Bank.

First USA's Corporate History. Born out of a series of bank mergers and acquisitions, First USA emerged to become a Delaware-based entity with both a national and international focus, and it is justifiably proud of this forward-thinking tradition. First

USA became a privately held, independently operating credit card bank in 1989, as the result of a leveraged buyout. The management team, headed by John Tolleson and Dick Vague, led this leveraged buyout, which was done in conjunction with Merrill Lynch Capital Partners.

First USA operated independently from 1989 until 1992, when the company completed an initial public offering of its stock, which was the beginning of a leveraged buyout exit strategy. As part of this exit strategy, three additional equity offerings totaled $1.1 billion over the next three years. In addition, the company had four dividend increases; two two-for-one stock splits and completed a $1 billion initial public offering of First USA Paymentech. During this time, First USA became the fastest-growing credit card company in the United States. In 1997, Bank One Corporation acquired First USA, in one of Wall Street's largest financial services acquisitions. As a result of this acquisition, First USA became the credit card issue subsidiary of Bank One, responsible for all credit card activities. Today, First USA has a 16 percent market share of the credit card services industry.

First USA's Future: Looking to Stay in First. The future for First USA

looks bright, but challenging. The entire banking industry is facing new, non-traditional competitors, as banks merge with other types of organizations, and as the rapid development of the internet's on-line banking and brokerages continues. First USA today is well-equipped to meet these challengers, by maintaining its low-cost, high-value leadership in the industry. First USA is developing partnerships, market segments and customized products, to offer greater benefits to each and every one of its customers. First USA also leads its industry in taking advantage of internet technologies to service clients. By focusing on internet portals, First USA offers instant credit, customized products and services, on-line statements and payments and full customer-service relationships.

First USA also continues to develop a strong international strategy. With enormous growth expected in worldwide charge volume over the next decade, such a strategy is imperative for any globally-minded company. First USA opened its first international offices and booked its first international accounts in December 1998. First USA's entry into the United Kingdom and Canada increases the company's target market by 44 million people.

One of most important keys to First USA's success has been hiring and retaining the right people – the best people. With its philosophy on hiring, First USA built one of the strongest management teams in the consumer lending business, and has positioned itself to continue to be an industry leader well into the future.

"We look forward to continuing our growth and expanding our customer services," says Vague. "And, as we continue to develop as a company, we will do so hand-in-hand with Delaware. Delaware has a long tradition as the 'First State,' and we would like to establish our own enduring tradition—of being *first* in serving our customers and our community."

1450 WILM NEWSRADIO

1450 WILM NEWSRADIO is Delaware's only broadcasting station (radio *or* television) dedicated to locally-originated all-news & information, seven days a week, including holidays.

For that reason, the station is unique among 1,000 watt, A.M. radio stations in the United States or Canada today; unique among A.M. "stand alone" stations (those without a sister station); and unique among stations in markets under a million people! WILM is one of America's only family held and operated news radio stations.

Listeners typically tuning in Friday night, Sunday morning, or Sunday evening still hear locally-executed all-news product (and some complementary news shows).

Northern Delaware is America's corporate capital, with scores of corporate employees, scientists, bankers, academics, and retirees in the area. 1450 WILM NEWSRADIO is not afraid to provide more in-depth news coverage to this market. The audience

Far atop Wilmington's skyline, (from left) John Watson, Delaware's #1 talk show host; Sally V. Hawkins, president; and Allan Loudell, program manager, take Delaware's pulse. Photo by Bob McClain/McClain Imagery

expects *and* respects this commitment.

The station maintains full-time business, city/county political, state legislative and court reporters. 1450 WILM NEWSRADIO's "beat" system more closely parallels the organization of a newspaper than the typical broadcast news department. Indeed, the vast majority of stories aired each day originate with WILM staff or sources, not a wire service or rewritten newspaper copy.

The station maintains its own "network" of some 350 journalists and experts around the world, for live reporting and interviews on breaking national and international news stories. This network is in addition to affiliations with CBS News, The Wall Street Journal Radio Network, The Associated Press, and Radio Deutsche Welle, from Cologne, Germany.

The recipient of nine national Marconi nominations in the 1990s, a Crystal award, and several Crystal nominations, 1450 WILM NEWSRADIO averages 40 to 50 awards each year for excellence in broadcast journalism and community service.

The FCC licensed WILM in 1923, when two young entrepreneurs, Brandt Boylan and his brother, Donald, went on the air under the

WILM NEWSRADIO Chairman of the Board and President, Sally V. Hawkins.

call letters WTBQ. Commercial radio broadcasting had only begun in North America in 1919. A newspaper account of their endeavor described Don, at age 16, and Brandt, at 22, as "the youngest men in their line of work in the country."

1450 WILM NEWSRADIO is the second-oldest, continuously-licensed broadcast station in Delaware. Over the years, it has moved up the radio dial from 1210, to 1420, and now, to 1450.

The Boylans began broadcasting through a transmitter at the top of the Equitable Trust Company building at Ninth and Market Streets, in Wilmington and the call letters changed from WTBQ to WILM.

In 1949, Ewing B. Hawkins purchased Delaware Broadcasting Company, taking over as president and general manager. By 1959, Sally V. Hawkins joined her husband's company as treasurer. She has served as president since 1972.

The Hawkins' have earned their reputation as innovators in the broadcast industry. Over the years, they have taken extraordinary steps in the development of radio as we know it today. For example, WILM had one of the first two-way telephone-talk programs in the country. Many older Delawareans will remember the controversial and flamboyant Joe Pyne, who hosted a two-way talk show as early as 1949. Pyne was on the WILM staff for some five years, and stands today as the accepted originator of controversial talk radio.

In 1976, WILM became 1450 WILM NEWSRADIO—a primarily locally-originated, all-news station— backed up by N.I.S., the old NBC Radio news and information service. N.I.S. represented the first attempt at an all-news, national radio network.

To be sure, CBS and Group W (Westinghouse Broadcasting Company) had converted many of their A.M. radio stations (mostly 50,000 watt, "clear channel" stations) to all-news in the 1960s, but those were stations in the nation's biggest markets.

N.I.S. allowed stations in medium and smaller-sized markets to attempt an all-news format. This first attempt at a national all-news radio network collapsed after a couple of years. However, nearly alone among the nation's former N.I.S. affiliates in markets outside the Top Twenty, Sally Hawkins made the strategic decision to keep WILM primarily all-news. In most other markets, former N.I.S. stations became primarily telephone-talk stations, or reverted to music formats.

This kind of gutsy decision illustrates the Hawkins' approach to broadcasting. The naysayers said it couldn't be done: Philadelphia's 50,000-watt KYW Newsradio was too close. They were wrong.

In 1992, E.B. Hawkins, son of Ewing and Sally Hawkins, entered the family business as general manager. Sally remains president of the company. E.B.'s first task was to redesign the marketing department to match the excellence of WILM NEWSRADIO'S award-winning news department. Today, the news and marketing departments both, have reached a level of integrity, accuracy and reliability unmatched in the nation!

Today, 1450 WILM NEWSRADIO remains the major news player on the Delaware media scene. Even the

Financial Times of London compared WILM NEWSRADIO to the venerable BBC!

Whether it be a Delaware election, snow closings, a major trial, the Gulf War, the Soviet coup and break-up, or the Kosovo crisis—1450 WILM NEWSRADIO keeps Delaware informed!

Above
E. B. Hawkins, Sally Hawkins and Allan Loudell on the scene of the Kalmar Nyckel launch. Whatever the vantage point—1450 WILM NEWSRADIO captures the news, whenever or wherever the story may be! Photo by Bob McClain/McClain Imagery

Below
Program Manager Allan Loudell, who is also morning and midday news co-anchor.

CARL M. FREEMAN COMPANIES

Sea Colony has been called the most successful development on the eastern shore. It includes nine waterfront mid-rise condominiums and an additional 1,000 homes in what is known as Sea Colony West. With an additional 55 acres under construction today, Sea Colony is innovatively planned, creatively designed and well-run. But it came close to never getting off the drawing board. The giant spector of Sea Colony struck cold fear and indignation in the hearts of long-time Bethany Beach residents, and many of them banded together to defend their turf. Due to the dream and perseverance of founder and creator, Carl M. Freeman, combined with preservation issues that surfaced from the community, Sea Colony became a model for community/developer partnerships. The Freeman respect and concern for the environment is evidenced by the Governor's Conservation Award received from the State of Delaware in 1996 and the sponsorship of the Center for the Inland Bays partnership to provide observation towers and a boardwalk through a local, preserved wetland. Sea Colony supplies the fireworks for Bethany's Fourth of July celebration, furnishes canned goods to St. Ann's Church for use in their food-for-the-needy programs and hosts an annual Triathlon to support the Make-A-Wish Foundation.

The Carl M. Freeman Companies' roots go back more than 50 years, with nearly three decades committed to the Delaware eastern shore. Due to its reputation of stability and history of success, the Carl M. Freeman Companies will have a continuing impact on Delaware through several new developments in 1999. To understand the legacy of the Carl M. Freeman Companies and its current position as a commercial, residential, resort and golf course developer, one can first look at its founding by Carl M. Freeman in 1946.

Freeman recognized the housing shortage in the Washington-area in the immediate post-war boom. He began as a single-family homebuilder, designing the award-winning California Cottage. It didn't take long, though, for Freeman to become frustrated with the escalating price of land in the real estate market. He was using up his profits on one house to buy the land for his next project. He resolved that issue by creating the widely successful garden apartment. As quoted in *Washingtonian*, "Freeman forever altered the appearance of the Washington suburb during the '50s when he created the garden apartment."

Carl Freeman's professional signature quickly became "Americana—You'll Live Better," as he named each of his apartment communities that still exist in today's market. He pioneered such innovative concepts as apartment balconies and interior bathrooms. The Carl M. Freeman Companies developed more than 20,000 apartment homes, townhouses and single-family homes in over 50 residential communities. Today, the company continues its traditional purpose to innovatively help people live better.

Carl M. Freeman 1910 - 1998. Founder and visionary of the companies bearing his name. Joshua M. Freeman has been carrying the torch as president since 1992.

Sea Colony, 1972. Carl M. Freeman's vision to create a beach and tennis community on the Bethany Beach shores began in 1972 with the construction of nine mid-rise condominiums and a handful of beach villas. Today, the community continues to grow.

In an effort to bring professional standards to the home-building industry, Carl Freeman was a founder and served as the first president of the Suburban Maryland Home Builders' Association, which essentially legitimized the Washington home-building industry. In 1964, just before the Sea Colony vision came to life, Freeman was recognized as one of the top 12 builders in the nation by *House & Home* magazine.

Long before other developers, Freeman's single vision was to create communities, rather than build houses. Carl Freeman added amenities such as pools and tennis courts to each of his developments, while maintaining the natural landscaping. Sea Colony offers 28 tennis courts, numerous swimming pools and community shuttles to the beach. Trails for biking, walking, jogging and roller-blading, as well as parks for sharing a picnic are special amenities that were included in Sea Colony since its inception in the early 1970s. It is a neighborhood resort—a place where Carl Freeman was able to "grow families" and help people to live better.

The Carl M. Freeman Companies quickly grew to understand that enhancing the quality of life involves more than creative living spaces and resort communities. They began developing and managing neighborhood shopping centers. According to Carl Freeman, neighborhood shop-

Sea Colony 1997. Sea Colony West allows another 1,000 homeowners to enjoy the amenities provided within this master-planned resort community envisioned by Carl M. Freeman. The Sea Colony West homes begin at Westway Drive and Route 1 and continue west across Kent Avenue to the Assowoman Canal.

ping centers are a natural outgrowth of community development. Under the dynamic leadership of Joshua Freeman, Marketplace at Sea Colony was added to the Sea Colony neighborhood, which allows both vacationing guests and year-round residents alike to benefit from the shopping center convenience. Today, the companies own, manage and have plans to redevelop eight neighborhood shopping centers totaling more than 800,000 square feet of retail and office space.

Given the Carl M. Freeman Companies' commitment to creating quality communities and responding to community based needs, they have recently expanded into the golf business. Bear Trap Dunes Golf Club in Ocean View, DE, is Freeman Golf's first course, which will act as the heart

of yet another Freeman community. Freeman Golf plans to operate 10 courses within the next five years— primarily in the Delaware resort markets and the Greater Metropolitan Washington area.

In line with the founder's vision, the golf course is a small piece of the community planned for Ocean View, DE. Freeman Communities plans to develop The Village at Bear Trap— 700 homes on the golf course and a village green that will provide retail access for the nostalgic neighborhood. The houses will reflect Delaware's history by modeling the Georgetown and Lewes home designs, but will live like tomorrow, using state-of-the-art technological features.

The newest Delaware project on the boards, proposed just west of Fenwick Island, is a culmination of all the Carl Freeman Companies have learned since 1946. The plans call for a Jack Nicklaus Signature Golf Course on the Assowoman Bay within a master planned community of approximately 2,000 homes and numerous recreational facilities. Healthcare is a planned cornerstone of the community. Ground breaking for the new golf course is anticipated for the year 2000.

The Carl M. Freeman Companies hire energetic and loyal people that continually challenge themselves both professionally and personally. They want to understand both internal and external customer expectations and strive to exceed them. The Carl M. Freeman Companies sponsored an employee skydiving adventure, and encourage participation in many athletic events, such as the Marine Corps Marathon and the Sea Colony Make-A-Wish Triathlon. In the 1998 Marine Corps Marathon alone, 15 Carl M. Freeman employees, coached by their associates, entered the Marathon and finished it.

The Carl M. Freeman Companies placed a stake in the Delaware land in the early 1970s and look forward to an enduring relationship with the residents and improving the communities they touch for many years to come.

Bear Trap Dunes 1998. Continuing to help people live better on Delaware's eastern shore, representatives from the Freeman Companies and various Delaware organizations break ground for a new championship golf course opining in summer 1999. Left to right: Rick Jacobson, golf course designer; Beryl Craft, president of Delaware Women's Golf Association; George Cole, Sussex County council member; Danny Stovall, vice president Carl M. Freeman Communities; Robert Stickles, county executive; Shirley Price, Sussex representative; Michael Nally, executive vice president, Carl M. Freeman Associates; George Bunting, Sussex County senator; Patti Grimes, vice president Sea Colony; and Bob Orem, mayor, Ocean View, DE.

GENERAL CHEMICAL'S DELAWARE VALLEY WORKS

General Chemical's Delaware Valley Works was a landmark facility when it opened in 1913. It pioneered new production methods, was a model for integrated chemical complexes, and even built a planned town for hundreds of workers.

Grand in scope, it produced the essential materials that America needed to win two world wars, and has consistently provided basic chemicals for almost every industry. Today, its influence extends far beyond its boundaries. The plant's products are used for hundreds of everyday items that make life safer, cleaner, more convenient and more satisfying.

The concept of a modern General Chemical plant in Delaware took form in 1910, when the company bought about 80 acres in Claymont. The site bordered Pennsylvania Pike on the north and had 1,600 feet of Delaware River frontage to the south. Within a few years, it had become one of the company's most varied and important sites, serving industry throughout the United States.

The plant's initial process unit made sulfuric acid by the first commercial

Aerial view of Delaware Valley Works looking toward the Delaware River.

use of the contact process in the U.S. The unit began operating in February 1913 and was expanded rapidly. The plant also made oleum (a strong form of sulfuric acid), and soon grew to be the nation's largest oleum producer. This proved important during World War I, because oleum was essential for explosives. Sulfuric acid and oleum were also used for petroleum, storage batteries, fertilizers, alum, iron, copper and many other products.

The emphasis of the sulfuric acid operation has shifted over the years.

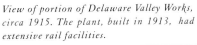

View of portion of Delaware Valley Works, circa 1915. The plant, built in 1913, had extensive rail facilities.

Beginning in 1955, it became as much an environmental facility as a commercial one. In addition to manufacturing acid for sale and as a feedstock for chemicals made on site, it also recycles spent acid from nearby companies, especially from an adjoining refinery. At this time, the 1,500 ton-per-day plant keeps more than 200,000 tons of acid from having to be treated and landfilled each year.

By 1920, the Delaware Valley Works was supplying more than a dozen chemicals to industries ranging from water treatment, drugs and paper to glass, textiles and photography. Its diversity has continued, and it is now an 11-area complex that creates dozens of products (see box), some of which have been made here since before 1920.

The plant's success rests to a great extent on the infrastructure it built early in the century. This included a dock for ocean-going vessels, a railhead and locomotives that assembled finished product loads. In an era of horse-drawn vehicles, it operated without horses, using an elevated train, 5½ miles of electrically driven trams, and electric cranes to unload vessels. It also generated its own

electricity in a central powerhouse and had extensive repair shops.

Many other facilities were added over the years, including a 100,000–square-foot warehouse, a well-equipped quality assurance laboratory, and many pollution control and prevention installations. The latter include a multimillion-dollar electrostatic precipitator for the sulfuric plant and a million-gallon-per-day water treatment facility. The plant also houses the Delaware Development Laboratory, one of the company's premier product development labs.

In order to meet the growing demand for specialty chemicals, the plant expanded across Pennsylvania Pike with the addition of about 50 acres, in the early 1940s.

During its first decade, the plant added many amenities for its workers, including a large dining hall, locker facilities, boarding houses, a hospital and even bowling alleys, playing fields and a movie theater.

Its most ambitious undertaking for its workforce was Overlook Colony. This was a planned village for workers and their families that included open spaces, shops, and recreational, educational and public facilities. The impetus to develop it came from the extreme scarcity of housing near the plant, especially during and right after World War I, when many workers were attracted to the area.

General Chemical purchased 216 acres for the village about a mile from the plant. The land had a view of the river a half-mile away, hence the "overlook" in its name. It was a picturesque, undulating site with a creek, precipitous spots, large boulders and woods containing oak, maple, chestnut and sycamore.

Sketch of "A" type house at Overlook Colony.

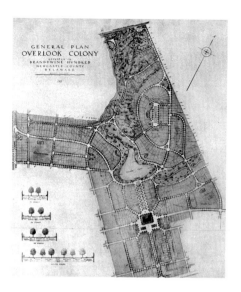

General plan of Overlook Colony

The company built light, airy row houses that were easy to maintain and drew heat from a central station. It installed sewers, water lines, gas, electricity and telephone lines, and even provided 100-square-foot garden plots. The village also had a four-room schoolhouse and boarding houses with single and double-occupancy furnished rooms, and a dormitory for single men.

Delaware Valley Works, which occupies 130 acres and employs nearly 300 people, is still one of the largest facilities in General Chemical's plant network. The facility is unique in many ways. For example, it is the largest U.S. producer of photo salts, sodium bisulfite, caustic pellets and fluoborates. It is also the largest sulfuric acid regenerator on the East Coast and the largest East Coast facility for liquefying soda ash.

The plant places an ongoing emphasis on quality, and continually strives to improve its products and services. Its commitment in this area is expressed in many ways; it is certified under the rigorous ISO 9002 quality standard and its state-of-the-art quality laboratory evaluates nearly every lot of product.

The plant continues to uphold the traditions it formed in the early 1900s. For instance, it remains a good corporate neighbor with strong ties to the community. And it continues to evolve as a highly-integrated chemical facility making a diverse slate of products that touch nearly every aspect of our lives.

Chemicals Basic to Our Way of Life

Chemicals made at the Delaware Valley Plant are basic ingredients and processing aids for hundred of every day items. Here are some of the products it makes and how they are used:

• Sulfuric acid: fertilizers, petroleum, steel, detergents, paper, storage batteries, titanium pigments, alum and medicinals.

• Sodium bisufite and sodium metabisulfite: water and wastewater treatment, food, beverages, flavors, polymers, textiles, dyes, paper, photography, medicinals, soaps, toiletries and surfactants.

• Sodium sulfite: flue gas desulfurization, leather, papermaking, food, photography, wastewater treatment and oil well drilling.

• Fluoboric acid and fluoborate

salts: printed circuit boards, bearings and wire.

• Potassium fluoride and potassium bifluoride: organic syntheses, welding and brazing fluxes, and fluorine.

• Sodium and potassium hydroxide pellets: analytical chemistry, food, pharmaceuticals, semiconductors and photography.

• Potassium nitrite: heat treating and heat transfer salts, corrosion inhibitors, catalyst regeneration and analytical reagents.

• Soda ash solution: waste stream neutralization, storage tank cleaning, municipal waste handling and papermaking.

• Sodium thiosulfate: photographic chemicals, water treatment and electric power.

GLOBE ELECTRIC COMPANY, INC.

Globe Electric Company, Inc. is a true success story. In 1961, two brothers, James F. Ciarlo and Vincent J. Ciarlo, dreamed of having their own business and making a success of it with hard work. Thus, a small electrical business was conceived.

Globe Electric began with the concept of providing good quality electrical service as its focal point, and this is still true today. Having been in business for 38 years, Globe Electric has gone through many stages of growth. Having only themselves as employees, and their wives Mena and Ginny performing the tasks of secretary, bookkeeper, file clerk and all other necessary jobs, they set out to succeed.

Globe's first place of operation began in their mother's basement, where they stored their materials and tools. Work was acquired by word-of-mouth of satisfied neighbors and friends. Nineteen sixty-one was not a good year in the construction industry, so they relied on service calls and small repair jobs, never forsaking their idea of quality work for a fair price. Jim and Vinny were able to build a close relationship with the community in which they grew up. The kindness and goodheartedness of the general population and the community's business leaders were very influential in their success.

After struggling for a few years, the brothers were awarded a large

James Ciarlo (left) and Vincent Ciarlo.

Original offices of Globe Electric Company, Inc.

suburban custom home development in North Wilmington, and in January 1964, Globe Electric was incorporated in the state of Delaware.

In a matter of a few years, they were able to purchase 20 garages just a few blocks away on Ninth Street in the city of Wilmington. The two front garages were redesigned to house their first "real" office, and the rear garages were converted into a small shop and warehouse. They were able to hire a bookkeeper, and with a workforce of eight electricians, they were "on their way."

During this time, Globe Electric continued to grow, and as they outgrew their space on Ninth Street, they purchased an old burned-out IGA grocery store, which they gutted and renovated into a two-story office

building and warehouse. In 1974, they moved into their new offices, where their employee-base grew to 22 in number. The office & warehouse on Ninth Street was then converted to nine townhouses which the brothers developed and sold in 1989. Their work eventually changed from mostly residential and service work to 70 percent commercial work.

In the early '80s, they were fortunate enough to land a contract with Bellevue Holding Company for the electrical work on a building being renovated by MBNA America Bank to accommodate 250 employees. Globe Electric continued to do electrical work for Bellevue and MBNA as the bank grew from one building to a complex in Newark, a complex in Christiana, a beautiful site known as Deerfield, and their headquarters surrounding Rodney Square in the City of Wilmington.

Along the way to Globe's growth, there were many other projects which were completed with the same integrity as their very first job. There were shopping centers, apartment complexes, office buildings, warehouses and the Harmony and Southgate Industrial Parks for the Mattei Corporation, Bellevue Holding Company, Snyder Crompton

Present offices of Globe Electric Company, Inc.

Associates and many other local companies.

There was the Union Park family of automobile dealerships, which includes a complex of 10 or more new and used car buildings and service departments. There were also the custom homes of Barley Mill, Fairthorne, Limerick and many others.

In 1993, Globe Electric relocated to their present offices in Southgate Industrial Center in New Castle. This 18,000 square-foot building was built to accommodate the equipment, trucks, and 60 plus office force and field personnel. The builder and developer was a contractor with whom Globe had worked with for over 20 years.

As the business grew, so did their families. Each brother has a son, Vincent (Rick) Ciarlo and Dane Ciarlo, in the business. Rick and Dane started in the business as young boys each summer, learning the trade from the bottom up. Much progress has been made since they

joined the company and they now handle most of the work.

Globe Electric grew and progressed from residential electrical work to commercial and industrial work, upholding a reputation for quality, thanks in part to the hard work and dedication of their employees, many of whom have been with the company for over 25 years. Jim and Vince have always stressed customer satisfaction to their employees. Neatness, cleanliness and safety have been the rule on every jobsite. And, because their company was always willing to "bend over backwards" to give good service, Globe's expert employees have traveled to Maine, Georgia, Maryland, and Pennsylvania for special customers.

Globe's philosophy has always been honesty and a striving for excellence in every endeavor. They are most proud of their humble beginnings and how they have grown through the years to be the reputable business they are today.

When they think back and reminisce on those beginnings, the Ciarlo brothers are very proud of their contribution to the City of Wilmington. They feel honored to have been part of the construction of some of the most beautiful buildings in Delaware.

Globe Electric has progressed from working out of their mother's basement with just one very old, beat-up truck, to a fleet of trucks and equipment that is state-of-the-art for electrical work.

The owners of Globe Electric are proud of the fact that even though they have grown to a large company, they are still a family-owned business. Jim and Vince hope that their sons will go into work with all of the values that have been passed on to them—hard work, perseverance, dedication, and honesty—to take Globe Electric to an even greater level than it has achieved today.

HOPKINS CONSTRUCTION, INC.

In 1988, Hopkins Construction, Inc. began with three men, five dump trucks, and first year sales of $225,000. Today, they have over 30 full-time employees and a vast fleet of heavy equipment, trucks, and tools with yearly gross sales of $8 to 10 million. Hopkins Construction operates as a general contractor specializing in wastewater treatment plants, utility construction, and site development.

Raising the Standard in every aspect of operation and business is part of what has made them successful, and what continues their growth today. Raising the standard of their workforce to the highest quality of skilled and dedicated workers has been an area of concentration since the beginning. Its core ideology is that challenged, fulfilled employees, coupled with satisfied customers, produces positive results for everyone.

They are very fortunate to have retained people who are both hard workers and keen thinkers. The strong character of their employees affords them a real advantage in their ability to be competitive at bidding, completing jobs in a timely manner, and maintaining a high level of quality service. With customer satisfaction as their highest priority,

The Hopkins team.

employees are challenged to go that extra mile everyday.

Hopkins Construction, Inc. specializes in turnkey projects. Turnkey is a complete package approach where the requirements of development and installation are coordinated into a single, unified operation. With this approach, they are able to include design, procurement, construction, and other related services in a single purchase order—at a single price. Unlike other companies who offer turnkey services as an outlet for their process equipment, they have no obligation to a specific equipment line. Hopkins Construction offers turnkey as a service to

their custmers, and equipment selections are based only on their specific needs.

The success of their turnkey service is the result of a consistent team effort. Hopkins Construction brings a select group of skilled professionals together on every project. This combination works, together with their customers throughout the development of the facility.

Wastewater Treatment Plant under construction. Allen's Family Foods Poultry Processing Plant, located in Cordova, Maryland.

Drawing on the contractor's construction expertise, the engineer's design expertise, and the customer's first-hand knowledge, the team determines the facility best suited for its client's specific needs. Together, they work to select the most appropriate treatment process equipment and construction methods. Before any construction begins, Hopkins Construction presents the final facility design and pricing to the client for approval.

Hopkins Construction, Inc. has become a recognized name among the local poultry processing industry with their proven record of quality workmanship and skilled professionals. The company's first project with the poultry industry was for Mountaire Farms of Delmarva. They have since completed projects for Perdue, Townsends, and in 1998 completed a $3.5 million state-of-the-art WWTP for Allen's Family Foods.

Hopkins Construction is excited about what the future holds for them, and will continue to improve all aspects of their company and services while they strive towards *"Raising the Standard."*

South Coastal Wastewater Treatment Plant, owned by Sussex County Council.

PROJECT LIST

- *Allen Family Foods WWTP-* Cordova, Maryland. $3.4M wastewater treatment facility including design/build work tasks. First of a kind project that exceeds all Federal and State requirements for treatment.
- *Mountaire Poultry-*Lumber Bridge, North Carolina $2.1M wastewater treatment facility with 390,000 square-foot lagoon. Project was completed in record time.
- *Town of Delmar WTP-* Delmar, Delaware. $1.5M state-of-the-art water treatment facility including new water and sewer distribution system.
- *Town of Vienna WWTP-* Vienna, Maryland. $1.5M wastewater treatment facility including sanitary collection system and new pump station.
- *Town of Rock Hall Pump*

*Station-*Rock Hall, Maryland. $1.2M pump station improvement project including seven new deep excavation pump stations.
- *Lighthouse Sound WWTP -* Bishopville, Maryland. $1.4M wastewater treatment facility including 200,000 square-foot lagoon, 15,000 L.F. of 8" sanitary sewer and new pump station.
- *Rt. 50 Stormwater Improvements-*Ocean City, Maryland. $317,000 stormwater/intersection improvements including 10,000 L.F. of 24" and 30" R.C.P. and HDPE storm pipe, basins, and stormwater structures. Work was done in record time.
- *Perdue, Inc. WWTP-* Salisbury, Maryland. $620,000 wastewater treatment plant upgrade including design/build work tasks and plant upgrades.
- *Allen Family Foods Aeration*

*Lagoon-*Harbeson, Delaware. $500,000 Aeration Lagoon including 400,000 square-foot lagoon and high diffusion aeration system.
- *Kent County WWTF Upgrades-* Frederica, Delaware. $1M wastewater treatment plant upgrades including new grit removal facility and required 25MGD temporary sewage bypass operation.
- *SCI Site Utilities-*Georgetown, Delaware. $3.3M project to install 20,000 L.F. of water, sewer, stormdrain, gas line, and forcemain. Installed 1,000 L.F. of bores under fencing and railroad.
- *Harrington Pump Station-* Harrington, Delaware. $1.1M project to install deep pumping station and five lift stations. Also included deep sheeting, shoring, 1.5MGD dewatering system.

W. L. GORE & ASSOCIATES, INC.

While consumers recognize the Gore name for the company's products—GORE-TEX® fabric and GLIDE® floss, among them—the Delaware community has known Gore for over forty years as a neighbor, innovator, and employer.

The beginnings of W. L. Gore & Associates, Inc., in 1958, were not particularly unusual. It began like many family businesses: founders Bill and Vieve Gore started small, operating out of the basement of their Newark home. Their focus was what set them apart: they chose to pursue applications for fluoropolymers, versatile materials that they believed held great, unexplored potential.

Their son, Bob, who was then a chemical engineering student at the University of Delaware, suggested the idea for an electronic cable insulated with the fluoropolymer polytetrafluoroethylene (PTFE). His suggestion became the company's first product, and resulted in its first patent.

The company's first decade was marked by steady expansion. In 1961, the company moved out of the Gores' basement and into the first manufacturing plant, located on Paper Mill Road in Newark. By 1967, manufacturing had expanded to Germany, Scotland, and Flagstaff, Arizona.

A joint venture to manufacture products with a Japanese company followed in 1969. That same year a Gore product found its way to the moon: the Apollo 11 astronauts used a temperature-resistant Gore cable to conduct seismographic experiments on the moon's surface.

Microscopic view of GORE-TEX® membrane.

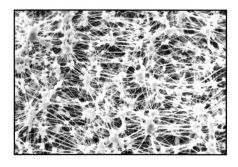

From left to right; Bob Gore, Genevieve Gore and Bill Gore at the corporate offices in 1982.

The year 1969 also saw a breakthrough that dramatically expanded the company's offerings and opened a wealth of new opportunities. Bob Gore discovered that rapidly stretching PTFE resulted in a remarkable material that offered many desirable new properties. Extremely strong, porous, waterproof, breathable, and possessed of excellent dielectric properties, Bob's discovery was named GORE-TEX® expanded PTFE.

In the early and mid-1970s, resulting new businesses sprang up in widely diverse markets. From sealant products for industrial pipes to implantable medical products for restoration of blood flow in the human body, Gore associates found uses for the new GORE-TEX® membrane and fibers in myriad applications.

GORE-TEX® fabric, the first waterproof yet breathable outerwear on the market, was born in that same period. It remains the highest-performing fabric available, enabling wearers at work and play to stay dry in even the worst weather conditions.

The Gore name is now found on thousands of high-performance products. They range from filtration products for virtually any environmental challenge to patches that repair heart defects and hernias. Gore chip modules and venting materials are found in the most sensitive components of computers, and the company's fibers are used in the outer layer of astronauts' space suits. No matter what the application, Gore products continue to be known today for their quality and technical benefits. The company is committed to invention and the challenge of bringing ever-better products to its customers.

That commitment is supported by another unique Gore creation: a work environment that lacks the barriers that sometimes impede more traditionally organized companies in their pursuit of innovation. Gore's corporate culture lacks titles and hierarchy. It is built upon direct, person-to-person communication rather than chains of command.

Because the culture gives Gore "associates" (not employees) the freedom to explore new ideas, it contributes directly to the generation of the company's product successes. It's also the reason the company has been repeatedly named one of the "100 Best Companies to Work For in America."

Today, Gore is a worldwide presence, posting sales of well over $1 billion annually and employing thousands of associates in its 50 facilities around the world. While the company outgrew the basement workshop long ago, the same commitment to technical innovation that inspired Bill and Vieve Gore remains a constant among associates today.

HOTEL DU PONT

The Hotel du Pont might have opened a century too late for George Washington to sleep there, but the prestigious hotel on Rodney Square lists no less than eight other U.S. presidents on its register since opening its doors in 1913.

The elegant Hotel du Pont, housed in the DuPont Company headquarters in downtown Wilmington, has hosted dignitaries and entertainers from around the world, including General Douglas MacArthur, First Ladies Eleanor Roosevelt and Rosalyn Carter, and entertainers Bob Hope and Elizabeth Taylor.

But, regardless of a guest's station or destination, the hotel staff of more than 400 rolls out its red carpet for thousands of business travelers and tourists each year. And, although its timeless attention to detail calls to mind an era of unhurried elegance, Hotel du Pont offers state-of-the-art business and communication facilities through its Conference Center.

Conference facilities were expanded from 5,000 square feet to 30,000 square feet in 1992. Other extensive renovations made that year at a total cost of $40 million, included expanding the size of the average guest room, thus reducing the number of rooms from 296 to 217.

More recent renovations include the resdesign of the front of the hotel

Deluxe guest-room honored with "Best Guest Room Design in the World," following 1992 renovation.

in September 1998. The old revolving doors were replaced with two beveled glass and brass entrances, including a renovated access for handicapped visitors.

Courteous and discreet service to everyone who enters through those doors, old and new, has been the standard set since the first planning meetings held in 1911. In that year, Pierre du Pont de Nemours was appproached by developers looking for financial support to construct a hotel in downtown Wilmington.

DuPont Company executives stressed the importance of "high quality (service) with no compromises" as their primary objective in establishing the Hotel du Pont. Two years later, on January 15, 1913, that idea became a reality when 295 men and women dined for the first time in the new hotel's dining room.

Careful attention to detail and maintenance of unusual architectural details such as the lobby ceiling, which was patterned after a Venetian ducal palace, still draw many visitors to the hotel's public rooms. Guests can relax in a variety of settings from yesteryear as they enjoy food and entertainment.

In 1913, the Playhouse Theatre was opened at the the Hotel du Pont in what had been known as Pinkett's Court. The 1,200-seat theater, housed entirely within the hotel, still presents quality theater to Wilmington residents and guests.

Magnificent Green Room.

In the Gold Ballroom, which was opened in 1919, visitors admire the craftsmanship of the 30 artisans who traveled from Italy to construct the walls of sgraffito (hand-cut or scratched designs made through multiple layers of colored plasters).

The walnut-paneled Brandywine Room, opened in 1941 in a space that had served over the years as a brokerage office, writing room and telephone exchange. The Christina Room, originally the hotel's Club Room for reading, relaxing and afternoon tea, was reopened in 1964 and today boasts a priceless collection of three generations of Wyeth family art.

The high-ceilinged Green Room, reopened in 1984, continues to be a model of elegance and refinement. Noted for its elaborately carved, beamed ceiling and beautifully restored mosaic floor, it draws many admirers. Guests looking for a more intimate experience can visit the Lobby Lounge, completed in 1983 as a "cafe with a living room atmosphere."

For many travelers, a trip to Wilmington is synonomous with a stay at the Hotel du Pont, where hotel staff continue to meet the goal set by its founders of "high quality service with no compromises."

KIRBY AND HOLLOWAY PROVISION COMPANY

Take one old family recipe. Add quality and a philosophy of giving customers what they need—perhaps before they even know they need it. Cook for 50 years, and you have a Mid-Atlantic States tradition.

Harrington, Delaware-based Kirby and Holloway, "the Sausage and Scrapple People," is still led by Russell R. Kirby, its 90-year-old chairman and co-founder, and his wife, Blanche, as the company's secretary. The company started in 1946, when Kirby and John B. Holloway decided to form the K & H Company. This later became Kirby and Holloway Provision Company.

At the time, Kirby owned a small meat market in Milford where he sold and delivered groceries and the highest quality meats, including homemade sausage and scrapple. Having been raised on a small farm near Big Stone Beach, he had learned the fine art of scrapple making, which dates to the earliest days of the American Republic. When the Dutch arrived in the New World, they brought their sausage-making skills. Once here, they developed a new dish, which they called "Scrapple," generically made with cornmeal, pork and seasonings, and often served fried.

Kirby and Holloway fleet in 1953.

Aerial view of the plant in 1953.

For years in the Milford area, scrapple making was a major annual event. Says Kirby:

"Every year, when it got cold, we'd have hog killing time. You'd make your sausage and your scrapple, and you always had plenty of help. Everyone would post the time they wanted their hog killing done, and the neighbors would all come over.

"Everyone seemed to want my mother to come in and help, because they all liked the way she seasoned the scrapple. So when I got to making scrapple myself, that's the recipe we used."

At his little market, Kirby, his mother, Carrie, and two dedicated and trusted employees, would make scrapple and sausage each Friday, for sale on Saturday. More than 50 years later, that same closely guarded recipe produces hundreds of thousands of pounds of scrapple each year, with production still done traditionally, in cast iron pots.

Holloway, meanwhile, worked as a bookkeeper for a company in Dover that sold ice cream during the summer and Kirby's sausage and scrapple in the winter. He and Kirby bought a slaughterhouse in Harrington, some second-hand sausage-and-scrapple-making equipment and a used truck, which refrigerated its cargo using a fan blowing from an ice bunker.

Ready for business, the partners turned to their next key tool: a coin. They flipped to see who would go on the road to sell, and who would stay in the plant and oversee operations. They flipped to see who would be president and who would be secretary, and to see who would do the hiring. All of their decisions were made by a flip of a coin.

Kirby ended up selling. He hit the road carrying a basket filled with

sausage and scrapple. The company's first strategy was to give merchants samples on Saturdays. The idea was for them to try the products for Sunday breakfast, appreciate the unique quality, and order for their customers.

Back at the plant, Carrie Kirby mixed the seasoning for the first 500-pound pot of Kirby and Holloway scrapple. She did it as she always had, with a pinch of this and a cup of that. This, the entrepreneurs soon realized, would not work as Kirby's selling generated greater and greater demand. They needed to maintain a uniform taste, so they prevailed on her to write it down.

After a short time, Kirby and Holloway decided to discontinue their slaughtering operations, turning instead to a large pork operation in Virginia, where they could select the finest pork for their products. Kirby returned to the plant, turning sales over to his brother, Joe, who quickly extended the company's customer-base to Wilmington.

In 1952, with all of Delaware enjoying Kirby and Holloway products, the company opened a restaurant in Dover. They soon had three restaurants there (two Kirby and Holloways and the Dutch Pantry). Their usual coin flip had Russell running them, leaving Holloway, again, in charge of the meat business. The restaurants sold a lot of sausage and scrapple; diners ate them and enjoyed them so much that they took them home, as well.

This lasted until 1963, when Holloway decided to retire. They sold the restaurants and Kirby took charge of production.

Over the years, the company added additional products, both meat goods that it manufactures, and foods from a select few of the higher-quality manufacturers on the East Coast, to distribute.

Additions to its own production ranged from hot and sweet Italian sausages, which were immediate hits when introduced in 1960, to 96% fat-free and additive-free premium smoked hams (available whole and in

Mr. Russell Kirby checking on the finished link sausage product in 1950.

halves, quarters and steaks) and a new spicy Hot Sausage. These were introduced in 1999, extending Kirby and Holloway's traditions of quality.

The other products included fresh and smoked pork, domestic and imported hams, beef, cheeses, soups, freezer products and salads—a total of more than 2,000 separate food items.

Its customer-base expanded beyond Delaware, with its products served in restaurants and hotels and available in retail chains in Maryland, Virginia, Pennsylvania and New Jersey. Moreover, consumers who have moved away from the area have been so loyal, that the company regularly fills orders from around the world.

Along the way, Kirby and Holloway has expanded and modernized its plant. Their facility was the first meat packing plant in Delaware inspected under a 1968 federal law. It received the highest possible rating, a level it has since maintained.

In 1981, Russell Rudy Kirby II entered the business, representing the third generation of Kirbys to participate and carry on the families' pride in products well done. Today, he is company president.

As the 20th century neared its end,

Kirby and Holloway remained a premier manufacturer and supplier with a large and loyal customer-base. Its success is built on quality and customer service.

Kirby and Holloway manufactures with consistently pure and top-grade ingredients, using time-tested methods and sacrosanct recipes, and it distributes foods which meet those same high standards.

It serves its customers by supplying them with what they need, even if Kirby and Holloway cannot stock the product. It will work with other suppliers to provide it, meeting the customers' needs and maintaining their loyalty.

Thus, Kirby and Holloway Provision Company has grown from one pot of scrapple to millions of pounds of sausage and scrapple a year, and from one old truck to a large fleet delivering quality products in five states. Its growth has been conservative and sound, based in the enthusiastic acceptance of its products and adherence to its foundations.

"I've always said, `Our customers get 16 ounces in every pound they pay for,'" says the company chairman. "You sell a good product, and you give good service. That's the way I've always done things, and the way we always will."

MBNA CORPORATION

Now one of Delaware's most prominent corporations, MBNA actually
traces its history back to the credit
card division of a Maryland bank and
the First State law that created a
home for an industry pioneer.

In the late 1970s, the U.S.
economy was sluggish, and for credit
card companies, especially those
companies based in Maryland, that
was an optimistic appraisal. State law
prohibited them from generating
revenue through annual fees and
severely limited interest rates—
severely limiting the chances for
success in the credit card business.
Then in 1981, legislators in neighboring Delaware threw credit card
companies a lifeline—the Financial
Center Development Act.

Signed on February 18 by
Governor Pierre S. du Pont, the law
enabled banks based in Delaware to
do business in any state, without
many of the restrictions imposed by
other states. Recognizing the opportunity, Maryland National Bank Vice
President Charles M. Cawley, along
with Bruce Hammonds and John
Cochran, spearheaded a move to the
First State and found an abandoned
supermarket on Route 4 in Newark.

*MBNA senior managers Al Lerner, Bruce
Hammonds, Ron Davies, Scot Kaufman, John
Cochran, and Charlie Cawley on the floor of
the New York Stock Exchange in 1991.*

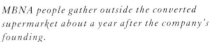

On March 17, 1982, MBNA America
opened in that building with a staff
of 155 people.

From those humble beginnings
came an impressive story of innovation, perseverance, and commitment.
That offshoot of a top Maryland
bank has evolved into a global leader
among financial institutions. As this
book takes shape, MBNA Corporation is an international company of
20,000 people working in offices in
England, Ireland, and Canada and
across the United States. They have
dedicated themselves to offering top-
quality products backed by peerless
customer service. The company's

*MBNA people gather outside the converted
supermarket about a year after the company's
founding.*

history is filled with breakthroughs
in both.

Less than a year after it opened its
doors; in fact, MBNA made industry
history by introducing the Gold
MasterCard. The card was an instant
success. At the end of 1983, more than
100,000 MBNA Gold MasterCard
accounts had been opened; less than
six years later, MBNA would become
the first company to issue one million
Gold MasterCard accounts.

In that first year, MBNA also
introduced a new concept to a
blooming industry. An endorsement
from the Georgetown University
Alumni Association pioneered one
of the credit card industry's most
significant developments—affinity
marketing. The Georgetown agreement enabled MBNA to market
credit cards bearing the university name to Georgetown's alumni
and students and paved the way for
relationships with additional schools,
sports teams, professional associations, charities, financial institutions,
and other organizations. Today,
thousands of organizations endorse
MBNA products.

Through those endorsements and
the company's innovative marketing
techniques, MBNA soon acquired

thousands, then hundreds of thousands, then millions of customers each year. In the blink of history's eye, MBNA developed one of the most desirable customer bases in the industry. Even today, typical MBNA customers earn above-average salaries, own their homes, and have a long history of paying bills on time.

Retaining those customers, of course, means ensuring their satisfaction. To that end, MBNA became in 1986 the first credit card issuer to offer customer service 24 hours a day, seven days a week to all of its customers. While others have since followed suit, MBNA has been serving customers round the clock longer than any other credit card issuer.

In 1996, MBNA pioneered what has since become another industry staple—the platinum credit card. Featuring higher credit lines and enhanced service and benefits, the MBNA *Platinum Plus* card remains one of the credit card industry's most successful products.

While MBNA recorded a number of successes in the 1980s, parent company MNC Financial encountered severe difficulties in real estate lending. To avoid a financial crisis, MNC decided to generate additional revenue by spinning off its most valuable asset—MBNA America. In January 1990, MBNA filed a registration statement with the Securities and Exchange Commission, the first step in the process of becoming a publicly traded company.

With that groundwork complete, MBNA senior managers traveled the country to speak to potential stockholders. Finally, on January 22, 1991, the first shares of stock in MBNA Corporation were sold on the New York Stock Exchange. A few days later, Cawley introduced to the people of the company MBNA Corporation Chairman and CEO Al Lerner, without whom, Cawley said, "the rescue of MNC Financial and creation of MBNA Corporation would not have been possible." By the time this book went to print,

MBNA had recorded nearly 18 consecutive years of financial growth.

That growth has expanded the company well beyond Delaware's borders. In 1993 alone, MBNA opened offices in Camden, Maine; New York City; and Beachwood, Ohio; and founded MBNA International in Chester, England. In the years that followed, MBNA expanded to include offices in Dallas; Chicago; San Francisco; Boca Raton, Florida; and Hunt Valley, Maryland, not far from Maryland National's old offices in Baltimore. A short time later, a Dublin office was opened, and MBNA Canada was created.

Through all of its evolution, however, one thing has remained constant—MBNA's commitment to customers, the people of the company, and the communities in which those people work. In countless places throughout each MBNA office appear the words "Think of Yourself as a Customer." Since its creation, MBNA has been repeatedly recognized by *Working Mother*, *Business Week*, and *FORTUNE* magazines as one of the best companies in the country for which to work. When they are not working, MBNA people

are often volunteering for nonprofit organizations near MBNA offices. In 1998 alone, they donated more than 200,000 hours of their personal time to charities and education initiatives.

The MBNA Education Foundation was created in 1997 as a result of the company's dedication to the education of young people in the community. Funded by contributions from MBNA and MBNA people, the Foundation committed $60 million over five years to scholarships for economically disadvantaged students and grants for schools and educators. It was only fitting that the first recipients of the foundation's scholarships and grants were from Delaware.

MBNA remains committed to the First State. Today, MBNA Corporation has offices in Dover, Greenville, Wilmington, and the original Newark location. It was in Delaware that the company started, and in Delaware that the company has grown to become the largest independent credit card issuer in the world.

Just a few minutes down from MBNA's first office in Newark, the Bracebridge Center in downtown Wilmington is the international headqurters of MBNA Corporation.

MEALEY FUNERAL HOMES

In 1878, in County Mayo, Ireland, Patrick O'Malley and new bride, Winifred Togher, started life together. They left Ireland and came to Wilmington, DE, where Patrick was employed as a farmer. During the naturalization and emigration process, *O'Malley* was transformed to *Mealey*, and Winifred bore ten children, all given the surname *Mealey*. Three of the children died before adulthood. Of the seven remaining children, only the oldest, Michael, remained in Delaware.

At the turn of the century, the nation was being ravaged by a viral illness, felling thousands. Michael Mealey was a furniture upholsterer as a young adult. Among his duties, he furnished casket linings for the cabinetmakers who were overwhelmed with the tragic results of the virus. Many Irish were impoverished and socially scorned, with little ability to provide dignified burial for their departed. From a desire to help ease their grief, Michael opened a funeral home in 1912, at the corner of 3rd and Jackson Streets. His com-

Michael A. Mealey, 1881 to 1945, founder of Mealey Funeral Homes. The company is now owned and operated by his great grandson, Charles F. Mealey, Jr.

The administative office and preparation room are located at the 7th and Broom Streets location. It was purchased by Michael A. Mealey in 1935. The area is now considered an historical section of Wilmington.

passion and service to his clients is the foundation upon which Mealey Funeral Homes were established and continue to grow today.

Michael was a fiddler, known and liked in many social circles. His honest approach to business quickly earned him a reputation for integrity and fairness among families of all income levels. His stature in the community was growing, yet Michael kept his unpretentious demeanor. An old friend recalls that, on hot summer days, Michael would doze

in front of the funeral home with his hairpiece flipped up to give his scalp access to the breeze.

Michael married a local lass, Susan E. Mulhern. They had five children: Frances, John (Jack), Mary, Daniel and Margaret. In 1935, Michael sold the Jackson Street funeral home and purchased a building on the corner of 7th and Broom Streets. He converted the lower floors to funeral facilities, and used the other two floors for his home.

In acquiring the new facility, Michael incorporated the business, naming the company Michael A. Mealey & Sons, Inc. His sons, Jack and Daniel were then active in the company and community. Jack married an Elkton, Maryland woman, Ann Romanek, and had seven children: Jack Jr., Michael II, Charles, Joseph, Susan, Patricia and Robert. The boys helped around the funeral home from the time they were youths. They graduated from Salesianum High School, then mortuary college, and received their funeral licenses. Daniel married Mary Donohue and had two children, Daniel Jr. and Susan. Like his cousins, Dan Jr.'s education was geared towards the funeral industry. However, he declined to join his family's business. In 1958, Daniel Sr. died, leaving the company to his brother and nephews.

The company prospered under the leadership of Jack and his four oldest sons. In 1957, Jack, Jr. was offered a career in the Army and left the family business. By the mid-1960s, Jack Sr.'s health was beginning to deteriorate. He retired, leaving his second son, Michael, as the president of the company, and Charles and Joseph as officers. Jack Sr. died from heart disease in 1970.

In the 1970s, the Wilmington suburbs expanded dramatically. Pike Creek Valley, once mostly farmland, burst with new developments and townhouses. Michael and his brothers saw in this area an excellent opportunity to serve their clients who had relocated from the city. Construction for a new funeral

home began on the corner of Limestone and Milltown Roads. In December 1972, the first funeral was held. The Mealey family was welcomed into the community.

Like his grandfather Patrick, who left Ireland to toil the land in Delaware, Joseph had a longing to be a farmer. In 1976, Joseph moved his family to Kentucky, leaving Michael and Charles to run the business. Around this same time, youngest brother Robert joined the firm, and worked for several years before leaving to pursue other interests.

Michael and Charles had growing families. Michael lived in North Wilmington with wife, Eleanor Kelley and five children: Michele, Maureen, Michael III, Mark and Kelley. Charles married Mildred Bradley and fathered four children: Charles Jr., Lori, Kathleen and Jane. Charles moved his family from the city to the Milltown-area in 1973 to join the community surrounding his new building. In the family tradition, Charles Jr. graduated from Salesianum High School and the University of Delaware, and worked summers and weekends, when needed, at the funeral homes. After earning a degree in business, he attended mortuary school in Pittsburgh, and graduated cum laude.

During this same time, Michael II was diagnosed with cancer. Though undergoing several years of treatments and procedures, he still worked when he could. He was an encouragement to many of the families he served during this time. His battle with his illness only deepened his commitment and compassion to the people he served. On August 23, 1982, Michael succumbed to his disease at age 47, leaving his family members grieving, and his family legacy with his younger brother.

When his father died, Michael III was prompted to reevaluate his future. He enrolled in college to earn the necessary credits for funeral licensing. He then entered mortuary school in Catonsville, Maryland. He worked mornings at the funeral home,

and commuted to classes in the afternoons. On September 24, 1987, en route home, Michael III was tragically killed in an auto accident. The entire Mealey family was devastated by this loss.

In the ensuing years, the business continued to grow as Charles Jr. assumed a larger role, and hired his sister, Lori, to run the business office. Charles Sr., in his forty years as a funeral director, planned funerals, comforted the grieving, buried his father, mother and brother, and guided the business through financial difficulties. He had confidence in his son and daughter, and consequently, gave consideration to his own future. In 1996, Charles Sr. sold the business to his son, though he continued to work until his retirement in 1998. He now resides primarily in Florida, though he stays in close contact with his children, offering advice from his years of experience.

Now at the helm, Charles Jr.'s primary goal is to serve his clients in every way possible. From this

The Limestone Road facility was designed by brothers Michael II, Charles Sr. and Joseph. The design was so innovative at the time, it was the subject of a funeral industry magazine in 1973. The funeral home opened in December 1972.

commitment came the First Annual Mealey Memorial Service. In December 1998, every family who had lost a loved one throughout the year was invited to the Pike Creek facility for a ceremony of reflection, song and refreshments. The lives of the departed were commemorated with a personalized Christmas ornament. Many family members hung the ornament on the Tree of Remembrance—a huge Christmas Tree outside the funeral home—where it remained on display throughout the Christmas season. Some 250 people attended, appreciative of the strength they gained to help them through a difficult holiday.

Charles Jr. now has his eye on the future. The Bear-area is now a thriving community, and plans are drawn for a new Mealey Funeral Home. The new facility will include many community-oriented features, such as a walking trail and meeting rooms. If zoning is approved, the brick funeral home and crematory will reside on 10 acres just south of Route 7. To date, meetings with local civic associations have generated tremendous community support.

Charles Jr. sees the future of the company in the eyes of his children, Rachel, Amelia and Patrick. Many family-owned funeral homes are being purchased by large corporations. Yet, the Mealey family is committed to serving the families in need—personally, professionally, and with the compassion that led Michael A. Mealey to the funeral profession at the turn of the 20th century.

Charles Mealey, Sr. stands by the gravesite of his ancestors at Cathedral Cemetery in Wilmington.

THE INDEPENDENCE SCHOOL

The Independence School spirit born in 1978 pervades every aspect of school life. Independence was founded around a kitchen table, by a group of concerned parents, as a non-profit elementary and middle school that would provide a challenging and sequential education. It opened in rented facilities under a karate studio, with 190 students, grades one through eight.

The concept of a solid, affordable independent elementary education fueled the vision and set the standard for the mission, spirit and conviction that is The Independence School today. Without a major donor, but with vigor and a sense of community, parents created a school founded on the philosophy that educational excellence results from outstanding teachers, a moderate class size, a pleasant, yet disciplined classroom environment, a sequential arts and science curriculum, Judeo-Christian values and a strong parent-school partnership. Under the governance of a Board of Trustees and the leadership of founding headmaster, Dr. Kenneth Weinig, Independence employs a faculty and staff of over 87.

With a recent bequest of 16 acres and 1900s farmhouse, The Independence School is a 90-acre campus in the Pike Creek Valley, and home to 720 students. Serving students from early childhood through grade eight in the tri-state area, Independence is a resource to the local community and a feeder school for approximately 15 area high schools. The school holds a Certificate of Accreditation from the Middle States Association of Colleges and Schools, and most recently has experienced the pride and joy of having an alumnus as its first Rhodes Scholar.

Recently, Independence successfully concluded construction of a middle-school wing and a gym/performing arts building, and completed a current long-range planning study. Independence's initial building sat on a 16-acre campus, but 1987 added 57 adjoining acres, and the Gore Outdoor Classroom and

Conservancy was constructed. At the same time, Independence built the Early Childhood Division to accommodate an extended-care program and pre-school through kindergarten classes.

Independence offers four foreign languages, three beginning in grade one, and an extensive arts and music program, including strings study. Students are involved in such extra-curricular activities as Math Counts, Math and Science Olympiad, and Odyssey of the Mind. They participate actively in outreach programs for area charities and community needs. Tennis courts, a cross-country trail, several fields and a track, are available for physical education, team sports, summer camp and extended-care. Year-round extra-curricular activities include 12 sports. Many community groups such as scouts, civic associations, adult sports leagues, churches, and youth soccer use Independence's facilities, athletic fields, and nature trails.

The extended Independence family visibly supports the school. Parent participation in annual giving has

The parent commitment, the vitality and enthusiasm, and the quest for excellence that gave birth to Independence are still very much a part of the Independence spirit. Now, as in 1978, Independence strives to educate students who will be leaders for tomorrow's world.

reached over 90% each year, since 1995. Area foundations, friends and grandparents help generously in support of capital projects. Additionally, at least 92% of parents volunteer for a variety of activities such as the Auction, Independence Parents' Association and May Fair, and serve as classroom, library, and field-trip aides.

The parent commitment, the vitality and enthusiasm, and the quest for excellence that gave birth to Independence are still very much a part of the Independence spirit. Now, as in 1978, The Independence School strives to educate students who will be leaders for tomorrow's world.

MITCHELL ASSOCIATES, INC.

Over three decades ago, in November 1965, Louis B. Rosenberg collaborated with Trudy O'Brien and the late Don Mitchell to establish Mitchell Associates Design Consultants. The three-person team embarked on their vision from rented space in local sculptor Charles Parks' farmhouse studio in Hockessin, Delaware. Their first design project was a bank in upstate Pennsylvania. As small projects grew and they began achieving national recognition, the firm was compelled to relocate to a larger office in the Independence Mall on Concord Pike. In 1979, shortly after the untimely death of Don Mitchell, they moved again to become the first tenants in Trolley Square, just above the Happy Harry's store.

By the early 1980s, under the management of Rosenberg and three other principals, William L. Endicott, Sheree L. Jones and Kim W. LeBorys, the firm had developed a national reputation in the corporate, educational and healthcare industries. The company continued to expand staff and clients, which again presented office space issues. They decided to renovate an abandoned rendering plant site on the Christina Riverfront into Mitchell Associates' present office—One Avenue of the Arts. This site has been increasingly exciting and prosperous, especially as the Wilmington Riverfront develops. In recent years, the office has been joined by neighbors such as Frawley Stadium, Kahunaville (another local client), and the First USA Riverfront Arts Center.

Today, Mitchell Associates has grown to a staff of over 50 architects and designers doing creative architectural interior design, programming/planning, donor recognition displays, signage and wayfinding projects. In fact, most Delawareans have stepped into or seen at least one of Mitchell Associates' designed environments. Interiors created by the firm include: First USA Bank; Beneficial Bank; Household International; Morris Nichols Arsht &

Mitchell Associates' office with the Kalmar Nyckel.

Tunnell; Morris James Hitchens & Williams; Delaware Technical and Community College's Stanton Campus; Christiana Healthcare Systems—Preventative Medicine Rehabilitation Institute; Christina Cultural Arts Center; Mellon Bank Center; Port of Wilmington; Delaware Theatre Company; and the Delaware College of Art & Design. The firm's donor recognition and graphic designs attract attention in the lobbies of Winterthur Museum & Gardens, Delaware Art Museum, First USA Riverfront Arts Center, and Christiana Healthcare Systems. Delawareans have also found their way through the state by following Mitchell Associates' signage systems, including the Brandywine Trailblazers, Wilmington Riverfront, Concord Mall, and WILMAPCO, as well as the rooftop signage for First USA Bank and Beneficial Bank. The firm has completed many assignments in the First State, representing only a portion of its diverse client list across the United States.

In addition to phenomenal corporate and client success, the late 1990s marked an exciting milestone, as the firm recognized the hard work and dedication of five staff members, through their appointment as the first associate principals—Robert R. Agosta, SEGD; Patricia A. Damiri, IIDA; Erik R. Dressler, Vicky J. Newton and John K. Raftery, AIA.

Rosenberg feels the reason for such outstanding success is simple, "We have built a design staff that is committed to service and believes that a close working relationship with clients produces designs of distinction." Each assignment is approached as a new challenge with the needs, desires, and financial commitment of the client providing the direction. Mitchell Associates applies the common principle that the creative design must fit the people, —those who work in the space, and those who visit it.

NEW PROCESS FIBRE COMPANY, INC.

New Process Fibre is one of the best-kept secrets in the tiny town of Greenwood, in Sussex County. Many of the townspeople are unaware of its existence, and even many longtime residents couldn't tell you what goes on there.

In fact, the products made in this little factory are an everyday part of modern life, and while many of the residents of Greenwood may be unaware of the company's existence, there are few Americans that don't come into daily contact with the products made here. Washers and gaskets used in plumbing and sealing applications; electrical insulation parts used in small appliances, hand tools, electronics equipment and electrical distribution; and component parts for the automotive industry are just a few of the places where New Process Fibre's parts can be found. New Process Fibre ships parts all over the United States as well as to many foreign countries.

New Process Fibre began as a manufacturer of vulcanized Fibre, sometimes referred to early on as chemical Fibre. New Process not only manufactured the material itself, but also fabricated items from it. Today, New Process no longer manufactures vulcanized Fibre; its main focus is to produce non-metallic, stamped parts. Materials today are mainly thermoplastics such as polypropylene, polyethylene, and nylon. Vulcanized Fibre is still fabricated, accounting for a lesser percentage of parts than the thermoplastics. Also fabricated is phenolic, or thermoset plastic parts. This material is commonly known for its use in circuit boards, although there is a wide variety of applications, mainly electrical. In addition to stamped parts, New Process also extrudes thermoplastic sheet, mainly for it's own consumption in the production of parts, but also for sale as material as well.

Vulcanized Fibre is an invention first patented by Thomas Taylor in England in 1859. The U.S. Patent was issued in 1871 and the Vulca-

Francis Carl Porter , about 1943.

nized Fibre Company was established in Newark in 1873. Many other companies sprang up before 1900 to produce Vulcanized Fibre. It is interesting that the Vulcanized Fibre industry was largely centered in and around Wilmington. There were also a few companies in Ohio and New York, but most were in Delaware or nearby, in Pennsylvania. By the late

1960s, only three Fibre companies remained in the United States and today National Vulcanized Fibre, or the NVF Company in Yorklyn, Delaware, is the only remaining producer of Vulcanized Fibre in the United States.

Francis Carl Porter founded new Process Fibre in 1927. F. Carl Porter was born in Greenwood in 1896. His father, J. Frank Porter was a well-known merchant in Greenwood and, most notably, was one of three local businessmen who founded the Greenwood Trust Company in 1911. Greenwood Trust enjoys worldwide recognition today as issuer of the Discover card.

Carl Porter left Greenwood to attend Goldey College in Wilmington, graduating in 1914. He went to work for Wilmington Fibre in New Castle at a time when Wilmington Fibre was one of the largest Vulcanized Fibre producers in the country. By 1923, Carl was supervising the Fibre making at Wilmington Fibre. He wrote a paper entitled, "A Prospectus On the Starting of a Company for The Manufacture and Sale of

New Process Fibre Company, Inc., Greenwood, Delaware, about 1964.

From left to right: Carl W. Peters, President, Henry W. Peters and Hans M. Peters.

Vulcanized Fibre and Fibre Products," and in 1927, he left Wilmington Fibre to come home to Greenwood to do just that.

Carl, his father, J. Frank, and William Leslie Cramer of New Castle formed the board of directors for the new venture. They called the company New Process Fibre, after the "new process" that Carl Porter had devised to produce Fibre. The "new process" proved to be a failure, but the name stuck.

The company incorporated in Delaware on October 11, 1927 and the plant was operational by March 1928. From October 1927 until that time, payroll records show the wages of various employees who were actually engaged in the building and setting up of the plant. The wages ranged from 30 to 60 cents per hour, although some received up to a dollar an hour, as they were hired with the use of a truck. When the plant became operational, employees worked up to 60 and sometimes 80 hours per week, with no time and a

A Welex 38" wide extruding nylon.

Below
Many of the products manufactured by New Process Fibre Company, Inc.

half for overtime. Once the plant was operating, 10 to 15 people were employed regularly.

From 1927 until 1950, New Process Fibre produced Vulcanized Fibre material in sheets, rod and tubing and fabricated parts from the materials as well. The company experienced prosperity, really only during the period around World War II, mostly due to the war effort. They had large government contracts for parts that required 1/4" thick sheet and two shifts were needed. Carl Porter's brother, Lester, ran the Fibre making and became quite adept at running the difficult, thicker material, as well as being able to run it quickly. A brick building was added in 1939 to house the punch press and fabrication operation. Production of Fibre was so great at times that the material had to be hung outside to dry. In 1950, production of Fibre ceased, and New Process had to buy raw material to continue fabrication operations.

Other than during the war, New Process Fibre experienced many financial troubles. Carl Porter's thesis was that the large Fibre companies were overcharging and fixing prices, and that he was going to produce Fibre cheaper. The harsh reality was that for a small company without the economies of scale, he couldn't compete even with their artificially high prices. In order to do so, he frequently lost money. The company sold stock and borrowed from banks frequently. After the war, the company fell back into this cycle and was seriously in debt by the time of Mr. Porter's death in 1962.

Carl Porter's son-in-law, Henry Peters had grown up on a farm in a small rural community near Hamburg, Germany. At 23, he left Germany for unknown opportunities in the United States. He married Nancy Porter and began working for New Process in 1957. When he took over the operation in 1962, he faced a short-term debt that was half of annual gross sales.

Henry Peters worked 18-hour days with a crew of three or four to get the company out of debt. At the end of 1962 his hard work had paid off. The company netted a profit that year, and has increased profits in almost every year since. By 1966, New Process Fibre was operating in the black. During those years, Henry Peters made frequent trips across the United States, "chasing smokestacks" to gain customers and acceptance. From that time, sales have increased dramatically. Today, New Process ships more in a single day than was shipped the entire year of 1962. Some of the customers that New Process serves today go back as far as the 1930s and earlier. Many of today's customers, however, began doing business with New Process during the early '60s.

In 1966, a new shipping room was added to the 1939 structure. For 10 years, New Process experienced solid growth. In 1976 it became necessary to add a new building to house the growing number of punch presses. This space was doubled in 1978, and a sheet extrusion line was added. The addition of the thermoplastic sheet extrusion line gave New Process more control over its raw material require-ments, regaining leverage similar to what it had when NPF produced Vulcanized Fibre prior to 1950. An addition with new shipping facilities and offices was added in 1980. More warehouse space and a second extrusion line was added in 1982. A remote warehouse was added in 1994. With the addition of a third extru-sion line in 1995, a new building to house the extruder operation was added. By this time New Process was producing sheet and coil stock not just for it's own production, but for sale as finished goods as well. Cur-rently, New Process is looking for the best place to add more floor space and plans to build again in 2000.

By 1962, employment had fallen to a mere three people. This grew to 20 by 1970. There were about 30 employees in 1990 and 50 in 1999. It should be noted that the hiring

New Process Fibre Company, Inc., today.

practices have been much more conservative than the sales growth and, consequently, New Process Fibre has never laid off an employee due to lack of work. Turnover is low, and many employees today have better than 15 years of service with the company.

New Process Fibre as it exists today is a far cry from the company it was when it was founded. The great success of New Process Fibre can be

The valued employees of New Process Fibre Company, Inc.

directly attributed to the hard work and perseverance of Henry W. Peters. Upon his retirement in 1997, that mantel was passed on to his sons, Carl and Hans, and his son-in-law, William Rust. Today, New Process Fibre is a leading supplier of non-metallic stampings and extruded thermoplastic sheet. This small Delaware company supplies impor-tant fabricated parts to many of the world's largest multinational corpora-tions in all types of industries.

NANTICOKE HOMES

The Mervine family of Greenwood, owners of Nanticoke Homes Inc., one of America's top 100 builders and recognized leaders in off-site new home construction, have roots set deep in the soils of Delaware.

A successful chicken-brokerage business, operated by John and Peggy Mervine, had its beginnings in 1936 when John's father created the family business. That entrepreneurial spirit was to lead to the birth of Nanticoke Homes. In 1971, a chance investment with a local contractor would change the housing industry and the lives of thousands across the Delmarva Peninsula. The use of an abandoned chicken feeding station behind the Mervine home, allowed for the indoor construction of a new home without the typical concerns for the elements. The first 28 x 46 foot ranch home was started in February without concern about temperature or frozen ground.

Later that year the new home, complete with paint, paper, kitchen and more, was moved to its site in Seaford. That was only the beginning for Nanticoke Homes and the Mervines.

The "Garrett" by Nanticoke Homes. A custom two-story Center Hall colonial.

By year's end the contractor-partner was gone, but 17 houses had become home for 17 families. Today, Nanticoke Homes is a major factor in the new home market, not only on Delmarva but north to New Jersey and Pennsylvania, west into Maryland and Virginia, and south to the Carolinas. With recent expansion into Indiana, Nanticoke is now a recognized name in the midwest as well. With construction in Green-

Custom-built Nanticoke three-bedroom ranch home.

wood as well as the Indiana facility and a Maryland location, Nanticoke continues to develop even greater flexibility. Custom single-family homes are built with care and craftsmanship, as are townhomes, apartments, offices and light-commercial buildings.

Today's Nanticoke Homes with John Mervine Sr. as CEO and John "Mcky" Mervine Jr. as president, has grown not only in capability but in sheer size as well. A three-plant complex employs over 800 and has a building capacity of 30 homes per week. A far cry from the first plant, which was destroyed by fire in 1979. A visit to Nanticoke Homes will afford one the opportunity to view the construction facilities, offices and model home center. It also allows one to see drive and imagination resulting in success, not for Nanticoke Homes alone, but for the nearly 17,000 who have placed their trust and confidence in one of Delaware's, and America's, leading homebuilders.

ROBERT C. PEOPLES, INC.

The story of Robert C. Peoples, Inc., begins with the determination of a young man, Bob Peoples, whose foresight and vision built both a reputation and a successful business. His life story is the American dream of earning success through hard work, persistence and honest dealing. Communities built by Robert C. Peoples, Inc., have distinctive features which reflect the philosophy of the company: a quality product at a fair price will ensure a reputation that is the best advertising. From the very beginning in 1954, Peoples-built houses have spoken for themselves. The principles laid down by founder Robert C. Peoples have been the keys to the success of the present-day company.

Born in the Cedars, an area of modest homes near the city of Wilmington, Bob Peoples undertook private enterprise at an early age. When he was 12 years old, he used the money he made from caddying to buy 25 chickens; he then began selling eggs to neighbors. At an age when children are expected to learn responsibility from taking care of a pet, Bob was learning to keep records and satisfy customers. This early success in the business world was a prediction of things to come.

While in high school, Bob continued his chicken business, but self-improvement was always his goal; therefore, he set his sights on obtaining a college degree. Family finances, however, were not strong enough to pay his college tuition. Undeterred, Bob achieved his goal through a football scholarship at the University of Delaware. His choice of a major—agricultural education—was a natural one because of his love for the land. Another love was fulfilled soon after he finished college when he married his high school sweetheart, Dorothy Mettenet.

For several years after college, Bob Peoples was a teacher of agriculture, but true to his enterprising spirit and the needs of a young family, he operated a side venture. In the summer months, along with students

Youthful Bob Peoples practicing his first business venture.

on the high school football team, he landscaped houses in the growing developments around the city of Wilmington. After purchasing some used equipment, he began paving the roads in these areas; and finally, he purchased land on which to build houses. For Bob Peoples, the lure of business, a sense of accomplishment, and the feeling of purpose came together in the home-building industry. From just a few lots to thousands of acres and thousands of houses, Bob Peoples realized his dream.

Providing large lots for landscaping, privacy, and safe places for children to play is an ongoing characteristic of R.C. Peoples, Inc. Such advantages are due to the builder's foresight in choosing to buy vast areas of undeveloped land in the area south of Newark, known as the Bear/Glasgow corridor. On these lots are quality constructed homes, with first stories of masonry, hardwood flooring, and carefully trimmed interiors. One of the first communities is Caravel Farms, now 35 years old— beautifully shaded and lovingly maintained—where resales have consistently been higher than the previous sale.

Thousands of houses of similar quality characterize this growing area. Peoples' houses are found in Shelly Farms, Rolling Meadows, Dutch Neck Farms, Marabou Meadows, Pine Valley Farms, Grande View Farms and Melody Meadows. Communities of homes built exclusively by R. C. Peoples are Caravel Woods, Hickory Woods, Caravel Hunt, and Mansion Farms, the newest venture, with seven hundred and fifty homes. In addition,

An aerial view of Peoples Plaza illustrates the spacious positioning of the buildings. Photo by Eric R. Crossan

Above
Robert C. Peoples. Photo by Eric R. Crossan

Below
Bob Peoples proudly stands with his three sons: Bob, Harry and Tom. The family business has been carried on with the knowledge gained by first hand experience. Photo by Eric R. Crossan

Hockessin Valley Falls is a community of elegant Peoples-built homes close to the Pennsylvania line. Although there have been modifications in style, the aspect of quality construction on lots large enough for green landscaping and for children to play continues to be the philosophy of R. C. Peoples' home-building.

Peoples Plaza Shopping Center, another venture of R. C. Peoples, Inc., is no ordinary strip mall. Located on 75 acres convenient to the mushrooming developments around the Routes 896 and 40 intersection, the buildings are planned and executed in a manner distinctive to Peoples' construction. Brick Georgian-type buildings are the sites of two office facilities, many suites of which are occupied by medical and legal services. Stores such as Genuardi's Family Markets, Regal Cinema and Home Depot round out a variety of retail stores satisfying the needs of the community. Restaurants, sandwich and coffee shops serve the needs of shoppers and diners. An array of specialty shops, arranged in a semi-courtyard pattern, make shopping convenient and pleasant for the growing number of residents. Today Peoples Plaza proudly boasts of being the fourth largest shopping center in the state of Delaware.

Trained as an educator, Bob Peoples believed that an important part of every community is a school. He had strong feelings about providing children with a good education in a safe environment. In 1979, Bob Peoples founded and built Caravel Academy, a non-profit, college preparatory school that now serves children from preschool to 12th grade. Many parents have held views similar to Peoples, and Caravel Academy has grown in both physical size and school population since its inception.

Enrichment of the community in multiple ways has been more than a commercial endeavor. The Peoples family provided land for use by the Canal Little League for over 30 years on property adjacent to Peoples Plaza Shopping Center. Thousands of young people have benefited from the use of these playing fields—through learning team play, skills and sportsmanship. The Robert C. Peoples and Dorothy M. Peoples Library at Wilmington College is evidence of the philanthropy of the Peoples family, and Dorothy Peoples continues to serve on the Board of Trustees of Wilmington College.

One of the qualities most admired about Bob Peoples was his love of family. Not only did he train his four children to take part in his many ventures, but also he considered his wife, Dorothy, a partner in business as well as in marriage. Fortunately, this aspect of his character also reflected his foresight, since his sudden death in May of 1990 left the business without single leadership. Now, Dorothy and children Bob, Harry, Tom and Carol run the many enterprises of R. C. Peoples, Inc. Whereas in the beginning one man ran it all, now those responsibilities are shared among the family members—all of whom had the advantage of having a great teacher.

POLYMER TECHNOLOGIES

Polymer Technologies incorporated on February 15, 1989 as a Delaware Corporation. The founders, Robert and Suzanne Prybutok, like many industrious entrepreneurs, engaged in this monumentally risky venture as a result of a negative life-cycle event.

Robert Prybutok had joined a small Delaware firm in 1972 that was in the polyurethane foam lamination and fabrication business. He joined that firm as a marketing representative and eventually became vice-president in charge of marketing, research and development and quality control. This company had significant growth from 1986 through 1989 under his leadership in the marketing area. In 1989, the company was acquired by an out-of-state competitor, and Mr. Prybutok was asked to resign his position. This was a great loss since much of his creative energy had been poured into developing this company's product line, marketing focus and national image. In evaluating options and with careful council from his wife, Suzanne, he decided that what he had helped build for others he could build for his family. The outcome of that decision was the launch of Polymer Technologies, Inc., a manufacturing company whose principal business focus was the lamination and fabrication of noise control composites for the national, and eventually global, industrial equipment markets.

Forming a corporation on February 15, 1989, the next eight months of frantic activity involved drafting a detailed business plan, searching for investors and securing bank financing. In the summer of 1989, the Prybutok's removed all the furniture from their dining room, set up desks, file cabinets and phone lines, and turned their dining room into the corporate offices of Polymer. The first employees were hired in August, and were two former associates of Mr. Prybutok's previous company. One was destined to be his operation's manager, Aaron Horsey, and the other his key customer service and

Polymer Technologies, Inc. headquarters built September 1995 and expanded to 70,000 square feet in 1999.

materials manager, Danielle Charron. The four developed the computer software systems, accounting systems, product line, literature, raw material sources and equipment process line details, as well as the office and plant layout. Most of this monumental task was accomplished in 60 days, culminating in the move into the company's first manufacturing site, on October 1, 1989.

During the summer of 1989, the Prybutoks purchased a small black poodle with a white chest, and suitably named him "Oreo." This was done as a diversion from the stress of the venture the Prybutoks had undertaken. Oreo became the company's mascot and to this day comes to the office every day, spending time with all of the employees. He is the official greeter, and usually the first one visitors meet at Polymer Technologies.

The first offices were 17,000 square feet of leased manufacturing space in the Pencader Corporate Complex in Glasgow, Delaware, a suburb of Newark. Through unique circumstances and hard negotiation, the company occupied 17,000 square feet of industrial space but only paid for 10,000 square feet. They did not pay for the aisles or areas they did not

actually occupy with inventory or manufacturing equipment! An interesting but useful arrangement for a young company wtih no customers and negative cash flow!

In 1989, three of the major companies in the OEM noise control industry were acquired by major conglomerates, and Mr. Prybutok realized that the key to the company's success was focusing on customer service and dedicating the organization to providing the best service and support available within their industry. This quality had been lacking within the industry, due to acquisitions of competitors by larger conglomerates that were less service-oriented. Through that first year, tremendous energy was spent on the phones to prospects throughout the country in a broad and diverse range of industrial, transportation, recreational and medical markets. In the first year Polymer Technologies had six employees that included the owners, Robert and Suzanne Prybutok. Revenues were a mere $272,000. Days were spent on the phone selling, and evenings and weekends working on equipment and developing products. At times the challenge seemed almost impossible, and success a distant reality.

In 1991, Carl Wolaver invested in Polymer Technologies, Inc. and joined the company as executive vice president. Mr. Wolaver had been an executive with a competitor and brought significant industry, technical and marketing knowledge to Polymer. In these immediate years the company was able to hire many former associates of Mr. Prybutok, all of whom added to the depth of knowledge and capability of the company.

From the onset of this entrepreneurial venture the corporate philosophy and corporate culture was one of being people and family oriented and providing customers with the best value within the marketplace.

The owners in a photo taken in 1999. Seated is Robert Prybutok; Suzanne Prybutok and Carl Wolaver are standing.

Throughout these early years and up to the present, the key to Polymer's success was dedicating itself to excellent customer service. This obsession for excellence in service is reinforced by management on a daily basis.

In spite of having limited resources, Polymer Technologies provided employees with company paid healthcare, vacation pay, sick pay, and holidays—benefits usually relegated to much larger companies. As Polymer Technologies grew and prospered, more company-paid and company-sponsored benefits have been initiated, including: long and short term disability; life insurance; and a 401K retirement program. Each month there is a party to celebrate the birthdays of employees whose birthdate falls in that month. Polymer is truly an employee-oriented company.

In 1995, several significant events took place. The company hired Cathy Vance, who was instrumen-

tal in developing administrative procedures and improving the organization for the company. Since 1995, Mrs. Vance has been an important influence in the success and growth of Polymer. That year, the company's revenues had reached approximately $4 million dollars, and the company purchased 4 acres of land in the same industrial park and built a 30,000 square-foot manufacturing facility. At this point the owners and employees felt they had leapt the first hurdle of becoming a real corporation and a major force within their industry.

Polymer Technologies, Inc. always maintained that its employees were its most valuable resource. With low unemployment in the state, Polymer had difficulty hiring employees with adequate english and math skills. In 1997, they contracted with a local university to assess Polymers' employees and conduct remedial education classes in the company cafeteria to strengthen employees skills in math and english. The company made these classes mandatory, but paid employees their regular wages to attend.

Today, Polymer Technologies has over 60 employees, and is approaching $10 million dollars in revenue. It is planning for an expansion in the Newark, Delaware location that will add an additional 40,000 square feet of manufacturing and warehousing space, along with an additional 5,800 square feet of office space.

Polymer Technologies has gained recognition under the International ISO 9002 quality standards, which is a significant achievement for a small company and is a sign of their dedication to quality and excellence. They continue to be an employee-oriented manufacturing force in Delaware and one of the fastest growing companies in their industry. Over the past 10 years of growth one of the proudest accomplishments of the owners of Polymer Technologies was to provide a vehicle for its employees' professional and financial growth. They have given back to the community through setting a standard of excellence and accomplishment.

QUALICON, a DuPont Subsidiary

Dwarfed by its giant parent, the DuPont company, tiny Qualicon has a big vision that it's well on the way to realizing: to create a new universal language for microbiology.

It's a vision of profound importance to everyone. Bacteria are everywhere on earth and are essential to our life processes. Understanding bacteria is essential to improving the quality of life, through such critical areas as preventing and controlling disease and assuring better quality, more abundant and safer food.

Qualicon technologies look at bacteria through their genetic code. Qualicon products make these technologies easy to use and accessible, greatly increasing the probability that they will enter routine use to benefit mankind.

Qualicon products help the food industry obtain a better understanding of the microbial composition of food. These products use breakthrough genetic technologies to address the industry's most important safety and quality management problems. Qualicon customers also include other industrial users with microbiological concerns, such as pharmaceutical and cosmetics manufacturing as well as hospital

The entrance to Qualicon, Inc. headquarters at the DuPont Experimental Station in Wilmington, Delaware.

epidemiology, veterinary diagnostics and research organizations. And by creating networks that exchange Qualicon-technology-generated genetic information about bacteria, Qualicon is writing a new universal language for microbiology.

Qualicon began as Food Quality Management Systems, an initiative in DuPont Central Research and Development.

Founder Vinay Chowdhry, a DuPont manager for corporate strategy and business development, envisioned anticipatory markets to apply advanced technologies to address future needs of industries.

DuPont had been very successful doing this in the past, with revolutionary products such as nylon. The food industry, whose spending on research and technology was far outstripped by other industries such as pharmaceuticals, was the first target. The fast-emerging field of genetic information provided the right focus.

By creating a small, entrepreneurial group within the giant company, DuPont had the flexibility to develop products on a schedule suited to the fast-paced biotechnology industry.

During the next few years, an experienced, interdisciplinary DuPont team worked together closely on a fast-track schedule to create a powerful patented technology platform specifically designed for the food industry. To develop a product that automated the generation and interpretation of genetic information—an impossibility, many said —it was necessary to draw on a diverse blend of disciplines: molecular biology, engineering, mathematics and information technology. To increase the possibility of success, multiple solutions for automating each step of the biochemical process were investigated simultaneously. At the same time, the team developed alliances with leading food processors as well as pharmaceuticals and personal products manufacturers and research associations around the world. The result was a several-years' jump on the competition.

In May 1995, the first Qualicon product was introduced. Four months later, Qualicon was formed.

Today, Qualicon, Inc., a DuPont subsidiary, is headquartered at the DuPont Experimental Station in Wilmington. It has customers in more than a dozen countries, including industry leaders such as Kraft Foods and Silliker Labs; prominent research organizations such as the Institut Pasteur and DSMZ (German National Culture Collection); and government organizations such as the USDA and the National Center for Food Safety and Technology. The Qualicon team numbers more than

The Qualicon RiboPrinter® system generates genetic fingerprints, called RiboPrint® patterns, to identify the culprit in a food contamination problem. The three patterns identify three strains of Listeria monocytogenes bacteria found in a plant. Variations in the patterns, clearly visible even to the naked eye, make it possible to pinpoint the exact bacterial strain causing the problem.

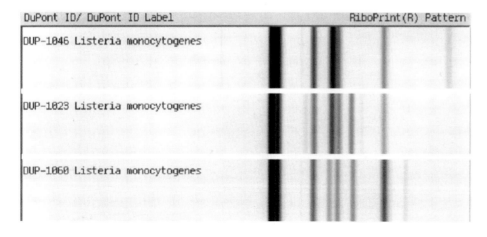

120 members around the world. A subsidiary, Qualicon Europe Ltd., was opened in England in 1997. Among Qualicon's assets are 35 U.S. patents. In addition, Qualicon has been awarded a development grant from the U.S. Department of Commerce NIST program to develop next-generation technologies.

Qualicon products grew out of the recognition that traditional microbial testing methods—labor-intensive, time-consuming, unreliable, highly subjective and virtually unchanged since the days of Louis Pasteur—are inadequate for doing truly thorough and definitive microbial analysis. Qualicon products resolve this problem through the use of genetic information, resulting in an automated, standardized approach to microbial identification.

The Qualicon RiboPrinter® Microbial Characterization System is the world's first and only automated instrument that can generate a genetic "fingerprint" from a bacterium. Since its introduction in May 1995, it has won four major industry awards. The RiboPrinter® system provides concurrent identification of bacterial genus and species, and also

provides characterization below the species level. It does this using a patented DNA-based approach to create a genetic fingerprint of a bacterium, known as a RiboPrint® pattern. This "Universal Product Code" for bacteria is just as versatile as its supermarket counterpart: it can be electronically stored for reference and analysis, compared to a database of patterns, sent over phone lines and compared to patterns generated by RiboPrinter® systems anywhere in the world.

The RiboPrinter® system is the basis of several worldwide networks of microbial information, performing functions such as tracing the path of antibiotic-resistant strains of bacteria in hospitals or identifying an outbreak of listeriosis caused by food.

The Qualicon BAX® Screening System, a family of tests, is the first commercial product to use the Nobel prize-winning technique, Polymerase Chain Reaction (PCR), to establish the presence or absence of specific bacteria in food and environmental samples. The BAX® systems were named to the 1996 R&D 100 for their technological significance. These products can accurately detect

even a tiny amount of a target pathogen, because they use PCR to rapidly multiply a specific segment of that bacterium's DNA—an extremely reliable indicator of the presence of the bacterium.

For example, BAX® for screening *Salmonella* provides a yes-or-no answer to the question, "Does this sample contain *Salmonella*?" Using the BAX® systems, food processors can ship products soon after production, minimizing inventory costs without jeopardizing consumer safety. Currently, there are BAX® systems for detecting *Salmonella, Escherichia coli* O157:H7, *Listeria monocytogenes* and *Listeria* genus.

Just as changes brought about by the computer information revolution have dramatically improved our lives, future advances will come from applying genetic information to solving real world problems. Qualicon will continue to create the innovative products that can greatly enhance the quality of our lives.

Qualicon founder Dr. Vinay Chowdhry and technician Dorothy Fields examine a report printed by the automated RiboPrinter® Microbial Characterization System (shown on the left) in a Qualicon laboratory.

RICHARDS, LAYTON & FINGER, P.A.

Robert H. Richards, founder of Richards, Layton & Finger, P.A.

Richards, Layton & Finger, P.A. is Delaware's largest law firm, with approximately 100 attorneys. It is also the oldest Delaware law firm practicing under its original name. The firm conducts a local, regional, national and international transactional, corporate, and litigation practice. It maintains its only office in Wilmington, Delaware.

The originator of the firm, Robert H. Richards, began practicing law in Georgetown, Delaware, in April 1897. Two years later, he moved his practice to Wilmington. In 1906, Richards hired as his secretary Aaron Finger, the 16-year-old son of a recently deceased Russian immigrant, with the promise of training him for the bar. After passing a college equivalency examination and the Delaware bar examination, Finger became the first Jewish lawyer in Delaware, and a partner with Richards in 1912. Caleb Layton joined Richards and Finger as a partner in 1929, at which time the firm became known by its present name of Richards, Layton & Finger.

Over the next 70 years, Richards, Layton & Finger became nationally and internationally recognized for its corporate and commercial practice. The firm has served as primary outside counsel or Delaware counsel in many of Delaware's most significant corporate cases. Delaware corporate litigation has helped to shape corporate law, affecting most of the United States' major corporations. In recent years, the firm has represented clients in such important Delaware corporate cases as: *Paramount Communications v. QVC Network, Inc.; Moran v. Household International, Inc.;* and *Unocal Corp. v. Mesa Petroleum Co.* Members of Richards, Layton & Finger have served as the principal draftspersons and members of the Delaware Bar Corporate Law Committee responsible for enacting major revisions to the Delaware General Corporation Law.

Richards, Layton & Finger is also nationally and internationally known for its transactional practice. The firm regularly serves as Delaware counsel on highly sophisticated financial transactions and corporate mergers and acquisitions. The firm ranks as one of the top law firms in the country in mergers and acquisitions work, and is among the top 10 firms for transactional work. Examples of the firm's transactional work include: advising on multibillion dollar mergers; structuring billion dollar leveraged buyouts and joint ventures; handling auctions and sales of companies; counseling companies on corporate governance issues; recommending the adoption or modification of "poison pills" and other defensive measures; and assisting with the securitization of various revenue streams generated by businesses, ranging from credit card and mortgage receivables to the music royalties of internationally known rock stars. Members of Richards, Layton & Finger have been responsible for creating and amending Delaware's innovative business statutes and laws involving limited partnerships, limited liability companies, alternative entities, business trusts, and a wide variety of other business ventures.

Richards, Layton & Finger is also well known for its bankruptcy and intellectual property practice. Since 1995, more than 50% of the nation's largest bankruptcy filings have been in Delaware, and Richards, Layton & Finger has been involved in each of these major bankruptcies. The firm ranks among the top firms in the United States for appearances in large bankruptcy cases. The firm has also represented parties in major patent and trademark litigation in the federal court in Delaware, which is emerging as one of the principal courts for trial of intellectual property matters. In addition, the firm is active in general commercial and tort litigation.

Over the years, members of Richards, Layton & Finger have been active in the Delaware community and politics. Former members of the firm have served in the Delaware Legislature. A former Delaware governor is currently of counsel to Richards, Layton & Finger. The present Chief Justice of the Delaware Supreme Court is a former partner of the firm. The first woman to become a partner in a major Wilmington firm thereafter left Richards, Layton & Finger for the federal court, where she now serves as a member of the Third Circuit Court of Appeals.

Richards, Layton & Finger will continue providing expert and diverse legal services across the globe, while maintaining its pride and presence in its home state of Delaware.

RLC CORP.

RLC Corp. was founded in 1954 as Rollins Fleet Leasing Corp., Inc., to incorporate the automobile leasing business established in 1946. It operated as a sole proprietorship in Lewes, Delaware by John W. Rollins, who continues to serve as RLC's chairman of the board of directors and chief executive officer.

The automobile leasing business was started by Rollins, a pioneer in the industry, to help corporate America build its sales forces after World War II. He recalls that, "until that time nearly all want ads for salesmen specified that job applicants had to own a car, but I convinced companies that owning a car should no more be a condition of employment for a salesman than owning a typewriter should be for a secretary."

The scope and significance of the transportation needs of companies that operate their own transportation systems indicated that those needs

RLC Corp. headquarters in the 15 story building on Concord Pike, north of Wilmington, since 1972.

Rollins Leasing Corp. founded in 1954 in Lewes, Delaware by John W. Rollins.

should be filled only by a full-service transportation organization. This organization would be dedicated to ensuring the efficient and economical operation of any type and size of truck fleet. Rollins' management was confident that the company could not only become such an organization, but could and *would* become a leader in the industry. Their confidence was bolstered by the proven effectiveness of the company's principal business philosophy which was then, is now, and always will be: the attainment of 100% customer satisfaction must be the first priority of every employee.

In 1968, the company became publicly held and its common stock was listed on the American Stock Exchange. Since 1978, the firm's common stock has been listed on the New York Stock Exchange.

RLC Corp. is headquartered in the fifteen-story Rollins Building (opened in 1972) on Concord Pike north of Wilmington. In the four decades since its incorporation, RLC has become one of the nation's leading highway transportation companies. RLC currently employees nearly 4,000 men and women at over 200 locations throughout the United States and has more than 37,000 vehicles in operation on the nation's highways.

Today Rollins Leasing Corp. services the transportation industry with Commercial Rental, Maintenance Leasing, Full Service Truck Leasing, Dedicated Carriage and a full line of Logistic Systems and Solutions.

Since 1954, Rollins has evolved into a major national company and has grown to become one of the top three Full Service Transportation Companies.

The best part is that Rollins' story doesn't end here. RLC steadily continues to grow by matching and bettering the competition in every major market area. Whatever challenges the company may face from its competition and the economy, that growth will continue because, as they always have, its competent, dedicated employees— the Rollins people—again, will make the difference.

ST. FRANCIS HEALTHCARE SERVICES

Its 75th anniversary in 1999 proved an ideal time for St. Francis Hospital and its related healthcare services to reaffirm their commitment to providing quality health care for the entire community.

As the only Catholic hospital in Delaware at the turn of the millennium, St. Francis celebrated under Dr. M. Eileen Schmitt, its new president and CEO, by emphasizing its tradition of gentle, high-touch excellence in patient care.

Dr. Schmitt, a family physician, began admitting patients to St. Francis in 1983, becoming an officer of its medical staff in 1990. By 1999, the medical staff numbered nearly 800. Dr. Schmitt is known for her commitment to the spiritually-based values of the hospital's founders, the Sisters of St. Francis of Philadelphia.

"Their mission and their ministry is entrusted to us and it is a sacred trust," Schmitt reflected. "Ultimately, what makes us different is our spiritual heritage."

The Order of the Sisters of St. Francis was founded in 1855, by three immigrant women who answered a calling to serve those in need. They opened their first hospital, St. Mary's in Philadelphia, in 1860. St. Mary's thrived on the courageous spirit of the Sisters and their trust in God's providence.

In 1924, the Sisters opened a 60-bed hospital in Wilmington that was dedicated to the patron saint of their order, the gentle Saint Francis of Assisi. This facility was built on a hilltop in Wilmington that had once been considered as a site for the U.S. Capitol. Two years later, in 1926, the School of Nursing at St. Francis opened.

Since its founding, St. Francis has periodically renewed its commitment to serving Wilmington and its inner city. This included a decision not to use a tract of land it had purchased in the 1950s in Christiana as a possible new location. The Sisters decided instead to keep the hospital where it was, and sold the land.

In 1964, an expansion—the DuPont Building—brought the hospital's capacity to 200 beds, and renovation in 1969 accommodated intensive care and pediatric units, and private rooms. A few years later, the original building was razed, and the seven-story Clayton Street Building was put on its site. When this opened, the hospital capacity was 289 beds with two floors available for future growth.

In the early 1980s, another phase of expansion added a Medical Office Building with physician offices, a family practice center and residency program. Another development in the '80s was the creation of the Franciscan Health System by the Sisters of St. Francis, in response to growing challenges in healthcare delivery.

In 1992, the Medical Services Building opened as a new home for family practice, the laboratory, home care, outpatient rehabilitation and physician and administrative offices.

That same year saw two milestones in the hospital's outreach programs. The St. Clare Medical Outreach Van, in partnership with the Ministry of Caring, began serving the poor and homeless of Wilmington with the first of the more than 30,000 visits it

The original St. Francis Hospital building opened on Clayton Street in 1924 with 45 beds. In 1937, the number of available beds doubled with the completion of the 7th Street annex. Today, the Hospital is licensed for 395 beds.

would make through the rest of the decade. Tiny Steps, a prenatal program for low income and uninsured women, began in collaboration with West End Neighborhood House, also opened. Seven years later it relocated to Westside Health Services, a federally-qualified healthcare center near St. Francis.

St. Francis Hospital's outreach ministry expanded in 1996 to serve Hispanic migrant workers with the opening of a Center of Hope satellite office in Newark, and in 1997 with the opening of the House of Joseph II, a hospice north of downtown Wilmington, for men with AIDS.

In 1998, St. Francis again collaborated with West End Neighborhood House, this time in an effort to revitalize the community. Their Cornerstone West strategy is moving more than 50 houses owned by either St. Francis or West End to private ownership.

In 1996, Catholic Health Initiatives (CHI) was formed by the

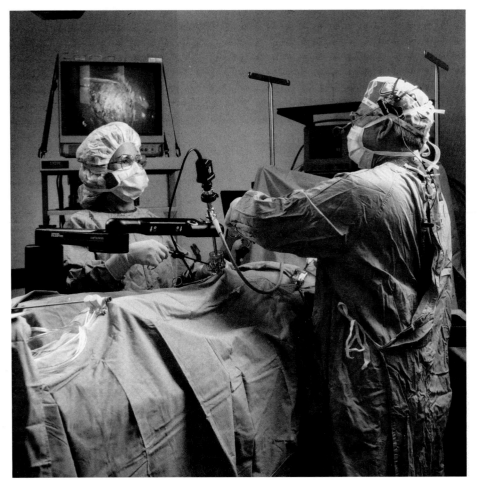

Dr. Maris Luis Medenilla, surgical assistant, and Dr. Alexander Balan, surgeon, use the AESOP 2000 Robotic Arm, one of St. Francis Healthcare Services' new technological advances, during a laparoscopic procedure.

consolidation of the Franciscan Health System with Catholic Health Corporation and the Sisters of Charity Health Care Systems. Catholic Health Initiatives is a national Catholic health system, which includes 68 hospitals and more than 50 long term care facilities in 22 states. In 1998, St. Francis' efforts in the community were recognized and supported with two substantial Mission and Ministry Grants from Catholic Health Initiatives. The Sisters of St. Francis of Philadelphia and St. Francis used these grants to collaborate with other community, educational and church organizations to create a women's health initiative and a Healthy Neighborhoods Project with

Christ Our King School/neighborhood.

By 1998, St. Francis' services had expanded to include a range of Family Care Centers, a Family Practice Center, two OB/GYN and midwifery centers, a pain center, several rehabilitation centers, extended care facilities, home care, and outreach programs and Select Specialty Hospital of Wilmington, a long-term acute care hospital. The hospital's primary location was its 395-bed facility at 7th and Clayton Streets, which in 1998 saw completion of a new state-of-the-art intensive care unit.

To reflect this breadth of services and locations, St. Francis adopted a new umbrella identity in 1998— St. Francis Healthcare Services.

The mission of CHI and St. Francis is to "nurture the healing ministry of the Church by bringing it new life, energy and viability in the 21st century. Fidelity to the Gospel urges us to emphasize human dignity and

social justice as we move toward the creation of healthier communities."

St. Francis shares with all Catholic Health Initiatives hospitals four core values:

• Reverence: Profound spirit of awe and respect for all of creation, shaping relationships to self, to one another and to God and acknowledging that we hold in trust all that has been given to us.

• Integrity: Moral wholeness, soundness, uprightness, honesty, sincerity as a basis of trustworthiness.

• Compassion: Feeling with others, being one with others in their sorrows and joy, rooted in the sense of solidarity as members of the human community.

• Excellence: Outstanding achievement, merit, virtue, continually surpassing standards to achieve/maintain quality.

These words serve to underscore the tender, loving nursing care for which St. Francis has long been known and the determination of its staff and administrators that the medical, nursing and spiritual needs of patients come first.

Statue of Saint Francis of Assisi.

UNIQEMA

Although the specialty chemical supplier Uniqema was launched in January 1999, the New Castle employer had its 1926 beginnings in an unlikely setting—the middle of the Atlantic Ocean. The plans for Uniqema's parent company, ICI (Imperial Chemicals Industries, plc.), were conceived onboard the Cunard vessel *Aquitania* on December 7, 1926, by Sir Harry McGowan, chief executive of Nobel Industries, and Sir Alfred Mond, later Lord Melchett, chairman of Brunner, Mond & Company.

ICI was the result of the merger of four of the largest chemical companies in the United Kingdom. It was formed to create a British company capable of competing in world markets against larger corporate players in the USA and Germany. During their trip from New York to Southampton, England, Sir McGowan and Sir Mond agreed upon the merger of Brunner, Mond & Company Limited, Nobel Industries Limited, British Dyestuffs Corporation Limited, and United Alkali Company Limited.

In its first year of business, the new company sold 27 million British pounds worth of products, including chemicals, explosives and accessories, fertilizers, insecticides, dyestuffs, domestic chemicals, leathercloth, printing materials, sporting ammunition and paint. With 33,000 employees worldwide in 1926, ICI's pre-tax profit reached 4.5 million British pounds.

Since its founding, Uniqema's parent company has remained at the forefront of scientific discovery and innovation with products such as fertilizers, plastics, manmade fibers, anaesthetics, heart drugs, herbicides, pesticides, commercial explosives, waterborne paints, reactive dyes and biodegradable plastics.

The Atlas Point plant has been a landmark at the Delaware Memorial Bridge since its construction in 1937. The Atlas Powder Company was created in Delaware in 1913, when the Wilmington-based Dupont Company was forced to sell the business as part of a federal antitrust settlement. ICI acquired the plant in 1971 as part of its purchase of Atlas Chemicals Industries, Inc., and moved its headquarters from Stamford, CT, to the Wilmington suburb of Fairfax. In 1992, ICI moved its headquarters several miles north to Concord Plaza, on Silverside Road in Talleyville.

In 1993, ICI demerged its bioscience businesses of pharmaceuticals, agrochemicals, specialties, seeds and biological products into the separate, publicly listed company, the Zeneca Group, plc. Four years later, ICI made its biggest acquisition to date with the purchase of four companies from Unilever: National Starch, Quest, Unichema and Crosfield, for a total of $8 billion. ICI merged the four companies into its operations to form the basis for ICI's transformation into the world's leading specialty products, coatings and materials company that makes up the ICI Group today.

The purchase of the four Unilever companies highlighted ICI's move away from bulk and industrial products toward specialty chemicals. With the addition of Mona Industries in 1998, the ICI group was ready to launch Uniqema, bringing together ICI's concentration in surfactants, oleochemicals, lubricants and other specialty chemicals. Uniqema is a global company with an annual turnover of more than $1 billion. With headquarters in London, it has approximately 10,000 products, 33 sites worldwide and more than 3,200 employees. Its main markets are personal and healthcare products, agrochemicals, polymers, lubricants, textiles and coatings. The company's broad portfolio of specialty chemicals and product solutions is supported by strong brands, applications expertise, world-class technical support and a flexible supply network.

Uniqema, along with the entire ICI Group, makes the safety and health of its workers and the environment its paramount concern, with a highly detailed ICI Group Safety, Health and Environmental Policy. "ICI will ensure that all its activities worldwide are conducted safely; the health of its employees, its customers and the public will be protected; environmental performance will meet contemporary requirements; and that its operations are run in a manner acceptable to the local communities." Executive Chairman Richard Stillwell, puts it more succinctly: "Nothing that we do is worth getting hurt for."

Uniqema's presence in Delaware includes the regional headquarters of North American operations in Talleyville. In New Castle County, Uniqema employs a total of nearly 300 workers at two locations, the headquarters at Concord Plaza and the Atlas Point plant, which is Uniqema's largest plant in the U.S. Although ICI's regional headquarters are scheduled to move to Bridgewater, New Jersey by 2000, Uniqema will retain its U.S. headquarters in New Castle County.

With a base of 10,000 customers, Uniqema offers products used in coatings, crop protection, health and personal care, lubricants and oilfield. Most consumers might not recognize a Uniqema product, even though they are found in hundreds of household items from baby shampoos and skin lotions, to diapers and colored soda bottles.

Uniqema recently completed expansions at Atlas Point, increasing the plant's capacity by 35%. Improvements include a new alkoxylation reactor that produces nonionic, alkoxylate-type specialty products. The new reactor is equipped with enhancements and new technology, in accordance with ICI's record as an industry leader in safety and produc-

tivity. The increased production capacity at Atlas Point benefits customers in the personal care, coatings, oilfield, agriculture, textile and other market segments.

"The expansion of Uniqema's alkoxylation capabilities positions us to better serve our expanding customer base," says Allan R. Coletta, operations manager at Atlas Point. "The new production unit utilizes the best of Uniqema's global technology and the latest control and safety systems. These modern processes will take Uniqema well into the 21st century." The expanded facility supplies products to North America and global markets. Products made at Atlas Point are primarily specialties, many of which are designed to specific customer requirements.

Local business and community leaders have always appreciated the positive impact that ICI, and now Uniqema, has had on New Castle County. "We look forward to working with Uniqema the way we have in the past with ICI, and we don't believe they'll miss a beat in that regard," says John Burris, president of the Delaware Chamber of Commerce.

Uniqema's President Pete Johnson also predicts a positive future: "Uniqema will be known for its consistent product quality, reliable service and outstanding capacity for problem solving and innovation. Our goal is to be the strongest and most innovative supplier in the specialty chemicals market. Uniqema has ambitious targets for growth."

Headquarters of Uniqema, in Delaware.

LEON N. WEINER & ASSOCIATES

Delaware beckoned. It was where opportunities were when Leon N. Weiner came out of the service after World War II. It was where opportunities continued to present themselves to him for the next 50 years.

Weiner, a third generation builder from Philadelphia, joined his uncle in Delaware in 1949, doing everything from sweeping the floors to laying bricks.

The company, then known as Franklin Builders, built houses under the GI Bill for soldiers returning from the fighting in Europe and Asia. The two key benefits under the Bill were help with higher education and with housing. Under the latter program, run by the Veterans' Administration, GI's could buy a house with no down payment and mortgages below the going interest rate.

"In 1949, you could buy a house with a four percent mortgage," Weiner recalls. "That's what my uncle was building and that's what I came down here to do with him."

The typical GI Bill house was a three-bedroom ranch-style building constructed over a crawl space. They sold for $9,800 and could include a full basement for another $800. Fifty years later, these houses were reselling for $145,000.

Franklin Builders built several hundred GI Bill homes into the early 1950s, and continued to concentrate on affordable housing in the years

The Adams Four Shopping Plaza stands as a reflection of Leon Weiner's commitment to urban renewal.

Left to right, Leon N. Weiner, founder of the firm, Kevin P. Kelly, and David W. Curtis.

that followed. These later homes were the same size or a bit larger and, as the years passed and customer demands changed, Weiner & Associates included air conditioning and other amenities. During its first 50 years, the company built and sold more than 5,000 single-family homes in Delaware and adjoining areas of Pennsylvania.

In the late 1950s, Weiner's uncle retired and Weiner continued the business, first as Franklin Industries and later as Leon N. Weiner & Associates.

In 1964, Weiner took his place as a visionary in the housing industry, joining in a consortium to develop a revolutionary mixed-use development of townhouses, single family houses, parks and commercial centers in Pike Creek Valley. Years later, honored as one of 30 people who changed Delaware, he was cited as changing not only where people lived, but also how they lived.

At about the same time, he became involved in developing the East Side of Wilmington, an area devastated by slum clearance. He built a mix of housing including high-rise apartments for senior citizens, and earned

the trust of all ethnic groups in that time of racial turmoil.

Weiner's leadership was readily recognized by his peers. He had joined and become active in the National Association of Homebuilders shortly after he arrived in Delaware, and in 1967, this representative of the smallest state in the Union was elected NAHB's president, an honor he places at the pinnacle of the many honors he and his firm have collected over the years. Today, the NAHB represents some 200,000 firms throughout the United States.

Weiner also served as president of the Home Builders Association of Delaware, chairman of the Executive Committee of the National Corporation for Housing Partnerships, president and chairman of the National Housing Conference and a director of the Home Loan Bank Board, Pittsburgh. He was appointed by President Lyndon B. Johnson to the Kaiser Commission which initiated much of the landmark Housing Act

The historic Jekyll Island Club in Jekyll Island, GA., was restored by Weiner & Associates in 1986.

of 1968. For this service and other activities dedicated to the betterment of the real estate industry, he received numerous awards, including induction into the National Housing Hall of Fame.

In the early 1970s, Weiner decided to dedicate himself to providing housing for low-to-moderate income families and senior citizens. He and his firm became experts in dealing with the maze of government programs, and in 1992, he and his senior team of David W. Curtis and Kevin P. Kelly were honored as the nation's top multi-family builder by the NAHB. By then, his firm had built 7,500 apartment units from the mid-Atlantic states to New England. The NAHB praised it as a leader in using state and federal housing programs to develop affordable communities.

"Leon drilled into us that you don't measure everybody by the amount of money they have," says Kelly.

Weiner's non-residential projects include shopping centers, such as Adams Four in Wilmington, and restorations such as the elegant Jekyll Island Club resort in Georgia. Adams Four is just one example that reflects the company's commitment to urban revitalization, which includes extensive experience establishing public/private partnerships and dealing with

federal, state and local housing and community development agencies and with a wide array of non-profit organizations. Jekyll Island demonstrates its interest in historic preservation.

Weiner & Associates is proudly a business that grew up and has, for the most part, operated in Delaware. As opportunities changed, it diversified, leaving no area unexplored and extracting from each, new measures of success. It has also done projects in New York, Connecticut, Pennsylvania, New Jersey, Maryland, Washington, D.C., Virginia, North Carolina and Georgia, and has expanded into financing and property development and management through LNW Investments and Arbor Management.

Arbor resulted from the merger of Weiner's North Delaware Realty Company (NDRC) with Konover Investments of Connecticut, with Weiner & Associates as operating partner. The entity continued NDRC's

One of many recent senior citizen apartment complexes constructed by Leon N. Weiner & Associates.

commitment to meeting the needs of residential and commercial rental tenants through energetic management and careful maintenance. NDRC, which had more than 4,000 apartment units, was among the top ten property management firms in the country, cited for excellence in property management by the National Center for Housing Management. Arbor manages some 7,600 units.

Kelly and Curtis are dedicated to continuing Weiner's legacy. Both are active in industry associations and with government agencies.

Kelly, who started with Weiner & Associates in 1979, was named 1998 Builder of the Year by the Home Builders Association of Delaware, Inc. He is completing his second term as president of the Home Builders Association of Delaware, serves as vice-chairman of the NAHB Multi-Family Council and was the national representative for Delaware.

Curtis' expertise in financing resulted in a pioneer restructuring of debt and reserves of three 15-year-old Delaware State Housing Authority properties, making additional funds available for financing new, affordable housing in the state. He started with Weiner in 1981. He is a board member of Home Loan Bank Board of Pittsburgh, heads up the Arbor Management operations and Weiner's involvement in HOPE VI programs for revitalization of public housing.

Throughout its existence, Weiner & Associates' major concentration remained housing, and its hallmarks remained fairness, quality and creativity in its work. "I've been in this business a long time and I've built many things, but none more important than the relationships with my clients, many of whom have become my friends," Weiner says. As one of the United States' preeminent home builders, developing and maintaining trust has been a crucial attribute. This has been bolstered by a sophisticated system of quality control, cost reporting and management procedures that allow the company to be responsive to a changing business environment.

WILMINGTON FRIENDS SCHOOL

Founded in 1748, Wilmington Friends School is the oldest school having continuous existence in the state of Delaware. It is the 11th oldest independent school in the United States.

The story of Wilmington Friends School begins in 1735, when a small group of Quakers (members of the Religious Society of Friends), led by William Shipley, settled in what is now known as Wilmington, Delaware.

Shipley and his wife, Elizabeth, purchased extensive property in Willingtown, as it was then called. On a site just below Fourth Street on the west side of what is now Shipley Street, they built a small, one-story brick house. It was in this house that the first Quaker Meeting for Worship was held in Willingtown.

Wilmington Friends School kindergarten class from 1902 forms a "Circle of Friends" in the school yard.

The size of the meeting grew, and by 1738 the group built their first meeting house across the street, on a site just beyond Tatnall Street on Fourth Street. The area soon became known as "Quaker Hill."

Only 10 years later, the increasing meeting membership outgrew the original 25 square-foot building. A new, larger meeting house was built across West Street from the original building, and the older building began to be used as a school in 1748. This is the date used to mark the founding of Wilmington Friends School.

The meeting's resolution to start its own local school resulted from the Quaker emphasis on moral and religious training for the young

within the Religious Society of Friends. With the value of practical education in mind, the Wilmington Monthly Meeting founded the school to teach the rudiments of reading, writing, and "ciphering," or arithmetic. The school was devoted almost entirely to educating the children of the poor in the neighborhood. This service to the community of providing education to the poor came directly from the meeting's

Above
Wilmington Friends School's graduating Class of 1900. Back Row, from left: Albert Marshall, J. Warren Marshall, J. Paul Cranston, Irving Warner; Middle Row: Anna J.E. Nichols, Mary E. Kent, G. Herschel Clark, Lorena Bates Emmons, James A. Hetherton; and Front Row: Edgar Q. Bullock, William H. Connell, Jr., Charles W. Bush, Edward G. Poole.

Below
An early 1920s Wilmington Friends School baseball team poses for a team photo with their coach and bat boy.

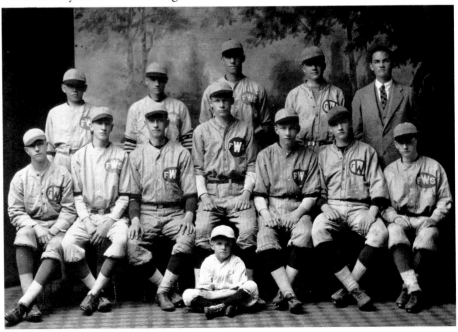

Friends first meeting house in Wilmington was built in 1738 on Fourth Street, just beyond Tatnall Street, on what is still known as "Quaker Hill."

Arthur Harmon, much-loved school bus driver and orchestra leader, stops the horse drawn school bus at Friends School's front door on West Street in 1908.

Quaker roots in England. Financial support for Friends School came from members of the meeting, usually in the form of bequests.

Like other Wilmingtonians of those days, many Friends hired tutors for their own children. In later years, dissatisfaction with the tutors and their system became apparent, and the trend toward instruction in formal classes at Friends School began.

When it was converted to a school, an additional room was added to the original building, nearly doubling its size. The two unlinked rooms housed the boy's and girl's schools. In 1829, the new portion was given a second story, and in 1846 the whole building was renovated and given two floors. Later additions included new classrooms, a science lab, and a gymnasium.

From those early beginnings, until 1937, the school operated at its original site. Additions and renovations continued throughout the years until a decision was made to move the school to its current location on School Road in Alapocas. After remodeling and a few years as an apartment building, the old school was torn down, removing the last bricks from the 1738 Quaker Hill Meeting House.

The new school in Alapocas originally housed grades kindergarten through 12. Later, in 1967, a pre-kindergarten was added. The school continued to grow, and on November 23, 1965, Wilmington Friends purchased land for a lower school campus. Construction of the lower school, which included grades pre-kindergarten through four, was completed in 1972. The lower school was again expanded in 1989, with the addition of a new wing, and it now includes grades pre-kindergarten through five.

Most recently, Friends School completed construction of a new $5 million athletic center, expanded and modernized its computer and science labs, and renovated its existing auditorium into a new performing arts center. Renovations for a new meeting room for regular meetings for worship, a 250-year tradition at the school, have also been completed.

Today, Wilmington Friends School is a private, co-educational, college-preparatory, day school with approximately 700 students in grades pre-kindergarten through 12.

Students work on their lessons inside a Wilmington Friends School classroom (circa 1914).

247

WILMINGTON TRUST

The year 1903 was a time of successful ventures for many Americans—the Wright Brothers made their first flight at Kitty Hawk, North Carolina, Henry Ford founded the Ford Motor Company, and the Boston Red Sox captured a victory over the Pittsburgh Pirates at the first World Series. It was also the year that T. Coleman du Pont and several other prominent Delaware businessmen joined together in the dining room and parlor of a former private residence in Wilmington to form the Wilmington Trust Company. The general assembly authorized capital of $1 million for the new venture, made up of 10,000 shares with a par value of $100. On opening day $500,000 was subscribed, with du Pont serving as the first president and chairman of the company.

By 1907, the banking industry was undergoing a time of financial and economic crisis marked by public loss of confidence in the financial struc-

Wilmington Trust Center rises 13 stories above the neo-classical frontage of the Old Post Office and serves as the company's corporate headquarters in Wilmington.

ture. Typically, such panics were characterized by a rapid fall of the securities market, resulting in bank failures and bankruptcies. Wilmington Trust remained strong through this period, having outgrown its quarters and relocating to the prestigious new DuPont Company building at Tenth and Market Streets. The building

Wilmington Trust in the early days of doing business.

remained Wilmington Trust's headquarters for 76 years. It wasn't until October 1983, that Wilmington Trust opened its doors at a new corporate headquarters on the site of the old Wilmington Post Office, on

North Market Street across from Rodney Square. This marked the first time in years that all of the bank's downtown operations were housed under one roof. In 1998, the bank celebrated the grand opening of a new operations facility on West 11th Street to accommodate a larger work force and additional office space, due to rapidly growing deposit operations and credit card processing activities.

In its first 50 years, the bank added only five branch offices. Today, Wilmington Trust has over 52 branch offices located throughout the state of Delaware and additional sales offices in its regional markets outside of the state. As the number of branch offices increased over the years, so did the success of the Company's trust business. Today, the Trust Department is one of the largest in the nation, with clients throughout the United States and in many foreign countries.

In 1982 Wilmington Trust became the first bank in Delaware to offer in-house discount brokerage services; the following year, Wilmington Trust Discount Brokerage Services was established. This same year saw the expansion of the company into Florida, with the establishment of its wholly-owned trust subsidiary, Wilmington Trust of Florida, NA, in Stuart. Since that time, Wilmington Trust of Florida has evolved into Wilmington Trust FSB, with offices currently located in Stuart, Vero Beach, and North Palm Beach. The success of the bank's expansion into Florida led to further movement into new regional markets throughout the 1990s, through the Wilmington Trust FSB affiliate, including Maryland, Nevada, New York, and California. In 1990 the bank applied for regulatory permission to establish a bank holding company to be known as Wilmington Trust Corporation. During the 10 years that followed, Wilmington Trust took its existing loan production office in Exton, Pennsylvania and created a commercial banking operation

that soon expanded to a full-service office in West Chester. In 1995 the bank also opened a personal trust and investment management office in downtown Philadelphia. Today, Wilmington Trust of Pennsylvania serves clients in southeastern Pennsylvania through locations in Haverford, Lionville, Media, Philadelphia, West Chester, and Villanova.

Along with increasing its office locations, the bank has formed strategic alliances with some of the nation's best investment firms to complement the strength of its asset management services. In 1996, Wilmington Trust acquired a 24 percent ownership in Clemente Capital, Inc., a global and international equity and fixed-income investment management firm headquartered in New York City. In 1998, Wilmington Trust and Cramer Rosenthal McGlynn, an investment advisory firm located in New York, formed an affiliation that allows both partners to offer their fiduciary and investment expertise to high net-worth clients. Later that same year, Roxbury Capital Management in Santa Monica, California also formed an affiliation with Wilmington Trust to serve high net-worth clients across the country.

Wilmington Trust has made great strides over the past 97

years—turning a two-room operation into a multi-billion dollar banking and wealth management company. The premiers of www.wilmingtontrust.com and Wilmington Trust's On-Line Banking service in 1998 and 1999 respectively, exemplify the Company's commitment to helping its customers succeed through alternative banking options such as electronic commerce.

Throughout the years, Wilmington Trust has earned a national reputation for reliability and stability, reflected in record earnings and paid increased dividends every year since 1982, and a return on shareholders' equity of 20% or more for 14 consecutive years. This strength led the company to move its stock listing from the NASDAQ National Market System to the New York Stock Exchange in early 1999. The listing of "WL" on the world's largest and most dominant equity market should help increase visibility for the company while directly supporting its corporate goals as it evolves into the 21st century.

Banners displaying the new trading symbol for Wilmington Trust hang from the top of the New York Stock Exchange Building, as "WL" commences trading on the "Big Board" on January 12, 1999.

WJBR-FM 99.5

WJBR-FM 99.5 was founded in 1956 by the father and son team of John B. Reynolds, Sr. and John B. Reynolds, Jr. John, Sr. was co-owner of a local service station. It was John, Jr., however, that had the knowledge of broadcasting and music. Jr. hosted a local TV dance program (before the days of American Bandstand), and was a recording pianist in the late 1940s. John, Sr. began the radio station due to John, Jr.'s strong belief in the future of FM radio.

The station operated with only five employees for the first few years. John Sr. did some selling and Jr. operated as general manager, program director and voiced many of the commercials. The other employees were booth announcers who also played the music.

The first offices, studios, and transmitter site for WJBR-FM were on Ebright Road in North Wilmington. The tower is located at the highest elevation in the state, approximately 400 feet above sea level, with the tower rising an additional 317 feet high. Offices and studio were moved to their current location, on Philadelphia Pike in Claymont, in 1993, although transmitting equipment and tower remained at Ebright Road.

WJBR-FM began broadcasting as a classical and light music format. Although the station had coined the phrase, "Just Beautiful Radio," the JBR in its name actually stands for the founders' initials. By 1985, "beautiful music" was a fading format, and new owners CRB Broadcasting believed the newer Adult Contemporary format would produce the audience makeup needed to maximize its market share. They created "Bright 99.5," which was renamed "Mix 99.5" approximately three years later. The "Mix" handle was phased out in 1993 and the station went back to identifying itself simply by the call letters that have become legendary in the Mid Atlantic—99.5/WJBR-FM. Currently, the station uses the slogan "Today's Hits and Yesterday's Favorites" to identify

Left to right: Paul Lewis, on-air talent and creative services director; Joe Robinson, public service director; Valorie Mack, news director; Michael Waite, morning show host, as well as program director and general manager; and J. Bear, celebrity mascot.

its format. Many listeners also know WJBR-FM as the station that plays, "the most music while you work."

WJBR-FM has also been a pioneer technically, recognized as one of the first to broadcast a 24-hour stereo format in the late '50s, and the first station to broadcast an all CD format in the late '80s.

The Reynolds family purchased WTUX in 1976, and changed over to WJBR-AM in 1978. The new "Bright" format was simulcast with the FM for several years, until it picked up a satellite nostalgia format and became what is known today as AM-1290.

John Jr. sold the stations in 1985, several years after his father passed away. The new owner, CRB Broadcasting, was a trio of men using their initials to name the company. The "B" in CRB belonged to Carter Burden, an heir to Commodore Vanderbilt's family. CRB began

aggressively seeking acquisitions in other markets, such as Allentown, PA; White Plains, NY; Norwalk, CT; Charlotte, NC; Huntington, WV; and Port St. Lucie, FL. These stations had a variety of formats, ranging from rock to country to adult contemporary, dictated by each market's needs. CRB eventually grew to about 20 stations before being sold and renamed as Commodore.

Progressive sales led to an eventual purchase by Capstar Broadcasting, of which Atlantic Star was a subsidiary. In September 1997, due to FCC restrictions, WJBR-FM was once again sold to its present owner, and is no longer affiliated with AM-1290.

Early personalities associated with the station include local celebrities: Del Parks, Ed Hunt, and Howard Gessner, all three during the "Beautiful Music" years. Doug Weldon was morning show host and operations director from 1985 to 1993, when Michael Waite joined WJBR-FM as morning show host, program director, and, (after the separation from Atlantic Star) general manager.

Currently, WJBR-FM hosts the "No Repeat Work Day" from 9am – 5pm daily. Every 10 minutes in the morning, and every 15 minutes in the afternoon, WJBR-FM presents the area's only airborne traffic reports of the tri-state roadways. The days are capped-off with Delilah taking your requests and dedications, playing that special song for your special someone.

A WJBR-FM program guide from the year 1963 with the front cover depicting Gordon MacRae and (left) the inside front cover showing the station personnel, at the time.

SECURITY INSTRUMENT CORP. OF DELAWARE

In June 1960, Donald K. Williams and Arthur J. Mattei, both from Wilmington, established Security Instrument Corporation of Delaware to meet the need for a local company that offered a personal touch for security systems and associated services.

In the '60s, crime and burglaries predominantly occurred in very affluent neighborhoods. So, in the beginning, Security Instrument specialized in custom home security systems, setting the benchmark for quality installations and providing a responsive, personalized service team. Eventually, this combination earned Security Instrument an excellent reputation in the area. While installing custom alarms in affluent homes, the company realized that many of their customers were highly involved in or owned their own business and were interested in utilizing the same type of systems and services for these locations. Thus, Security Instrument expanded its service to include the commercial security and fire alarm business.

In the early days, a typical security system consisted of magnetic contact switches on doors and windows to detect opening. As the market for alarm systems grew, Security Instrument saw the need to create a system that could detect movement inside a home or business, minimizing an intruder's ability to move throughout the premises undetected.

Corporate offices of Security Instrument Corp. of Delaware in Wilmington.

Frank Moley, an electronics enthusiast and highly creative individual in the security field, had been developing a radar detection unit. This unit could detect movement in open areas as well as through walls and floors. Security Instrument determined it might be very useful to its customers. Don't forget that this was in the '60s, when motion technology was in the early stages of its development.

The units worked so well, that after some testing and field evaluations, Frank, Don and Art created a second company, called MOWIMA Electronics, to manufacture these units. The company, named after the owners, MOley, WIlliams and MAttei, began producing these detectors under the trade name of Space Guard, while Security Instrument marketed the new detectors to its clients. As technology changed, ultrasonic and microwave detectors became available through national

distribution, using modern production techniques. The Space Guard detectors became too expensive to produce and MOWIMA electronics was phased out. Frank Moley continued his career with Security Instrument until he retired in the early 1990s.

As the company continued to expand, the owners realized that the need for monitoring service was growing. Initially, it utilized answering services and voice dialers to provide this service. In 1970, the company built a full-service, U.L.-approved central station to provide monitoring and a variety of enhanced services to its customers. Throughout the '70s and '80s, the need for home and business alarm services greatly increased. With its approved central station, reputation for quality workmanship, and responsive personalized service, the company continued to prosper.

In 1990, Don Williams sold his portion of the business to the Mattei family. Presently, the Mattei family and its dedicated, conscientious staff continue to operate the firm using the quality foundation built by its founders. Today, Security Instrument is Delaware's largest full-service, independently-owned security firm with over 95 employees, serving thousands of customers throughout the Delaware, Pennsylvania, and Maryland areas.

Space Guard System as distributed by Security Instrument Corp.

A TIMELINE OF DELAWARE'S HISTORY

1609 Henry Hudson is the first European to sail into the unnamed bay north of Cape Henlopen and establishes a Dutch claim to the Delaware Valley.

1610 Samuel Argall sails into the bay north of Cape Henlopen and names it for the Governor of Virginia, Lord De La Warr.

Corbit-Sharp House in Odessa was built in 1772-74 by Quaker tanner William Corbit. It harbored fugitive slaves in the antebellum era. Photo by Eric Crossan

1631 The Dutch establish the first temporary European settlement in Delaware.

1638 The Swedes establish the first permanent European settlement in Delaware at Fort Christina.

1639 Black Anthony, the first African, arrives in Delaware.

1655 The Dutch conquer the Swedish holdings on the Delaware River.

1666 The English conquer the Dutch holdings on the Delaware River.

1682 Delaware given to William Penn by James, Duke of York.

1698 Pirates plunder Lewes.

1704 Delaware gets its own legislature but continues to acknowledge the authority of the Penns or their appointed Lieutenant Governors.

1713 Large influx of slaves into Delaware begins.

1720s Large influx of Scots-Irish into Delaware begins.

1739 Willingtown renamed Wilmington.

1750 Tobacco is no longer a significant cash crop in Delaware.

1770 Slaves make up 20 to 25 percent of Delaware's population.

1776 On June 15, Delaware declares its independence from Great Britain. (Today June 15 is celebrated in Delaware as "Separation Day.")

On July 2, thanks to Caesar Rodney's ride, Delaware casts an important vote in Philadelphia for the collective independence of all thirteen colonies.

1777 Battle of Cooch's Bridge, the only Revolutionary War battle on Delaware soil.

"Jints," who lived southeast of Georgetown, holds her master's granddaughter Hanna Stockley, circa 1860-61. This is the only existing photo of a Delaware slave. Courtesy, Delaware State Archives

Early Swedish log cabin at the site of Fort Christina, the first Swedish settlement, now part of east Wilmington. Courtesy, Delaware Tourism Office

1781 Dover becomes Delaware's permanent capital.

1784 Barratt's Chapel near Frederica becomes the "Independence Hall" of American Methodism.

1787 On December 7, Delaware becomes the first state to ratify the U.S. Constitution. (Today December 7 is celebrated in Delaware as "Delaware Day.")

1802 DuPont Company's powder works begins operation along the Brandywine.

1810 All three Delaware counties have approximately the same population.

1813 Lewes bombarded by British fleet during War of 1812.

1816 African Union Church, the first independent black church in Delaware, is established by Peter Spencer in Wilmington.

1829 Completion of Chesapeake and Delaware Canal.

1832 Delaware enacts the first of a series of black codes to restrict the rights of free African-Americans.

Delaware's first commercial peach orchard is planted in Delaware City.

1840s Wilmington begins its extraordinary industrial and population growth.

1847 Bill to abolish slavery in Delaware fails by one vote in the state senate.

1859 Delaware Railroad reaches Delmar on Delaware's southern border.

The Allee House, located northeast of Dover, is representative of the homes of eighteenth-century Delaware gentry. Courtesy, Delaware State Museums

1861 Delaware chooses to remain within the Union during the Civil War.

Lincoln's plan to free Delaware's slaves is rejected by the General Assembly.

1865 In December the Thirteenth Amendment puts an end to slavery in the last two remaining slave states, Delaware and Kentucky.

1872 President Grant sends Federal troops to Delaware in an attempt to protect the right of black males to vote.

1889 John Edward O'Sullivan Addicks first becomes engaged in Delaware politics.

1890s Peach blight ends peach boom in southern Delaware.

1897 Present Delaware Constitution adopted.

1902 Three du Pont cousins, Alfred I., T. Coleman, and Pierre S., take over the DuPont Company.

1907 Commitment by the DuPont Company to make its corporate headquarters in Wilmington.

1920 Delaware refuses to ratify the Nineteenth Amendment but Tennessee's ratification gives women the right to vote in the U.S.

1921 A more centralized state public school system is adopted.

1923 Beginning of the national broiler industry in southeastern Sussex County.

1924 Completion of the DuPont Highway from Wilmington to Selbyville and Delmar.

1929 Beginning of Depression in Delaware.

1941-1945 World War II brings industrial boom to Delaware.

1954 Brown vs. Board of Education decision of U.S. Supreme Court causes aborted attempt at school integration in Milford.

1967 Jason School in Georgetown, the last all-black school in the state, is closed and its campus becomes Del Tech's first campus in Delaware.

Lewes Canal, just south of where the Dutch briefly established their Swanendael settlement in 1631. Courtesy of Delaware Tourism Office

1968 Race riots in Wilmington provoke Governor Terry to send in the national guard.

1971 Coastal Zone Act passed by General Assembly which protects Delaware's seacoast from industrial development.

1972 Completion of reapportionment of General Assembly districts which ends the control of the state legislature by Kent and Sussex counties.

1975 Plan Omega adopted which led to the construction of the Christiana Medical Center in suburban New Castle County.

1978 Court-ordered busing of public school children begins in northern New Castle County to combat de facto segregation.

1981 Financial Center Development Act passed by General Assembly which, subsequently, attracts a large number of banks to Delaware.

1984 Increasing feminization of Delaware's work force is reflected by the fact that 23 percent of DuPont's Delaware-based managerial and professional staff and 17 percent of the state's practicing physicians are now women.

1990 Delaware ranks sixth among states in per capita income.

1992 James Sills elected first black mayor of Wilmington.

1997 Secretary of Education created as a cabinet-level position in Delaware.

Delaware ranks fifth among states in per capita income.

1998 Banks employ 8 percent of Delaware's non-farm work force.

An Amish farm west of Dover in 1998. Courtesy, Delaware Tourism Office

BIBLIOGRAPHY

The best modern comprehensive histories of Delaware are John A. Munroe's *History of Delaware* (1984), which is a chronological treatment, and Carol E. Hoffecker's *Delaware: A Bicentennial History* (1977), which has a topical format. Also of interest is Roger A. Martin's *A History of Delaware Through Its Governors, 1776-1984* (1984). A two-volume, collaborative work edited by H. Clay Reed, *Delaware: A History of the First State* (1947), focuses on a number of topics important to understanding Delaware's past. J. Thomas Scharf's two-volume *History of Delaware, 1609-1888* is crammed full of facts, but they are not always accurate.

A History of Kent County, Delaware (1976) and *The History of Sussex County, Delaware* (1976), both written by Harold Hancock, give a brief look at downstate Delaware. A detailed analytical treatment of Wilmington's past is found in Carol E. Hoffecker's *Wilmington, Delaware: Portrait of an Industrial City* (1974) and in *Corporate Capital: Wilmington in the Twentieth Century* (1983).

For the history of Delaware during the colonial period, see John A. Munroe, *Colonial Delaware* (1978). Studies of the Delaware and Nanticoke Indians may be found among the assorted works of C.A. Weslager. John A. Munroe's *Federalist Delaware* (1954), Harold Hancock's *The Loyalists of Revolutionary Delaware* (1977), and William H. Williams' *The Garden of American Methodism: The Delmarva Peninsula, 1769-1820* (1984), all deal with the post-colonial era. John A. Munroe's *Louis McLane: Federalist and Jacksonian* (1973) and Harold Hancock's *Delaware During the Civil War* (1962) focus on the nineteenth century. For slavery in Delaware, see William H. Williams, *Slavery and Freedom in Delaware, 1639-1865* (1996); and for a look at social and legal practices in early nineteenth-century Sussex County, see Bernard L. Herman, *The Stolen House* (1992). A thorough study of the emerging Du Pont Company in the early twentieth century is *Pierre S. du Pont and the Making of the Modern Corporation* (1971) written by Alfred D. Chandler and Stephen Salsbury. For a look at downstate Delaware and Governor John G. Townsend during the same period, readers are advised to examine Richard Carter's *Clearing New Ground* (1984). A recent treatment of public school integration in New Castle County can be found in Part Four of Raymond Wolters' *The Burden of Brown: Thirty Years of School Desegregation* (1984). For an examination of the poultry industry on Delmarva, see William H. Williams' *The Delmarva Chicken Industry: 75 Years of Progress* (1998). For a comprehensive history of the University of Delaware, see John A. Munroe, *History of the University of Delaware* (1985).

A detailed bibliography of Delaware history can be found in the back of John A. Munroe's *History of Delaware*.

The information for chapter VIII came from a number of sources. More than 50 Delawareans in public and private life were willing to share their factual knowledge and personal opinions concerning Delaware in the years 1985-1999. The *News Journal* was an indispensable source. In addition, particularly helpful on the economy, population, and land development patterns in Delaware, were David Ames' *1997 Annual Assessment Report to the Cabinet Committee on State Planning Issues* (1998); Edward Ratledge's *Delaware, 1945-1998* (1998); *Delaware 1998 Statistical Overview* (1999); and Robert A. Glen's *Office of State Bank Commissioner Annual Report for the Year Ended Dec. 31, 1998* (1999). For facts on Delaware agriculture, see *1997 Census of Agriculture: Delaware State and County Data* (1999); and William H. Williams, *Delmarva's Chicken Industry: 75 Years of Progress*. For Delaware women in the late twentieth century, see Carol E. Hoffecker's *Beneath Thy Guiding Hand: A History of Women at the University of Delaware* (1994); and *Celebrating Seventy-Five Years of Women in the Delaware Bar* (n.d.). For education in Delaware, see *Delaware Student Testing Program: State Summary Report 1998 Administration* (1999); and *Expecting the Best for Delaware's Children: the Carper Administration's Plan to Raise Student Achievement* ....(1998).

NEWCASTLE AND FRENCHTOWN

RAIL-ROAD.

PASSENGER CARS,

PROPELLED BY A LOCOMOTIVE ENGINE,

Leaves the *Depot*, at NEW CASTLE, *for* FRENCHTOWN,

EVERY MORNING,

Upon the arrival of the Steam-boat from Philadelphia, at about

Half Past Eight o'clock,

RETURNING

Leaves Frenchtown at about Half-Past Ten o'clock.

ANOTHER TRAIN OF

PASSENGER CARS

Departs from New Castle. for Frenchtown, every evening, (except Sunday,) upon the arrival of the AFTERNOON BOAT, *from* Philadelphia, at about Six o'clock, and on return arrives about Nine o'clock.

Fare over the Road - - - - - - - 50 cents.
Do., for excursion over the road and back - - 50 cents.

New Castle, June 1st, 1833.

R. H. BARR *Ag't.*

The New Castle and Frenchtown Railroad began operations in 1831. The railroad at first used horses to pull its fancy coaches. The company imported an engine from England in 1832 and assembled it in its New Castle shops. Courtesy, Historical Society of Delaware

INDEX

CHRONICLES OF LEADERSHIP INDEX

American Life Insurance Company, 180
Artisans' Bank, 181
Ashby & Geddes, 182-183
AstroPower, Inc., 184-185
Bayhealth Medical Center, 186-187
Belfint, Lyons & Shuman, P.A., 188
Blue Cross Blue Shield of Delaware, 189
Caravel Academy, 190-191
Cohen's Furniture, 197
Corrado American, Inc., 192-193
DaimlerChrysler Corporation, 194-196
Delaware Hospice, 203
Delaware State Museums, 198-199
Division of State Service Centers-Delaware, 200-202
DuPont, 204-205
First USA, 206-207
1450 'WILM NEWSRADIO, 208-209
Freeman Companies, Carl M., 210-211
General Chemical's Delaware Valley Works, 212-213
Globe Electric Company, Inc., 214-215
Gore, & Associates, Inc., W. L., 218
Hopkins Construction, Inc., 216-217
Hotel du Pont, 219
Independence School, The, 226
Kirby & Holloway Provision Company, 220-221
MBNA Corporation, 222-223
Mealey Funeral Homes, 224-225
Mitchell Associates, Inc., 227
Nanticoke Homes, 231
New Process Fibre Company, Inc., 228-230
Peoples Inc., Robert C., 232-233
Polymer Technologies, 234-235
Qualicon, a DuPont Subsidiary, 236-237
Richards, Layton & Finger, P.A., 238
RLC Corp., 239
St. Francis Healthcare Services, 240-241
Security Instrument Corp. of Delaware, 252
Uniqema, 242-243
Weiner & Associates, Leon N., 244-245
Wilmington Friends School, 246-247
Wilmington Trust, 248-249
WJBR, 250-251

GENERAL INDEX
Italicized entries indicate illustrations

A
Adams, John, 50
Addicks, Edward Charles O'Sullivan, 99, *99*, 108, 256
African-Americans, 168, 169, 176, 255
Agribusiness, 163; integrated companies, 163, 164
Agricultural Lands Preservation Program, 162
Agriculture, 25, 26, 40, 72, 86, 92-94, 121-122, 162, 163; apples, 95; broilers, 162-165, *164,* 256; corn, 40, 122, 162, 164, 165; peaches, 93-95, 255, 256; poultry, 121-122, 163, 164, 165; soybeans, 122, 162, *163,* 164, 165; strawberries, 95; timber, 86; tobacco, 36, 40, 255; wheat, 40, 86
Allee, J. Frank, 101
Allee House, *256*
Allen's, 163
Alrichs, Peter Sigfredus, 148
American Anti-Slavery Society, 84
American Revolution, 51-53, 56, 68, 69
Ames, David, 167
Amish, *162, 257*
Antietam, battle of, 84
Argall, Samuel, 18, 254
Articles of Confederation, 54, 55
Asbury, Francis, *47,* 56-68, *65*
Assateague Indians, 17
Associated Charities, 78
Atlas Powder Company, 105, 120
Automobiles, *112,* 120, 125
AstraZeneca, 161

B
Babiarz, John, 115, 133
Babiarz, Stanley, 115
Baker, David W., 162
Baker, James, 169
Bancroft, Samuel, Jr., 155
Banks, 161, 162, 257
Barratt's Chapel, 66, *67,* 255
Bassett, Richard, 55, *59,* 68
Battle of Brandywine, 53, 56
Battle of Cooch's Bridge, 255
Baxter, Jim, 163
Bayard, James A., 68, *143*
Bayard, Thomas F., *86,* 86
Bay State Gas Company, 101
Becket, Reverend William, 36
Bedford, Gunning, Jr., 55, *59*
Bell Atlantic, Delaware, 169
Belton, Ethel, 131
Berger, Carolyn, *170*
Biden, Joseph, 154, 175
Big Quarterly, *130*
Bjork, Erick, 27
Black Anthony, 254
Blacks, 40, 75, 99, 111, 130-133; racial unrest, 125-126, 129, 133, *134;* segregation, 133; suffrage, 84-85, 86
Blue Hens Chickens, 53, *61*
Blunt-Bradley, Lisa, 171
Boggs, J. Caleb, 154
Bombay Hook, 43, *177*
Boston Tea Party, 46
Brady, Jane, 171
Brandywine River, *40,* 41, 71-73, 74

Broadkill, 40
Broom, Jacob, 55
Brown v. Board of Education, 256
Buck, C. Douglas, 116
Buena Vista, 82
Bulah, Shirley, 119, 131
Burton, Benjamin, 83, 84
Burton, William, 93
Byrd, Harry F., 131

C
Calvert, Cecilius, 31
Calvin, John, 37
Canby, Henry S., 75
Cape Henlopen, 11, 15, 18, 21, 26, 31, *33,* 254
Cape May, 26
Carper, Thomas, 154, *171,* 172, 173, 175
Carr, Robert, 30
Carter, Jimmy, 133
Carvel, Elbert N., 154
Castle, Michael, 154, 174, 175, *175*
Chadds Ford, 53
Chalkley, Rebecca, *63*
Chalkley, Thomas, *63*
Charles I, 31
Chase, 162
Child labor, *88-91*
Chrysler Corporation, 120, 161
Churches: African Union Church (Old Union), 127, 255; Asbury Methodist Episcopal, 126; Barratt's Chapel, 66, *67;* Bethel A.M.E., *126;* Ezion Methodist Episcopal, 126; Immanuel Church, *39, 63;* Old Swedes Church, 37-38, *63,* 114; Pencader Presbyterian, 39; Protestant Episcopal, 39, *65;* Sacred Heart, 114; St. Anthony's, 113, *113,* 114; St. Hedwig's, 114, 115; St. Peter's Anglican, 35-36, *37;* St. Stanislaus, 115; Welsh Tract Baptist, 39; Zion Lutheran, 114
Cities and towns: Belleview, *135;* Bethany Beach, 123, *124;* Bombay Hook, 43; Chicopee, 77; Claymont, 100; Clayton, 94; Delaware City, 93, 95, 255; Dewey Beach, 123, 166; Dover, 39, 53, 54, 94, 115, 254, *256, 257;* Fairfax, 161; Felton, 94, 162, *162, 167, 175;* Georgetown, 98, 163, *168,* 169, *255,* 256; Hagley, 105; Greenville, 162; Harrington, 94; Henry Clay Village, 105; Hockessin, *79;* Iron Hill, 51; Lewes, 14-15, 20, 35-36, *69,* 165, 166, 254, 255; Lowell, 77; Middletown, 94, 166; Milford, 159, 160, 256; Milton, *99;* Nassau, 166; New Castle, 23, 27, 28, *28,* 30, *30,* 31, *31,* 32, 36, 37, 39, 40, 41, 53, *54,* 69, 157, 166; Newark, 162, 166, *169,* 176; Newport,

107; Odessa, 39, 166, *254;* Philadelphia, 35, 36, 45, 46, 53, 54, 73; Rehoboth Beach, 122, *166;* Seaford, *70,* 94, 107; Selbyville, *164, 256;* Smyrna, 85; Squirrel Run, 105; Welsh Tract, 37, 39; Willingtown; 42, 255; Wilmington, 39, 51, 53, 71-78, 86, 101, 103, 106, 111-115, 120, 125, 133, 136, *139,* 157, *158, 160,* 161, *161,* 162, *165,* 166, *168,* 169, 170, 171, 172, *172,* 176, 255, *255,* 256, 257; Wyoming, 94

Civil rights, 169, 174
Civil War, 84, 85, 256
Clayton-Bulwar Treaty, 82
Clayton, John M., 82, *82*
Coastal Zone Act, 153, 257
Coke, Thomas, 66, *66*
Compton, Spencer, 42
Constitutional Convention, 55
Continental Army, 53
Continental Courthouse, *34*
Cooch's Bridge, 51
Cooch, Thomas, *51*
Corbit, William, *254*
Corbit-Sharp House, *254*
Counties: Kent, 73, 160, *162,* 163, 164, 167, *177,* 257; New Castle, 73, 160, 161, 166, 167, 171, 176, 256; Sussex, 73, 160, 163, 164, 165, 166, 167, *168,* 176, 256, 257

D
Davis, Samuel B., 69
Davis, Vera G., 157
Declaration of Independence, signing of, 47
Delaware Association for the Moral Improvement and Education of Colored People, 129
Delaware Bay, 15, 17, *33,* 53, 69, 177
Delaware Constitution, 68, 111, 256; creation of, 50
Delaware Day, 56, 255
Delaware Fire Company, *140*
Delaware Memorial Bridge, *176*
Delaware Park, 173
Delaware State Education Association, 173
Delaware State Federation of Women's Clubs, 155
Delaware State House, *60*
Delaware state seal, *7*
Delaware State Testing Program, 172
Delaware Theater Company, 172
Delaware Valley, 254
Delaware's State Police, 169
De La Warr, Lord, 12, 18, 254
Delmar, 255
Delmarva Peninsula, 163
Del Pesco, Susan, *170*
Department of Corrections, 173

Depression, the, 116-117, 162, 256
de Vries, David Peter, 11, 20, *20,* 21, 157, 177
Dickinson, John, 36, 42, *43,* 46, 47, *47,* 55
Dickinson, Samuel, 36
Dixon, Jeremiah, 31
Dover Air Force Base, 167, *167*
Dover Downs, 173
Dover's Hotel, 99
Dravu Corporation, 120
du Pont, Alfred I., 97, *98,* 105, 106, 115, 116, 256
DuPont Company, 97, 98, 101-107, *102, 103, 104, 106, 107,* 120, *144,* 156, 161, *161,* 162, 169, 170, 255, 256, 257
du Pont, Eugene, 105
du Pont family, 176
du Pont, Henry Belin, 136
du Pont, Henry Francis, 155
DuPont Highway, *112,* 256
du Pont, Irenee, 101-103, 105
du Pont, Pierre S., 97-98, 101, 105, 106, 107-108, *108,* 111, 115, 129, 133, *135,* 154, 256
du Pont, T. Coleman, 97-98, 105, 106, 111, *112,* 115, 256
du Pont, Victor, 101, 105
Dutch West India Company, *18, 20,* 18-21, 24, 25, 28

E
Economy, 41-42, 54, 73-77, *74,* 86, 98-99, 101, 106-107, 116-117, 120-122, 133-134, 160, 162, 163, 167, 174
Edgewood Sanitorium, *79*
Education, 39, 77-78, 81-82, 129, 136, 154-156, 169, 170, 172; reform, 107-111
Educational Advancement Act, 154
E.I. du Pont de Nemours, 105
Elk Neck Peninsula, 51
Employment, 28, 74, 75, 101, 103-105, 107, 116-117, 120-121, 133, 162, 171; child labor, 88-91
English Privy Council, 31
Evans, Oliver, *41*
Environmentalists, 164, 165

F
Fell, Jonathon, 138
Fenwick Island, Delaware, 123, 165
Feret, Mary, 114-115
Fertilizers, 164, 165
Financial Center Development Act, 133, 161, 257
Financial World (magazine), 160
First Continental Congress, 46
First U.S.A., 162
First U.S.A. Riverfront Arts Center, *160,* 172

Fisher, Henry, 15
Fort Casimir, 23, 27-28, *28, 29,* 30
Fort Christina, 25, 26, *26,* 27-28, *28,* 42, 254, *255*
Fort Delaware, 84, *85*
Fort Miles, *120*
Fort Nassau, 21, 27
Franklin, Benjamin, 35
Frawley Stadium, 172
Frederica, 255
French and Indian War, 45, 46
Fur trade, 13, *16,* 20, 25-26

G
Gallatin, Albert, *143*
Garrett, Thomas, 83, *83,* 115
Gause, J. Taylor, 78
Gause, Martha, 78
Gay and lesbian community, 171
General Assembly, 165, 170, 171, 173, 174, 177, 256, 257
General Foods Corporation, 121
General Incorporation Law, 101
General Motors Boxwood plant, *120*
General Motors Corporation, 120-121, 161
Georgetown High School, *123*
Getty Oil Company, 121
Gilpin's Paper Mill, *139*
Godyn, Samuel, 21
Grand Opera House, 133
Grant, Ulysses S., 85, 256
Great Awakening, 40
Great Britain, 255
Great Compromise, 55
Green and Wilson's Shop, *106*
Gristmills, 41, *41,* 42, 72, *138*
Gulcz, John S., 114

H
Haley, Thomas, *105*
Hall, David, 68
Hall, Willard, 81
Hanby, Florence M., 156
Harlan and Hollingsworth, 74
Harrington, Martha H., 78
Harrington Raceway, 173, *173*
Haskell, Harry, 133, 136
Haskell Indian Institute, 130
Haslet, Joseph, *61,* 68
Hercules Powder Company, 105, 120
Herrmann Court House, Daniel, *161, 162*
Higggins, Anthony, 100
Historical Society of Delaware, 172, *172*
Hoffecker, Carol, 74, 136
Holloway, Herman, Sr., 133
Holm, Johan Campanius, 26
Horse-racing industry, 173
Horse-Racing Preservation Act, 173
Hospitals: Bay Health (Kent General Hospital), 167; Christina Hospital,

136; Christiana Medical Center, 257;
Delaware Division, 136; Delaware
Hospital, 78, 136; Homeopathic
Hospital, 78; Medical Center of
Delaware, 136; Memorial Hospital, 78,
136; Wilmington General, 136;
Wilmington Hospital, 136; Wilmington
Medical Center, 136
Hossit, Gillis, 20, 21
Hotels: Dover's Hotel, 99; Hotel Du Pont,
106, 133; Hotel Richardson, *100;*
Raddison Hotel, 133
Howe, William, 51-53
Hudson, Henry, 17, 18, 254

I
Immigrants, 169; Africans, 37; Dutch, 37,
254, *256;* English, 37, 254; Finns, 37;
Germans, 37, 75, 114; Irish, 75, 84, 86,
105, 111, 113; Italians, 111-113; Poles,
113; Scotch-Irish, 36, 37, 68, 255;
Spanish-speaking, 164, 169; Swedes, 37,
254; Welsh, 37
Independence Hall of American
Methodism, 66, 255
Indians, 11, 12-18, *20, 21, 25,* 26, 129-
130; trade with Europeans, 13, 24, 25
Integration, 172, 256
International Latex Corporation, 121

J
Jackson, Andrew, 82
Jackson and Sharp, 74, 75, *116*
James, Duke of York, 28-32, 254
Johns, Kensey, *59*
Johnson's Canning Camp, *91*

K
Keene, William B., 155
Kickapoo Indian Medicine Company, *76*
King, Martin Luther, Jr., 125
King's Privy Council, 42
King Street Market, *92*
Kirtley, Donald R., 166
Ku Klux Klan, 130

L
Land development, 166, 167
Langford, Daisy, *89*
Lank, Lawrence, 166
Latimer, James, *59*
Latinos, *164,* 169, 170
Layton, Caleb, 130
Lee, Richard Henry, 47
Legislative Hall, *175*
Lenni Lenape, 10, 12, 13, 16, 17, 24, 26
Lincoln, Abraham, 84-85, 256
Lindestrom, Peter, 25, 157, 177
Lobdell Car Wheel Company, 74
Lockman, Norman, 172
Loqulla, James, *88*

M
McClellan, George, 84
McKean, Thomas, *45,* 46, 47
McKinly, John, 53
McLane, Alan, *59*
McLane, Lewis, 82
McLaughlin, William T., 133
McNadd, Albert, *88*
Macdonough, Thomas, 68, *69*
Madison, James, 55, 68
Magna Carta, 43
Majestic Theatre, *76*
Manufacturing, 160, 161
Martin, John, *58*
Martin, Joshua W., 169
Mason, Charles, 31
Massey, Bes, *124*
Massey, Liz, *124*
MBNA, *161, 162*
Memorial Hall, *169*
Mero, Michael, *90*
Metts, Iris, 169
Millsboro, 16
Minner, Ruth Ann, 159, 160, *170*
Minuit, Peter, 24
Mobley, Stacey, 169
Moors of Cheswold, 17
Morgan, Richard, 68
Morgan, William, 49, 50, *50,* 68
Mountaire, 163, *164*
Munroe, John, 82
Moyed, Ralph, 165
Museums: Delaware Art Museum, 155;
Hagley Museum, 155; Museum of
Natural History, 155; Winterthur
Museum, 155

N
NAACP, 130
Nanticoke Indian Association, 16
Nanticoke Indian Museum, 18
Nat Turner's rebellion, 84
New Castle Army Air Base, *120*
New Castle Courthouse, *33*
Newlin, Joseph, *60*
New Netherland, 27
Newspapers: *Baltimore Sun,* 92; *New
York Evening Post,* 101; *News Journal,*
171; *Sunday Star,* 106
New Sweden Company, 24, 25
Nichols, Joseph, 39
Nutrient Management Commission, 165

P
Pea Patch Island, 84
Penn, William, 30, *30,* 31, 32, 37, 39, 254
Penns, 254
Perdue, 163
Peterson, Russell, 133, 153-154
Pierce, Richard, *89*
Pirates, *57*

Plan Omega, 136, 257
Plockhoy, Peter, 32
Point to Point Race, *176*
Political parties: American, 84;
Democratic, 82, 84, 99-101, 115,
117, 153-154, 170, 174, 175;
Democratic-Republicans, 68, 82;
Federalists, 49, 68, 82; Loyalists, 50;
Regular Republicans, 101; Republican,
84-85, 99-101, 117, 153-154, 170, 174,
175; Tories, 50; Union Republican, 101;
Whig, 82, 84
Population, 27, 36, 42, 72-73, 92, 101, 160,
165, 166, 167, 169, 177, 255
Postles, Thomas, 130
Printz, Johan, 26, 27, 28
Prohibition, 115-116, 117
Protester, *166*
Public whipping, 177
Purnell, William, 155
Pusey and Jones, 74
Pyle, Howard, 155

Q
Queen Christina, *24,* 25

R
Race riots, 256
Railroads: Delaware, 94, 255; New Castle
to Frenchtown, 111; Philadelphia,
Wilmington and Baltimore, 74;
Wilmington and Baltimore, 73;
Wilmington and Western, 73
Read, George, 45, *45,* 46, *46,* 47, 55
Reapportionment, 136
Redding, Louis J., 131
Red Lion Camp Meeting, *140*
Reforms, 77-78, *79,* 108
Religions: Anglican, 32, 39, 65, 66;
Baptist, 39; Church of England, 39,
40, 65; Judaism, 114; Lutheran, 26,
27, 37; Mennonites, 32; Methodist,
65-68, 83, 95; Methodist Episcopal,
127; Presbyterian, 37, 39, 66;
Quaker, 32, 39, 83; Roman Catholic, 39,
111, 113, 114
Return Day, 9, *151,* 154, *168*
Revolutionary War, 255
Reybold, Philip, 93
Richardson, Henry, 99
Ridgely, Nicholas, *59*
Rising, Johan, 27, *29*
Rivers and canals: Brandywine, *40,* 41,
42, 71-72, 73, 74, 103, 255; Broadkill,
40; Chadds Ford, 53; Chesapeake
and Delaware Canal, *72,* 73, 74,
116, 117, 157, 166, *167,* 175, 255;
Christina, 42, *42,* 72, 73, 74, 101,
103, 120, *158,* 172, 177; Delaware,
21, 53, 103, *176,* 254; Duck Creek, 24,
40; Indian, 40; Lewes Canal, *256;*

Nanticoke, 40, *70;* St. Jones, 40; White Clay Creek, 40
Robinson, Thomas, 50
Robinson, Winifred, 155
Rodney, Caesar, 42, 45, *45,* 46, 47, *52, 64,* 255
Rodney Square, *161,* 162
Rodney, Thomas, 45
Roosevelt, Franklin D., 117
Ross, George, 39
Roth, William (Bill), 154, 175, *175*

S
Saulsbury, Eli, 86
Saulsbury, Gove, 86
Saulsbury, Willard, 84, 86
School Law of 1829, 82
School system, public, 256
Schools and colleges: Buttonwood School, *128,* Claymont High, 119, 131; Delaware College, 81, *108;* Delaware Law School, 156, 170; Delaware State College, 129, 155; Delaware Technical and Community College, 155, 256; Georgetown Colored School, *110;* Georgetown High, *123;* Hockessin's Elementary, 119, 131; Howard High, 129, *130;* Jason School, 256; Milford High, 131, 160; Newark Academy, 81; Newark College, 81; Pierre S. du Pont High, *110;* University of Delaware, 81, *108,* 133, 155, *169,* 170; Widener University School of Law, 170; Women's College of Delaware, 155
Seal of New Netherland, *18*
Second Continental Congress, 46, 47, 54
Secretary of Education, 257
Segregation, 257
Seitz, Collins J., 131
Separation Day, 47, 255
Service Citizens of Delaware, 108, 111
Shaw, Robert, 149
Shipbuilding: 74, 101, 120; Harlan and Hollingsworth, 74; Jackson and Sharp, 74, 75, *116;* Lobdell Car Wheel Company, 74; Pusey and Jones, 74
Shipping, 26, 27, 42, *44,* 69, 72, 93
Ships: *Doris, 94; Griffin, 22,* 24; *Half Moon, 17; Key of Kalmar, 22,* 24, *176; Lucy Ann, 58; Republic, 141; Thomas Clyde, 87*
Sikes, James, *59*
Sills, James, *168,* 169, 257
Slavery, 28, 30, 36, 66-67, 82-84, 86, 111, 255, 256
Slaves, 254, 255, *255,* 256
Slot machines, 173, *173*
Society for the Propagation of the Gospel, 39
Society of Friends, 39

Spencer, Peter, 126, 127, 255
Stamp Act, 46
Steele, Cecile A., 121, 122, *122*
Steele, Wilmer, 121, 122
Storm of 1962, 123
Streetcars, *153*
Stuart, Mary A., 115
Stuyvesant, Peter, 27, *29,* 30
Sunday Breakfast Mission, *116*
Swanendael, *20,* 20-21, 31, 32, *256*
Swanendael massacre, 21
Swedish log cabin, *255*
Swinger, Jacob, 114

T
Taney, Roger B., 83
Tatnall, Joseph, *62*
Temporary Emergency Relief Commission, 116
Terry, Charles L., Jr., 133, 155, 256
Theophilus, 83
Thirty Years War, 28
Thompson, Mary Wilson, 115
Thorne, Sydenham, 65
Tilton, James, 46, 71, *72*
Tinicum Island, 26, 28
Townsend Acts, 46
Townsend, John G., 107-111, *108,* 115
Townsend, Samuel, 148
Townsends, 163
Traffic, 166, 167, 176
Treat, Charles H., 99
Tribitt, Sherman, 154
Truitt, Glenn, *87*
Tubman-Garrett Park, 172
Tucker, John Francis, 113, *113*
Tyson, 163

U
Underground railroad, 83
U.S. Constitution, 55-56, *58,* 68, 176, 255; Thirteenth Amendment, 256; Nineteenth Amendment, 256
U.S. Environmental Protection Agency, 165
U.S. Freedmen's Bureau, 129
U.S. Supreme Court, 256

V
Valley of the Swans, 20
Veasey, Thomas, 66
Vietnam War, 174

W
Warner, Emalea Pusey, 78, *79,* 155
War of 1812, 255
War of the Roses, 115
Washington, George, 51-53, 56, *62*
Water Witch Steam Fire Company, *140*
Webb, Thomas, 65
Welsh Tract, 37
Wesley, John, 65, 66

West, Thomas, 12
Whaling, 21
Whann's Raw Bone Super-Phosphate, *144*
Whatcoat, Richard, 66
White Clay Creek, 40
White, Thomas, 66
Whitefield, George, 35-36, *36,* 39
Whiteleysburg, 66
Whorekill, 12, 32
Whore's Creek, 12
Wildlife, 176, *177*
Williams, John J., 131, *132,* 154
Williams, Ron, 167
Wilmington Country Club, 115-116
Wilmington Gas Works, *139*
Wilmington Marine Terminal, *102*
Wilmington Society of Friends, *38*
Wilson, Woodrow, 115
Winchester, William J., 130
Winterthur, *175*
Wolf, Jacob, 49
Women, significance of, 159, 160, 170, 176, 256, 257
Women's Christian Temperance Union, 115
World War I, 105, 106, 115
World War II, 120, 162, 256

Route 1 bridge over the Chesapeake and Delaware Canal unites upstate and downstate Delaware. Courtesy, Delaware Tourism Office

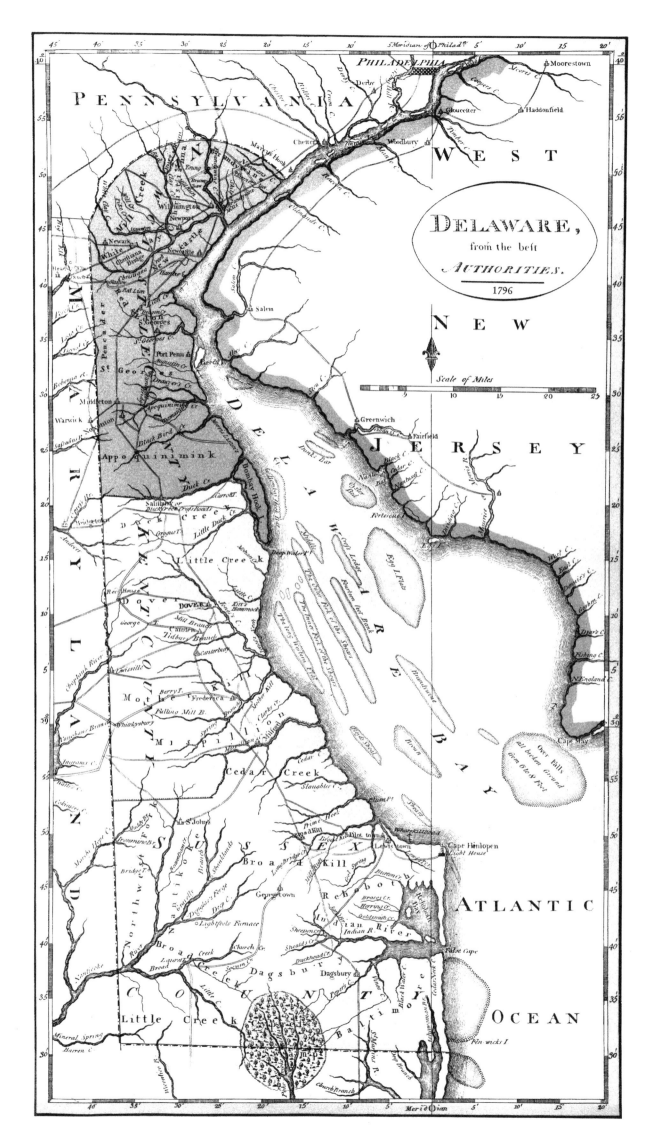